Slavery in American Society

Second Edition

Edited and with an introduction by

Richard D. Brown
University of Connecticut

Stephen G. Rabe
University of Connecticut

D. C. HEATH AND COMPANY
Lexington, Massachusetts   Toronto

CONTENTS

Slavery and American Society

INTRODUCTION

Slavery and its distinctive pattern of race relations have long exercised a decisive role in shaping American society. Although more than a century separates us from slavery as an established institution, its heritage remains a dynamic force of immense proportions. Our own attitudes, patterns of behavior, and institutions continue to reflect impulses that were generated in a system which has long since vanished. As a result this defunct social institution retains a profound continuity with our own times, possessing a special immediacy for contemporary society.

No one planned the creation of American black slavery. Like many American innovations it was a synthesis produced by interaction between the colonists and their environment. Ironically, the Englishmen who created slavery and who were responsible for modeling most colonial institutions came from a nation which boasted that it knew no law of slavery, and that English soil was synonymous with personal and political freedom. Nevertheless, social arrangements resembling a racial caste system emerged as a central feature of Anglo-American society.

The first challenge to English social conceptions came from the American Indians. Here, after some small efforts at assimilation, English colonists responded to the problems of ethnic heterogeneity by displacing or destroying the natives, ultimately rejecting them as alien enemies. This solution seemed to permit the development of a purely Christian society. But the racial homogeneity of European society in North America was never actually established. At the same time that Indians disappeared from English settlements, Africans entered. Their entry—first in small numbers, later by the thousand—

produced a variety of social and religious challenges to the societies of the scattered English settlements. Yet their solutions were remarkably uniform; everywhere they established the supremacy of Europeans and the subjection of the Africans.

Supremacy, by the early eighteenth century, meant that chattel slavery was the normal status of African immigrants in every colony. As chattels, Africans became articles of moveable property devoid of the minimum rights of English subjects. Unless they could show written proof of free status, hereditary lifelong servitude had become the fixed condition of any colonist with at least one African parent or grandparent. A servant caste was emerging, intimately connected with many phases of colonial social life, yet regarded with disdain and fear and excluded from sharing the social and economic mobility that was an essential condition of white men in a developing society. Blacks lived in the dynamic, competitive, exploitative society not as willing actors but largely as manipulated, often hostile, servants in—but not of—American society.

This pattern of white supremacy and black subjection has been so much a part of American life that it was long seen as inevitable. For many years historians believed that given the intensive colonial demand for labor, the physical and ethnic characteristics of the two races necessarily established white men as masters over black slaves. But since the end of World War II a new, consciously antiracist attitude has characterized inquiry into the development of American race relations. Now the particular pattern of white subjection of blacks—however natural and necessary it may have seemed to generations of Americans—demands explanation. Historians wonder why Englishmen invented a new slave status in their midst, and why they attached it to Africans. Moreover they wonder why slavery in Anglo- and Latin America produced different patterns of race relations. During the last three decades these historians have begun to answer such questions by examining the processes whereby captive Africans were transformed into the classic, antebellum American black chattel slave.

In Anglo-America the events of the seventeenth century were crucial. Winthrop Jordan's analysis, comparing the development of slavery in New England with its growth in both the Chesapeake Bay region and the British West Indies, reveals how a variety of ideas and experiences converged to establish the institution. Once created

North American slavery was a dynamic social force. As the studies by Morgan, Wood, Nash, Litwack, Stampp, and Genovese demonstrate, both the character of slavery and race relations experienced continuous mutation throughout the colonial and antebellum periods. In the North this included the peaceful abolition of slavery, while in the South, eighteenth- and nineteenth-century developments intensified the special character of American slavery and its impact on society.

This "special" character of American race relations stands out when slavery in Anglo-America is compared with its Latin American counterpart. There, it has been argued, the humanity of slaves was recognized and black people were not reduced to the subhuman status of chattels. Frank Tannenbaum explains these differences in terms of religion and tradition. He starts from the premise that the "humane" Roman legal and customary traditions of multiracial slavery had been preserved in the Iberian peninsula until the era of American settlement. Therefore when the Spanish and the Portuguese established slavery in the New World, it was tempered by these traditions, which were reinforced by the activities of the Catholic Church, a powerful institution whose concern for the salvation of souls embraced all races. By contrast, since the English lacked a slave tradition as well as a strong colonial establishment, they fitted slavery into their law of property. As a result Tannenbaum believes that North American blacks, who were not protected by a universal church, came to be regarded as objects.

Tannenbaum's argument has long exercised wide influence on interpreters of slavery and race. His comparative analysis of New World slavery helps account for the differences in contemporary race relations in the two Americas. But recently, historians such as Franklin Knight and Carl Degler have challenged Tannenbaum's thesis. Knight, in his study of Cuba's nineteenth-century slave society, argues that it would be foolhardy to accept the sets of laws and decrees promulgated in Spain as a conclusive description of life in the colonies. Local "checks and balances" limited the power of imperial officials. Changes in the economic basis of society, moreover, could place strains on laws and tradition. Cuba's slave codes became increasingly repressive as the slave-operated sugar industry came to dominate Cuba's nineteenth-century economy.

Degler criticizes Tannenbaum by specifically comparing slavery in Brazil and the United States. He finds that the slave personality received as little recognition on the Brazilian plantations as it did in the United States, and that the Catholic clergymen could be as callous toward the slaves as their Protestant counterparts. Degler agrees with Tannenbaum that manumission was easier and more common in Brazil than in the United States, but he disputes the assertion that the frequency of manumission demonstrated a Latin belief in the moral personality of the slave. Economic and demographic developments, not moral concerns, explain Brazilian manumission. In Degler's view, historians must look behind the practices of slavery if they wish to explain the diverging racial patterns of Latin America and the United States.

In the next essay Thomas Skidmore attempts to fulfill Degler's suggestion by comparing race relations in Brazil and the United States. Skidmore identifies the essential difference between the two societies to be the Brazilian acceptance of a multiracial social structure. The United States, on the other hand, has always exhibited a rigidly bi-racial system. Skidmore theorizes that variations in the political, economic, and demographic circumstances of the two countries produced the different racial classification systems. While his conclusions are only tentative, Skidmore has underscored a theme that Knight and Degler have emphasized—any interpretation of slavery and race must be placed within a nation's historical experience.

Historians of American slavery have been similarly concerned with analyzing slavery within the context of American society. By studying slavery's place in society, they hope to illuminate the nature of race relations. Leaning heavily on Tannenbaum's work, Stanley Elkins argues that chattel slavery was a consequence of capitalism applied to agriculture, and that race relations took their character from the positions of the white and black in a capitalist culture. Eugene Genovese replies by arguing that Southern society was more paternal and antibourgeois than it was capitalist, and that race relations, like the economy, followed patterns common to traditional societies.

Elkins and Genovese confine their analysis of slavery and race to Southern society. But the prominence of national race problems demonstrates that slavery and race had an impact everywhere. Eric Foner, in his study of the political party most opposed to the extension of slavery—the Republicans—shows how racial prejudice pervaded Northern society. The Republicans could never decide whether it was slavery or the slave's presumed mental deficiencies that led to the degradation of black people in American society. As do the works of Elkins and Genovese, Foner's study implies that the evolution of slavery and race relations are inseparable from the general character of American society.

Slavery should not, therefore, be examined in isolation. Throughout its history the institution and its internal characteristics were always enmeshed in larger patterns of social life. The traditional conception of America as a free society has put slavery and its patterns of behavior conveniently outside the mainstream, making them anomalies to be dealt with as special cases, since slavery did not become the general way of American life and was extinguished after 1865. But if patterns of behavior between white and black people, as between other ethnic groups, are part of the mainstream of American history, then slavery must be included. Examination of the origins and evolution of American black slavery becomes necessary for an understanding of American society, while a comparative approach adds a dimension of conceptual leverage frequently absent from historical analysis.

I THE EMERGENCE OF SLAVERY IN ANGLO-AMERICA

Winthrop D. Jordan

UNTHINKING DECISION: ENSLAVEMENT OF AFRICANS IN AMERICA TO 1700

In the following essay Professor Jordan provides a comparative analysis of the emergence of chattel slavery in the English colonies. Nearly a decade after its initial publication in White Over Black: American Attitudes toward the Negro, 1550–1812, *Jordan's study, revealing the interaction between social attitudes and social institutions, is still the most nearly definitive treatment available of the origin of slavery in Anglo-America. Professor Jordan teaches at the University of California, Berkeley.*

At the start of English settlement in America, no one had in mind to establish the institution of Negro slavery. Yet in less than a century the foundations of a peculiar institution had been laid. The first Africans landed in Virginia in 1619, though very little is known about their precise status during the next twenty years. Between 1640 and 1660 there is evidence of enslavement, and after 1660 slavery crystallized on the statute books of Maryland, Virginia, and other colonies. By 1700, when Africans began flooding into English America, they were treated as somehow deserving a life and status radically different from English and other European settlers. Englishmen in America had created a new legal status which ran counter to English law.

Unfortunately the details of this process can never be completely reconstructed; there is simply not enough evidence to show precisely when and how and why Negroes came to be treated so differently from white men. Concerning the first years of contact especially we have very little information as to what impression Negroes made upon English settlers: accordingly, we are left knowing less about the formative years than about later periods of American slavery. That those early years were crucial is obvious, for it was then that the cycle of Negro debasement began; once the African became fully the

From Winthrop D. Jordan, *The White Man's Burden: Historical Origins of Racism in the United States* (New York: Oxford University Press, 1974), pp. 26–54. Derived from *White Over Black*, by Winthrop D. Jordan, published by the University of North Carolina Press for the Institute of Early American History and Culture. Reprinted by permission. Footnotes omitted.

slave it is not hard to see why Englishmen looked down upon him. Yet precisely because understanding the dynamics of these early years is so important to understanding the centuries which followed, it is necessary to bear with the less than satisfactory data and to attempt to reconstruct the course of debasement undergone by Africans in seventeenth-century America.

The Necessities of a New World

When Englishmen crossed the Atlantic to settle in America, they were immediately subject to novel strains. A large proportion of migrants were dead within a year. The survivors were isolated from the world as they had known it, cut off from friends and family and the familiar sights and sounds and smells which have always told men who and where they are. A similar sense of isolation and disorientation was inevitable even in the settlements that did not suffer through a starving time. English settlers had undergone the shock of detachment from home in order to set forth upon a dangerous voyage of from ten to thirteen weeks that ranged from unpleasant to fatal and that seared into every passenger's memory the ceaselessly tossing distance that separated him from his old way of life.

Life in America put great pressure upon the traditional social and economic controls that Englishmen assumed were to be exercised by civil and often ecclesiastical authority. Somehow the empty woods seemed to lead much more toward license than restraint. At the same time, by reaction, this unfettering resulted in an almost pathetic social conservatism, a yearning for the forms and symbols of the old familiar social order. When in 1618, for example, the Virginia Company wangled a knighthood for a newly appointed governor of the colony the objection from the settlers was not that this artificial elevation was inappropriate to wilderness conditions but that it did not go far enough to meet them. English social forms were transplanted to America not simply because they were nice to have around but because without them the new settlements would have fallen apart and English settlers would have become men of the forest, savage men devoid of civilization.

For the same reason, the communal goals and values that animated the settlement of the colonies acquired great functional importance in the wilderness; they served as antidotes to social and individual disintegration. For Englishmen planting in America, it was of the utmost importance to know that they were Englishmen, which was to say that they were educated (to a degree suitable to their station), Christian (of an appropriate Protestant variety), civilized, and (again to an appropriate degree) free men.

It was with personal freedom, of course, that wilderness conditions most suddenly reshaped English laws, assumptions, and practices. In America land was plentiful, labor scarce, and, as in all new colonies, a cash crop desperately needed. These economic conditions were to remain crucial for many years; in general they tended to encourage greater geographical mobility, less specialization, higher rewards, and fewer restraints on the processes and products of labor. In general men who invested capital in agriculture in America came under fewer customary and legal restraints than in England concerning what they did with their land and with the people who worked on it. On the other hand their activities were restricted by the economic necessity of producing cash crops for export. Men without capital could obtain land relatively easily: hence the shortage of labor and the notably blurred line between men who had capital and men who did not.

Three major systems of labor emerged amid the interplay of these social and economic conditions in America. One, which was present from the beginning, was free wage labor. Another, which was the last to appear, was chattel slavery. The third, which virtually coincided with first settlement in America, was temporary servitude, in which contractual arrangements gave shape to the entire system. It was this third system, indentured servitude, which permitted so many English settlers to cross the Atlantic barrier. Indentured servitude was linked to the development of chattel slavery in America, and its operation deserves closer examination.

A very sizable proportion of settlers in the English colonies came as indentured servants bound by contract to serve a master for a specified number of years, usually from four to seven or until age twenty-one, as repayment for their ocean passage. The time of service to which the servant bound himself was negotiable property, and he might be sold or conveyed from one master to another at any time up to the expiration of his indenture, at which point he became a free man. (Actually it was his *labor* which was owned and sold, not his *person*, though this distinction was neither important nor obvious at the time.) Custom and statute law regulated the relationship between servant and master. Obligation was reciprocal: the master undertook to feed and clothe and sometimes to educate his servant and to refrain from abusing him, while the servant was obliged to perform such work as his master set him and to obey his master in all things.

Freedom and Bondage in the English Tradition

While in retrospect we can readily see these three distinct categories, thinking about freedom and bondage in Tudor England was in fact confused and self-contradictory. In a period of social dislocation there was considerable disagreement among contemporary observers as to what actually was going on and even as to what ought to be. *Ideas* about personal freedom tended to run both ahead of and behind actual social conditions. Both statute and common law were sometimes considerably more than a century out of phase with actual practice and with commonly held notions about servitude. Finally, both ideas and practices were changing rapidly. It is possible, however, to identify certain important tenets of social thought that served as anchor points amid this chaos.

Englishmen lacked accurate methods of ascertaining what actually was happening to their social institutions, but they were not wrong in supposing that villenage, or "bondage" as they more often called it, had virtually disappeared in England. In the Middle Ages, being a villein had meant dependence upon the will of a feudal lord but by no means deprivation of all social and legal rights. By the fourteenth century villenage had decayed markedly, and it no longer existed as a viable social institution in the second half of the sixteenth century. Personal freedom had become the normal status of Englishmen. Most contemporaries welcomed this fact; indeed it was after about 1550 that there began to develop in England that preening consciousness of the peculiar glories of English liberties. This consciousness was to flower in America as well.

How had it all happened? Among those observers who tried to explain, there was agreement that Christianity was primarily responsible. They thought of villenage as a mitigation of ancient bond slavery and that the continuing trend to liberty was animated, as Sir Thomas Smith said in a famous passage, by the "perswasion . . . of Christians not to make nor keepe his brother in Christ, servile, bond and underling for ever unto him, as a beast rather than as a man.'' They agreed also that the trend had been forwarded by the common law, in which the disposition was always, as the phrase went, ''in favor of liberty.''

At the same time there were in English society people who seemed badly out of control. From at least the 1530s the countryside swarmed with vagrants, sturdy beggars, rogues, and vagabonds, with men who *could* (it was thought) but *would not* work. They committed all manner of crimes, the worst of which was remaining idle. It was an article of faith among Tudor commentators that idleness was the mother of all vice and the chief danger to a well-ordered state. Tudor statesmen valiantly attempted to suppress idleness by means of the famous vagrancy laws which provided for houses of correction and (finally) for whipping the vagrant from constable to constable until he reached his home parish. They assumed that everyone belonged in a specific niche and that anyone failing to labor in the niche assigned to him by Providence must be compelled to do so by authority.

In response, Tudor authorities gradually hammered out the legal framework of a labor system which permitted compulsion but which did *not* permit so total a loss of freedom as lifetime hereditary slavery. And as things turned out, it was indentured servitude which best met the requirements for settling in America. Of course there were other forms of bound labor which contributed to the process of settlement: many convicts were sent and many children abducted. Yet among all the numerous varieties and degrees of nonfreedom which existed in England, there was none which could have served as a well-formed model for the chattel slavery which developed in America. This is not to say, though, that slavery was an unheard-of novelty in Tudor England. On the contrary, ''bond slavery'' was a memory trace of long standing. Vague and confused as the concept of slavery was in the minds of Englishmen, it possessed certain fairly consistent connotations which were to help shape English perceptions of the way Europeans should properly treat the newly discovered peoples overseas.

The Concept of Slavery

At first glance, one is likely to see merely a fog of inconsistency and vagueness enveloping the terms *servant* and *slave* as they were used both in England and in seventeenth-century America. When Hamlet declaims "O what a rogue and peasant slave am I," the term seems to have a certain elasticity. When Peter Heylyn defines it in 1627 as "that ignominious word, *Slave*; whereby we use to call ignoble fellowes, and the more base sort of people," the term seems useless as a key to a specific social status.

In one sense it was, since the concept embodied in the terms *servitude, service,* and *servant* was widely embracive. *Servant* was more a generic term than *slave.* Slaves could be "servants," but servants *should not* be "slaves." This principle, which was common in England, suggests a measure of precision in the concept of slavery. In fact there was a large measure which merits closer inspection.

First of all, the "slave's" loss of freedom was complete. "Of all men which be destitute of libertie or freedome," explained one commentator in 1590, "the slave is in greatest subjection, for a slave is that person which is in servitude or bondage to an other, even against nature." "Even his children," moreover, ". . . are infected with the Leprosie of his father's bondage." At law, much more closely than in literary usage, "bond slavery" implied utter deprivation of liberty.

Slavery was also thought of as a perpetual condition. While it had not yet come invariably to mean lifetime labor, it was frequently thought of in those terms. Except sometimes in instances of punishment for crime, slavery was open ended; in contrast to servitude, it did not involve a definite term of years. Slavery was perpetual also in the sense that it was often thought of as hereditary. It was these dual aspects of perpetuity which were to assume such importance in America.

So much was slavery a complete loss of liberty that it seemed to Englishmen somehow akin to loss of humanity. No theme was more persistent than the claim that to treat a man as a slave was to treat him as a beast. Almost half a century after Sir Thomas Smith had made this connection a Puritan divine was condemning masters who used "their servants as slaves, or rather as beasts." No analogy could have better demonstrated how strongly Englishmen felt about total loss of personal freedom.

Certain prevalent assumptions about the origins of slavery paralleled this analogy at a different level of intellectual construction. Lawyers and divines alike assumed that slavery was impossible before the Fall, that it violated natural law, that it was instituted by positive human laws, and, more generally, that in various ways it was connected with sin. These ideas were as old as the church fathers and the Roman writers on natural law. Sir Edward Coke, the great jurist, spelled out what was perhaps the most important and widely acknowledged attribute of slavery: ". . . it was ordained by Constitution of Nations . . . that he that was taken in Battle should remain Bond to his taker for ever, and he to do with him, all that should come of him, his Will and Pleasure, as with his Beast, or any other Cattle, to give, or to sell, or to kill." This final power, Coke noted, had since been taken away (owing to "the Cruelty of some Lords") and placed in the hands only of kings. The animating rationale here was that captivity in war meant an end to a person's claim to life as a human being; by sparing the captive's life, the captor acquired virtually absolute power over the life of the man who had lost the power to control his own.

More than any other single quality, *captivity* differentiated slavery from servitude. Although there were other, subsidiary ways of becoming a slave, such as being born of slave parents, selling oneself into slavery, or being adjudged to slavery for crime, none of these was considered to explain the way slavery had originated. Slavery was a power relationship; servitude was a relationship of service. Men were "slaves" to the devil but "servants" of God. Men were "galley-slaves," not galley servants.

This tendency to equate slavery with captivity had important ramifications. Warfare was usually waged against another people; captives were usually foreigners—"strangers" as they were termed. Until the emergence of nation-states in Europe, by far the most important category of strangers was the non-Christian. International warfare seemed above all a ceaseless struggle between Christians and Muslims. In the sixteenth and seventeenth centuries Englishmen at home could read scores of accounts concerning the miserable fate of Englishmen and other Christians taken into "captivity" by Turks and Moors and oppressed by the "verie worst manner of bondmanship and slaverie." Clearly slavery was tinged by the spirit of religious difference.

It is clear, therefore, that Englishmen did possess a *concept* of slavery, formed by the clustering of several rough but not illogical equations. The slave was treated like a beast. Slavery was inseparable from the evil in men; it was God's punishment upon Ham's prurient disobedience. Enslavement was captivity, the loser's lot in a contest of power. Slaves were infidels or heathens.

On every count, Negroes qualified.

The Practices of Portingals and Spanyards

Which is not to say that Englishmen were casting about for a people to enslave. What happened was that they found thrust before them not only instances of Negroes being taken into slavery but attractive opportunities for joining in that business. Englishmen actually were rather slow to seize these opportunities; on most of the sixteenth-century English voyages to West Africa there was no dealing in slaves. The notion that it was appropriate to do so seems to have been drawn chiefly from the example set by the Spanish and Portuguese.

Without inquiring into the reasons, it can be said that slavery had persisted since ancient times in Spain and Portugal, that prior to the discoveries it was primarily a function of the religious wars against the Moors, that Portuguese explorers pressing down the coast in the fifteenth century captured thousands of Negroes whom they carried back to Portugal as slaves, and that after 1500, Portuguese ships began supplying the Spanish and Portuguese settlements in America with Negro slaves. By 1500 European enslavement of Negroes had become a fixture of the New World.

There is no need to inquire into the precise nature of this slavery except to point out that in actual practice it did fit the English concept of bond slavery. The question which needs answering pertains to contemporary English knowledge of what was going on. And the answer may be given concisely: Englishmen had easily at hand a great deal of not very precise information.

The news that Africans were being carried off to forced labor in America was broadcast across the pages of the widely read Hakluyt and Purchas collections. While only one account stated explicitly that Negroes "be their slaves during their life," it was clear that the Portuguese and Spaniards treated Negroes and frequently the Indians as "slaves." This was the term customarily used by English voyagers and by translators of foreign documents. William Towrson was told by an African in 1556 "that the Portingals were bad men, and that they made them slaves, if they could take them, and would put yrons upon their legges." There were "rich trades" on that coast in Negroes "which be caried continually to the West Indies." The Portuguese in the Congo "have divers rich Commodities from this Kingdome, but the most important is every yeere about five thousand Slaves, which they transport from thence, and sell them at good round prices in . . . the West Indies."

Some Englishmen decided that there might be profit in supplying the Spanish with Negroes, despite the somewhat theoretical prohibition of foreigners from the Spanish dominions in the New World. John Hawkins was first; in the 1560s he made three voyages to Africa, the Caribbean, and home. The first two were successful; the third met disaster when the Spanish attacked his ships, took most of them, and turned the captured English seamen over to the Inquisition. This famous incident helped discourage English slave trading in favor of other maritime activities. English vessels were not again active frequently in the slave trade until the seventeenth century. But Englishmen learned, from the accounts published by Richard Hakluyt, that Hawkins had taken Africans in Africa and sold them as "marchandise" in the West Indies.

By the end of the first quarter of the seventeenth century it had become abundantly evident in England that Negroes were being enslaved on an international scale. Clearly an equation had developed between Africans and slavery. Primarily, the associations were with the Portuguese and Spanish, with captivity, with buying and selling in Guinea and in America. Yet there is no reason to suppose Englishmen especially eager to enslave Negroes, nor even to regard the traveler Richard Jobson eccentric in his response to an African chief's offer to buy some "slaves": "I made answer, We were a people, who did not deale in any such commodities, neither did wee buy or sell one another, or any that had our owne shapes." By the seventeenth century, after all, English prejudices as well as English law were "in favor of liberty."

When they came to settle in America, Englishmen found that things happened to liberty, some favorable, some not. Negroes became slaves, partly because there were economic necessities in America which called for some sort of bound, controlled labor. The Portuguese and Spanish had set an example, which, however rough in outline, proved to be, at very least, suggestive to Englishmen. It would be surprising if there had been a clear-cut line of influence from Latin to English slavery. Elizabethans were not in the business of modeling themselves after Spaniards. Yet from about 1550, Englishmen were in such continual contact with the Spanish that they could hardly have failed to acquire the notion that Negroes could be enslaved. The terms *negro* and *mulatto* were incorporated into English from the Hispanic languages. This is the more striking because a perfectly adequate term, identical in meaning to *negro*, already existed in English; of course *black* was used also, though not so commonly in the sixteenth century as later.

By 1640 it was becoming apparent that in many of their new colonies overseas English settlers had bought Negroes and were holding them, frequently, as hereditary slaves for life. In considering this development, it is important to remember that the status of slave was at first distinguished from servitude more by duration than by onerousness; the key term in many early descriptions of the Negro's condition was *perpetual.* Negroes served "for ever" and so would their children. Englishmen did not do so. Servitude, no matter how long, brutal, and involuntary, was not the same thing as perpetual slavery. Servitude comprehended alike the young apprentice, the orphan, the indentured servant, the convicted debtor or criminal, the political prisoner, and, even, the Scottish and Irish captive of war who was sold as a "slave" to New England or Barbados. None of these persons, no matter how miserably treated, served for life in the colonies, though of course many died before their term ended. Hereditary lifetime service was restricted to Indians and Africans. Among the various English colonies in the New World, this service known as "slavery" seems first to have developed in the internationa' cockpit known as the Caribbean.

Enslavement: The West Indies

The Englishmen who settled the Caribbean colonies were not very different from those who went to Virginia, Bermuda, Maryland, or even New England. Their experience in the islands, however, was very different indeed. By 1640 there were roughly as many English (and Irish and Scots) in the little islands as on the American continent. A half-century after the first settlements were established in the 1620s, many of the major islands—Barbados, and the Leeward Islands—were overcrowded. Thousands of whites who had been squeezed off the land by sugar plantations migrated to other English colonies, including much larger Jamaica which had been captured from the

Spanish in 1655. Their places were taken by African slaves who had been shipped to the islands, particularly after 1640, to meet an insatiable demand for labor which was cheap to maintain, easy to dragoon, and simple to replace when worked to death. Negroes outnumbered whites in Barbados as early as 1660.

In that colony, at least, this helpful idea that Negroes served for life seems to have existed even before they were purchased in large numbers. Any doubt which may have existed as to the appropriate status of Africans was dispelled in 1636 when the Governor and Council resolved "that *Negroes* and *Indians*, that came here to be sold, should serve for life, unless a Contract was before made to the contrary." Europeans were not treated in this manner. In the 1650s several observers referred to the lifetime slavery of Negroes as if it were a matter of common knowledge. "It's the Custome for a Christian servant to serve foure yeares," one wrote at the beginning of the decade, "and then enjoy his freedome . . . the Negroes and Indians (of which latter there are but few here) they and the generation are Slaves to their owners to perpetuity." As another visitor described the people of the island in 1655:

> The gentcroy heare doth live far better than ours doue in England: thay have most of them 100 or 2 or 3 of slaves apes whou they command as they pleas. . . . This Island is inhabited with all sortes: with English, french, Duch, Scotes, Irish, Spaniards thay being Jues: with Ingones and miserabell Negors borne to perpetuall slavery thay and thayer seed . . . some planters will have 30 more or les about 4 or 5 years ould: they sele them from one to the other as we doue shepe. This Illand is the Dunghill wharone England doth cast forth its rubidg: Rodgs and hors and such like peopel are those which are gennerally Broght heare.

Dunghill or no dunghill, Barbados was treating its Negroes as slaves for life.

Enslavement: New England

It was ironic that slavery in the West Indies should have influenced, of all places, New England. The question with slavery in New England is not why it was weakly rooted, but why it existed at all. No staple crop demanded regiments of raw labor. That there was no compelling economic demand for Negroes is evident in the numbers actually imported: there could have been no need for a distinct status for only 3 percent of the labor force. Indentured servitude was completely adequate to New England's needs. Why, then, did New Englanders enslave Negroes, probably as early as 1638? Why was it that the Puritans rather mindlessly (which was not their way) accepted slavery for blacks and Indians but not for whites?

The early appearance of slavery in New England may in part be explained by the fact that the first Negroes were imported in the ship *Desire* in 1638 from an island colony where Negroes were already being held perpetually. After 1640 a brisk trade got under way between New England and the English Caribbean islands. These strange Negroes from the West Indies must surely have brought with them to New England prevailing notions about their usual status. Ship masters who purchased perpetual service in Barbados would not have been likely to sell service for term in Boston.

No amount of contact with the West Indies could have by itself created Negro slavery in New England; settlers there had to be willing to accept the proposition. Because they were Englishmen, they were so prepared—and at the same time they were not. Characteristically, as Puritans, they officially codified this ambivalence in 1641 as follows: ". . . there shall never be any bond-slavery, villenage or captivitie amongst us; unlesse it be lawfull captives taken in just warrs, and such strangers as willingly sell themselves, or are solde to us. . . ." Thus as early as 1641 the Puritan settlers were seeking to guarantee their own liberty without closing off the opportunity of taking it from others whom they identified with the Biblical term, "strangers."

It would be wrong to suppose, though, that all the Puritans' preconceived ideas about freedom and bondage worked in the same direction. While the concepts of difference in religion and of captivity worked against Indians and Negroes, certain Scriptural injunctions and English pride in liberty told in the opposite direction. In Massachusetts the magistrates demonstrated that they were not about to tolerate glaring breaches of "the Law of God established in Israel" even when the victims were Africans. In 1646 the authorities arrested two mariners who had carried two Negroes directly from Africa and sold them in Massachusetts. What distressed the General Court was that the Negroes had been obtained during a raid on an African village and that this "haynos and crying sinn of man stealing" had taken place on the Lord's Day. The General Court decided to free the unfortunate victims and ship them back to Africa, though the death penalty for the crime (clearly mandatory in Scripture) was not imposed. More quietly than in this dramatic incident, Puritan authorities extended the same protections against maltreatment to Negroes and Indians as to white servants.

From the first, however, there were scattered signs in New England that Negroes were regarded as different from English people not merely in their status as slaves. In 1652, for example, the Massachusetts General Court ordered that Scotsmen, Indians, and Negroes should train with the English in the militia, but four years later abruptly excluded Negroes, as did Connecticut in 1660. Evidently Negroes, even free Negroes, were regarded as distinct from the English. They were, in New England where economic necessities were not sufficiently pressing to determine the decision, treated differently from other men.

Enslavement: Virginia and Maryland

In Virginia and Maryland the development of Negro slavery followed a very different course, for several reasons. Most obviously, geographic conditions and the intentions of the settlers quickly combined to produce a successful agricultural staple. Ten years after settlers first landed at Jamestown they were on the way to proving, in the face of assertions to the contrary, that it was possible "to found an empire upon smoke." More than the miscellaneous productions of New England, tobacco required labor which was cheap but not temporary, mobile but not independent, and tireless rather than skilled. In the Chesapeake area more than anywhere to the northward, the shortage of labor and the abundance of land—the "frontier"—placed a premium on involuntary labor.

This need for labor played more directly upon these settlers' ideas about freedom and bondage than it did either in the West Indies or in New England. Perhaps it would be more accurate to say that settlers in Virginia (and in Maryland after settlement in 1634) made their decisions concerning Negroes while relatively virginal, relatively free from external influences and from firm preconceptions. Of all the important early English settlements, Virginia had the least contact with the Spanish, Portuguese, Dutch, and other English colonies. At the same time, the settlers of Virginia did not possess either the legal or Scriptural learning of the New England Puritans whose conception of the just war had opened the way to the enslavement of Indians. Slavery in the tobacco colonies did not begin as an adjunct of captivity; in marked contrast to the Puritan response to the Pequot War, the settlers of Virginia did not react to the Indian massacre of 1622 with propositions for taking captives and selling them as "slaves."

In the absence, then, of these influences in other English colonies, slavery as it developed in Virginia and Maryland assumes a special interest and importance over and above the fact that Negro slavery was to become a vitally important institution there and, later, to the southwards. In the tobacco colonies it is possible to watch Negro slavery *develop*, not pop up full-grown overnight, and it is therefore possible to trace, very imperfectly, the development of the shadowy, unexamined rationale which supported it. The concept of Negro slavery there was neither borrowed from foreigners, nor extracted from books, nor invented out of whole cloth, nor extrapolated from servitude, nor generated by English reaction to Negroes as such, nor necessitated by the exigencies of the New World. Not any one of these made the Negro a slave, but all.

In rough outline, slavery's development in the tobacco colonies seems to have undergone three stages. Africans first arrived in 1619, an event Captain John Smith referred to with the utmost unconcern: "About the last of August came in a dutch man of warre that sold us twenty Negars." Africans trickled in slowly for the next half-century; one report in 1649 estimated that there were three hundred among Virginia's population of fifteen thousand—about 2 percent. Long before there were more appreciable numbers, the development of slavery had, so far as we can tell, shifted gears. Prior to about 1640 there is very little evidence to show how Negroes were treated. After 1640 there is mounting evidence that some Negroes were in fact being treated as slaves. This is to say that the twin essences of slavery— lifetime service and inherited status—first became evident during the twenty years prior to the beginning of legal formulation. After 1660 slavery was written into statute law.

Concerning the first of these stages, there is only one major historical certainty. There simply is not enough evidence to indicate whether Negroes were treated like white servants or not. At least we can be confident, therefore, that the two most common assertions about the first Negroes—that they were slaves and that they were servants—are *unfounded*, though not necessarily incorrent. And what of the positive evidence?

Some of the first group bore Spanish names and presumably had been baptized, which would mean they were at least nominally Christian, though of the Papist sort. They had been "sold" to the English; so had other Englishmen but not by the Dutch. Probably these Negroes were not fully free, but many Englishmen were not. It can be said, though, that from the first in Virginia Negroes were set apart from white men by the word *Negroes*. The earliest Virginia census reports plainly distinguished Negroes from white men; often Negroes were listed as such with no personal names—a critical distinction. It seems logical to suppose that this perception of the Negro as being distinct from the Englishman must have operated to debase his status rather than to raise it, for in the absence of countervailing social factors the need for labor in the colonies usually told in the direction of nonfreedom. There were few countervailing factors present, surely, in such instances as in 1629 when a group of Negroes were brought to Virginia freshly captured from a Portuguese ship which had snatched them from Angola a few weeks earlier. Given the context of English thought and experience sketched in this chapter, it seems probable that the Negro's status was not ever the same as that accorded the white servant. But we do not know for sure.

When the first fragmentary evidence appears about 1640 it becomes clear that *some* Negroes in both Virginia and Maryland were serving for life and some Negro children inheriting the same obligation. Not all blacks, certainly, for after the mid-1640s the court records show that some Negroes were incontestably free and were accumulating property of their own. At least one black freeman, Anthony Johnson, himself owned a slave. Some blacks served only terms of usual length, but others were held for terms far longer than custom and statute permitted with white servants. The first fairly clear indication that slavery was practiced in the tobacco colonies appears in 1639, when a Maryland statute declared that "all the Inhabitants of this Province being Christians (Slaves excepted) Shall have and enjoy all such rights liberties immunities privileges and free customs within this Province as any naturall born subject of England." Another Maryland law passed the same year provided that "all persons being Christians (Slaves excepted)" over eighteen who were imported without indentures would serve for four years. These laws make very little sense unless the term *slaves* meant Negroes and perhaps Indians.

The next year, 1640, the first definite indication of outright enslavement appears in Virginia. The General Court pronounced sentence on three servants who had been retaken after absconding to Maryland. Two of them, both white, were ordered to serve their masters for one additional year and then the colony for three more, but "the third being a negro named John Punch shall serve his said master or his assigns for the time of his natural life here or else where." No white servant in any English colony, so far as is known, ever received a like sentence.

After 1640, when surviving Virginia county court records began to mention Negroes, sales for life, often including any future progeny, were recorded in unmistakable language. In 1646 Francis Pott sold a Negro woman and boy to Stephen Charlton "to the use of him . . . forever." Similarly, six years later William Whittington sold to John Pott "one Negro girle named Jowan; aged about Ten yeares and with her Issue and produce duringe her (or either of them) for their Life tyme. And their Successors forever"; and a Maryland man in 1649 deeded two Negro men and a woman "and all their issue both male and Female." The executors of a York County estate in 1647 disposed of eight Negroes—four men, two women, and two children—to Captain John Chisman "to have hold occupy posesse and injoy and every one of the afforementioned Negroes forever."

Further evidence that some Negroes were serving for life in this period lies in the prices paid for them. In many instances the valuations placed on Negroes (in estate inventories and bills of sale) were far higher than for white servants, even those servants with full terms yet to serve. . . . Besides setting a higher value on Negroes, these inventories failed to indicate a last name and the number of years they had still to serve, presumably because their service was for an unlimited time.

Where Negro women were involved, higher valuations probably reflected the facts that their issue were valuable and that they could be used for field work while white women generally were not. This latter discrimination between black and white women did not necessarily involve perpetual service, but it meant that blacks were set apart in a way clearly not to their advantage. This was not the only instance in which Negroes were subjected to degrading distinctions not immediately and necessarily attached to the concept of slavery. Blacks were singled out for special treatment in several ways which suggest a generalized debasement of blacks as a group. Significantly, the first indications of this debasement appeared at about the same time as the first indications of actual enslavement.

The distinction concerning field work is a case in point. A law of 1643 provided that *all* adult men were taxable and, in addition, *Negro* women. The same distinction was made twice again before 1660. Maryland adopted a similar policy beginning in 1654. This official discrimination between black women and other women was made by white men who were accustomed to thinking of field work as being ordinarily the work of men exclusively. The essentially racial character of this discrimination stood out clearly in a law passed in 1668 at the time slavery was taking shape in the statute books:

> *Whereas some doubts, have arisen whether negro women set free were still to be accompted tithable according to a former act,* It is declared by this grand assembly *that negro women, though permitted to enjoy their Freedome yet ought not in all respects to be admitted to a full fruition of the exemptions and impunities of the English, and are still lyable to payment of taxes.*

Virginia law set blacks apart from all other groups in a second way by denying them the important right and obligation to bear arms. Few restraints could indicate more clearly the denial to Africans of membership in the English community. This first foreshadowing of the slave codes came in 1640, at just the time when other indications first appeared that blacks were subject to special treatment.

Finally, an even more compelling sense of the separateness of Negroes was revealed in early reactions to sexual union between the races. Prior to 1660 the evidence concerning these reactions is equivocal, and it is not possible to tell whether repugnance for intermixture preceded legislative enactment of slavery. In the early 1660s, however, when slavery was gaining statutory recognition, the assemblies acted with full-throated indignation against miscegenation. These acts aimed at more than merely avoiding confusion of status. In 1662 Virginia declared that "if any christian shall committ Fornication with a negro man or woman, hee or shee soe offending" should pay double the usual fine. Two years later Maryland regulated interracial marriages: "forasmuch as divers freeborne English women forgettfull of their free Condicion and to the disgrace of our Nation doe intermarry with Negro Slaves by which alsoe divers suites may arise touching the issue of such woemen and a great damage doth befall the Masters of such Negros for prevention whereof for deterring such freeborne women from such shameful Matches," strong language indeed if "divers suites" had been the only problem. A Maryland act of 1681 described marriages of white women with Negroes as, among other things, "always to the Satisfaccion of theire Lascivious and Lustfull desires, and to the disgrace not only of the English butt allso of many other Christian Nations." When Virginia finally prohibited all interracial liaisons in 1691, the Assembly vigorously denounced miscegenation and its fruits as "that abominable mixture and spurious issue."

From the surviving evidence it appears that outright enslavement and these other forms of debasement appeared at about the same time in Maryland and Virginia. Indications of perpetual service, the very nub of slavery, coincided with indications that English settlers discriminated against Negro women, withheld arms from Negroes, and—though the timing is far less certain—reacted unfavorably to interracial sexual union. The coincidence suggests a mutual relationship between slavery and unfavorable assessment of blacks. Rather than slavery causing "prejudice," or vice versa, they seem rather to have generated each other. Both were, after all, twin aspects of a general debasement of the Negro. Slavery and "prejudice" may have been equally cause and effect, continuously reacting upon each other, dynamically joining hands to hustle the Negro down the road to complete degradation. Much more than with the other English colonies, where the enslavement of Africans was to some extent a borrowed practice, the available evidence for Maryland and Virginia points to less borrowing and to this kind of process: a mutually interactive growth of slavery and unfavorable assessment, with no cause for either which did not cause the other as well. If slavery caused prejudice, then invidious distinctions concerning working in the fields, bearing arms, and sexual union should have appeared *after* slavery's firm establishment. If prejudice caused slavery, then one would expect to find these lesser discriminations preceding the greater discrimination of outright enslavement. Taken as a whole, the evidence reveals a process of debasement of which hereditary lifetime service, while important, was not the only part.

Certainly it was the case in Maryland and Virginia that the legal enactment of Negro slavery followed social practice, rather than vice versa. In 1661 the Virginia Assembly indirectly provided statutory recognition that some Negroes served for life: "That in case any English servant shall run away in company with any negroes who are incapable of makeing satisfaction by addition of time," he must serve for the Negroes' lost time as well as his own. Maryland enacted a similar law in 1663, and in the following year came out with the categorical declaration that Negroes were to serve "Durante Vita"—for life. During the next twenty-odd years a succession of acts in both colonies defined with increasing precision what sorts of persons might be treated as slaves.

By about 1700 the slave ships began spilling forth their black cargoes in greater and greater numbers. By that time racial slavery and the necessary police powers had been written into law. By that time, too, slavery had lost all resemblance to a perpetual and hereditary version of English servitude, though service for life still seemed to contemporaries its most essential feature. In the last quarter of the seventeenth century the trend was to treat Negroes more like property and less like people, to send them to the fields at younger ages, to deny them automatic existence as inherent members of the community, to tighten the bonds on their personal and civil freedom, and correspondingly to loosen the traditional restraints on the master's freedom to deal with his human property as he saw fit. In 1705 Virginia gathered up the random statutes of a whole generation and baled them into a "slave code" which would not have been out of place in the nineteenth century.

The Un-English: Scots, Irish, and Indians

In the minds of overseas Englishmen, slavery, the new tyranny, did not apply to any Europeans. Something about Africans, and to lesser extent Indians, set them apart for drastic exploitation, oppression, and degradation. In order to discover why, it is useful to turn the problem inside out, to inquire why Englishmen in America did not treat any other peoples as they did Negroes. It is especially revealing to see how English settlers looked upon the Scotch (as they frequently called them) and the Irish, whom they often had opportunity and "reason" to enslave, and upon the Indians, whom they enslaved, though only, as it were, casually.

In the early years Englishmen treated the increasingly numerous settlers from other European countries, especially Scottish and Irish servants, with condescension and frequently with exploitive brutality. Englishmen seemed to regard their colonies as exclusively *English* preserves and to wish to protect English persons especially from the exploitation which inevitably accompanied settlement in the New World. In Barbados, for example, the assembly in 1661 denounced the kidnapping of youngsters for service in the colony in a law which applied only to "Children of the *English* Nation."

While Englishmen distinguished themselves from other peoples, they also distinguished *among* those different peoples who failed to be English. It seems almost as if Englishmen possessed a view of other peoples which placed the English nation at the center of widening concentric circles, each of which contained a people more alien than the one inside it. On occasion these social distances felt by Englishmen may be gauged with considerable precision, as in the sequence employed by the Committee for Trade and Foreign Plantations in a query to the governor of Connecticut in 1680: "What number of English, Scotch, Irish or Foreigners have . . . come yearly to . . . your Corporation. And also, what Blacks and Slaves have been brought in." Sometimes the English sense of distance seems to have been based upon a scale of values which would be thought of today in terms of nationality. At other times, though, the sense of foreignness seems to have been explicitly religious, as instanced by a letter from Barbados in 1667: "We have more than a good many Irish amongst us, therefore I am for the down right Scott, who I am certain will fight without a crucifix about his neck." It is scarcely surprising that hostility toward the numerous Irish servants should have been especially strong, for they were doubly damned as foreign and papist. Already, for Englishmen in the seventeenth century the Irish were a special case, and it required more than an ocean voyage to alter this perception.

As time went on Englishmen began to absorb the idea that their settlements in America were not going to remain exclusively English preserves. In 1671 Virginia began encouraging naturalization of legal aliens, so that they might enjoy "all such liberties, priviledges, immunities whatsoever, as a naturall borne Englishman is capable of," and Maryland accomplished the same end with private naturalization acts.

The necessity of peopling the colonies transformed the long-standing urge to discriminate among non-English peoples into a necessity. Which of the non-English were sufficiently different and foreign to warrant treating as "perpetual servants"? The need to answer this question did not mean, of course, that upon arrival in America the colonists immediately jettisoned their sense of distance from those persons they did not actually enslave. They discriminated against Welshmen and Scotsmen who, while admittedly "the best servants," were typically the servants of Englishmen. There was a considerably stronger tendency to discriminate against papist Irishmen, those "worst" servants, but never to make slaves of them. And here lay the crucial difference. Even the Scottish prisoners taken by Cromwell during the English Civil Wars—captives in a just war!—were never treated as slaves in England or the colonies.

Indians too seemed radically different from Englishmen, far more so than any Europeans. They were enslaved, like Africans, and so fell on the losing side of a crucial dividing line. It is easy to see why: whether considered in terms of religion, nationality, savagery, or geographical location, Indians seemed more like Negroes than like Englishmen. Given this resemblance the essential problem becomes why Indian slavery never became an important institution in the colonies. Why did Indian slavery remain numerically insignificant and typically incidental in character? Why were Indian slaves valued at much lower prices than Negroes? Why were Indians, as a kind of people, treated like Negroes and yet at the same time very differently?

Certain obvious factors made for important differentiations in the minds of the English colonists. As was the case with first confrontations in America and Africa, the different contexts of confrontation made Englishmen more interested in converting and civilizing Indians than Negroes. That this campaign in America too frequently degenerated into military campaigns of extermination did nothing to eradicate the initial distinction. Entirely apart from English intentions, the culture of the eastern American Indians probably meant that they were less readily enslavable than Africans. By comparison, they were less used to settled agriculture, and their own variety of slavery was probably even less similar to the chattel slavery which Englishmen practiced in America than was the domestic and political slavery of the various West African cultures. But it was the transformation of

English intentions in the wilderness which counted most heavily in the long run. The Bible and the treaty so often gave way to the clash of flintlock and tomahawk. The colonists' perceptions of the Indians came to be organized not only in pulpits and printshops but at the bloody cutting edge of the English thrust into the Indians' lands. Thus the most pressing and mundane circumstances worked to make Indians seem very different from Negroes. In the early years especially, Indians were in a position to mount murderous reprisals upon the English settlers, while the few scattered Africans were not. When English-Indian relations did not turn upon sheer power they rested on diplomacy. In many instances the colonists took careful precautions to prevent abuse of Indians belonging to friendly tribes. Most of the Indians enslaved by the English had their own tribal enemies to thank. It became common practice to ship Indian slaves to the West Indies where they could be exchanged for slaves who had no compatriots lurking on the outskirts of English settlements. In contrast, Negroes presented much less of a threat—at first.

Equally important, Negroes had to be dealt with as individuals— with supremely impartial anonymity, to be sure—rather than as nations. Englishmen wanted and had to live with "their" Negroes, as it were, side by side. Accordingly their impressions of blacks were forged in the heat of continual, inescapable personal contacts. There were few pressures urging Englishmen to treat Indians as integral constituents in their society, which Negroes were whether Englishmen liked or not. At a distance the Indian could be viewed with greater detachment and his characteristics acknowledged and approached more cooly and more rationally. At a distance too, Indians could retain the quality of nationality, a quality which Englishmen admired in themselves and expected in other peoples. Under contrasting circumstances in America, the Negro nations tended to become Negro people.

Here lay the rudiments of certain shadowy but persistent themes in what turned out to be a multiracial nation. Americans came to impute to the braves of the Indian "nations" an ungovernable individuality and at the same time to impart to Africans all the qualities of an eminently governable subnation, in which African tribal distinctions were assumed to be of no consequence. More immediately, Indians and Africans rapidly came to serve as two fixed points from which English settlers could triangulate their own position in

America; the separate meanings of *Indian* and *Negro* helped define the meaning of living in America. The Indian became for Americans a symbol of their American experience; it was no mere luck of the toss that placed the profile of an American Indian rather than an American Negro on the famous old five-cent piece. Confronting the Indian in America was a testing experience, common to all the colonies. Conquering the Indian symbolized and personified the conquest of the American difficulties, the surmounting of the wilderness. To push back the Indian was to prove the worth of one's own mission, to make straight in the desert a highway for civilization. With the Negro it was utterly different.

Racial Slavery: From Reasons to Rationale

And *difference,* surely, was the indispensable key to the degradation of Africans in English America. In scanning the problem of *why* Negroes were enslaved in America, certain constant elements in a complex situation can be readily, if roughly, identified. *It may be taken as given* that there would have been no enslavement without economic need, that is, without persistent demand for labor in underpopulated colonies. Of crucial importance, too, was the fact that Africans in America were relatively powerless. In themselves, however, these two elements will not explain the enslavement of Indians and Negroes. The pressing need in America was labor, and Irish, Scottish, and English servants were available. Most of them would have been helpless to ward off outright enslavement if their masters had thought themselves privileged to enslave them. As a group, though, masters did not think themselves so empowered. Only with Indians and Africans did Englishmen attempt so radical a deprivation of liberty—which brings the matter abruptly to the most difficult and imponderable question of all: what was it about Indians and Negroes which set them apart from Englishmen, which rendered them *different,* which made them special candidates for degradation?

To ask such questions is to inquire into the *content* of English attitudes, and unfortunately there is little evidence with which to build an answer. It may be said, however, that the heathen condition of Negroes seemed of considerable importance to English settlers in America—more so than to English voyagers upon the coasts of Africa—and that heathenism was associated in some settlers' minds with the condition of slavery. Clearly, though, this is not to say that

English colonists enslaved Africans merely because of religious difference. In the early years, the English settlers most frequently contrasted themselves with Negroes by the term *Christian,* though they also sometimes described themselves as *English.* Yet the concept embodied by the term *Christian* embraced so much more meaning than was contained in specific doctrinal affirmations that it is scarcely possible to assume on this basis that Englishmen set Negroes apart because they were heathen. The historical experience of the English people in the sixteenth century had made for fusion of religion and nationality; the qualities of being English and Christian had become so inseparably blended that it seemed perfectly consistent to the Virginia Assembly in 1670 to declare that "noe negroe or Indian though baptised and enjoyned their owne Freedome shall be capable of any such purchase of christians, but yet not debarred from buying any of their owne nation."

From the first, then, the concept embedded in the term *Christian* seems to have conveyed much of the idea and feeling of *we* as against *they:* to be Christian was to be civilized rather than barbarous, English rather than African, white rather than black. The term *Christian* itself proved to have remarkable elasticity, for by the end of the seventeenth century it was being used to define a kind of slavery which had altogether lost any connection with explicit religious difference. In the Virginia code of 1705, for example, the term sounded much more like a definition of race than of religion: "And for a further christian care and usage of all christian servants, *Be it also enacted . . .* That no negroes, mulattos, or Indians, although christians, or Jews, Moors, Mahometans, or other infidels, shall, at any time, purchase any christian servant, nor any other, except of their own complexion, or such as are declared slaves by this act." By this time "Christianity" had somehow become intimately and explicitly linked with "complexion." The 1705 statute declared "That all servants imported and brought into this country, by sea or land, who were not christians in their native country . . . shall be accounted and be slaves, and as such be here bought and sold notwithstanding a conversion to christianity afterwards." As late as 1753 the Virginia slave code anachronistically defined slavery in terms of religion when everyone knew that slavery had for generations been based on the racial and not the religious difference.

It is worth making still closer scrutiny of the terminology which

Englishmen employed when referring both to themselves and to the two peoples they enslaved, for this terminology affords the best single means of probing the content of their sense of difference. The terms *Indian* and *Negro* were both borrowed from the Hispanic languages, the one originally deriving from (mistaken) geographical locality and the other from human complexion. When referring to the Indians the English colonists either used that proper name or called them *savages,* a term which reflected primarily their view of Indians as uncivilized. In significant contrast, the colonists referred to *negroes,* and by the eighteenth century to *blacks* and to *Africans*, but almost never to African *heathens* or *pagans* or *savages.* Most suggestive of all, there seems to have been something of a shift during the seventeenth century in the terminology which Englishmen in the colonies applied to themselves. From the initially most common term *Christian,* at mid-century there was a marked shift toward the terms *English* and *free.* After about 1680, taking the colonies as a whole, a new term of self-identification appeared—*white.*

So far as the weight of analysis may be imposed upon such terms, diminishing reliance upon *Christian* suggests a gradual muting of the specifically religious elements in the Christian-Negro distinction in favor of secular nationality: Negroes were, in 1667, "not in all respects to be admitted to a full fruition of the exemptions and impunities of the English." As time went on, as some Negroes became assimilated to the English colonial culture, as more "raw Africans" arrived, and as increasing numbers of non-English Europeans were attracted to the colonies, English colonists turned increasingly to what they saw as the striking physiognomic difference. In Maryland a revised law prohibiting miscegenation (1692) retained *white* and *English* but dropped the term *Christian*—a symptomatic modification. By the end of the seventeenth century dark complexion had become an independent rationale for enslavement: in 1709 Samuel Sewall noted in his diary that a "Spaniard" had petitioned the Massachusetts Council for freedom but that "Capt. Teat alledg'd that all of that Color were Slaves." Here was a barrier between "we" and "they" which was visible and permanent: the black man could not become a white man. Not, at least, as yet.

What had occurred was not a change in the justification of slavery from religion to race. No such justifications were made. There seems to have been, within the unarticulated concept of the Negro as a different sort of person, a subtle but highly significant shift in emphasis. A perception of Negro heathenism remained through the eighteenth and into the nineteenth and even the twentieth century, and an awareness, at very least, of the African's different appearance was present from the beginning. The shift was an alteration in emphasis within a single concept of difference rather than a development of a novel conceptualization. Throughout the colonies the terms *Christian, free, English,* and *white* were for many years employed indiscriminately as synonyms. A Maryland law of 1681 used all four terms in one short paragraph.

Whatever the limitations of terminology as an index to thought and feeling, it seems likely that the English colonists' initial sense of difference from Africans was founded not on a single characteristic but on a cluster of qualities which, taken as a whole, seemed to set the Negro apart. Virtually every quality in "the Negro" invited pejorative feelings. What may have been his two most striking characteristics, his heathenism and his appearance, were probably prerequisite to his complete debasement. His heathenism alone could not have led to permanent enslavement since conversion easily wiped out that failing. If his appearance, his racial characteristics, meant nothing to the English settler, it is difficult to see how slavery based on race ever emerged, how the concept of complexion as the mark of slavery ever entered the colonists' minds. Even if the English colonists were most unfavorably struck by the Negro's color, though, blackness itself did not urge the complete debasement of slavery. Other cultural qualities—the strangeness of his language, gestures, eating habits, and so on—certainly must have contributed to the English colonists' sense that he was very different, perhaps disturbingly so. In Africa these qualities had for Englishmen added up to *savagery;* they were major components in that sense of *difference* which provided the mental margin absolutely requisite for placing the European on the deck of the slave ship and the African in the hold.

The available evidence (what little there is) suggests that for Englishmen settling in America, the specific religious difference was initially of greater importance than color, certainly of much greater relative importance than for the Englishmen who confronted Negroes in their African homeland. Perhaps Englishmen in Virginia, tanning seasonally under a hot sun and in almost daily contact with tawny Indians, found the Negro's color less arresting than they might have in other circumstances. Perhaps, too, these first Virginians sensed how inadequately they had reconstructed the institutions and practices of Christian piety in the wilderness; they would perhaps appear less as failures to themselves in this respect if compared to persons who as Christians were *totally* defective. Perhaps, though, the Jamestown settlers were told in 1619 by the Dutch shipmaster that these "negars" were heathens and could be treated as such. We do not know. The available data will not bear all the weight that the really crucial questions impose.

Of course once the cycle of degradation was fully under way, once slavery and racial discrimination were completely linked together, once the engine of oppression was in full operation, then there is no need to plead lack of knowledge. By the end of the seventeenth century in all the colonies of the English empire there was chattel racial slavery of a kind which would have seemed familiar to men living in the nineteenth century. No Elizabethan Englishman would have found it familiar, though certain strands of thought and feeling in Elizabethan England had intertwined with reports about the Spanish and Portuguese to engender a willingness on the part of English settlers in the New World to treat some men as suitable for private exploitation. During the seventeenth century New World conditions had enlarged this predisposition, so much so that English colonials of the eighteenth century were faced with full-blown slavery—something they thought of not as an institution but as a host of ever-present problems, dangers, and opportunities.

II THE DEVELOPMENT OF AMERICAN SLAVERY

Edmund S. Morgan

SLAVERY AND FREEDOM: THE AMERICAN PARADOX

This selection by Edmund S. Morgan of Yale University both complements and expands upon Jordan's study of the origins of slavery. Morgan, who focuses on seventeenth-century Virginia, concedes Jordan's argument that racial prejudice predated the colonization process. But he believes that slavery became a fixed American institution only in the late seventeenth century when Virginia's harried ruling classes realized "the social benefits of an enslaved labor force." In Morgan's view, this solution may have paradoxically nourished representative government in colonial Virginia. This selection is drawn from Morgan's address to the Organization of American Historians.

The story properly begins in England with the burst of population growth there that sent the number of Englishmen from perhaps three million in 1500 to four-and-one-half million by 1650. The increase did not occur in response to any corresponding growth in the capacity of the island's economy to support its people. And the result was precisely that misery which Madison pointed out to Jefferson as the consequence of "a high degree of populousness." Sixteenth-century England knew the same kind of unemployment and poverty that Jefferson witnessed in eighteenth-century France and Fletcher in seventeenth-century Scotland. Alarming numbers of idle and hungry men drifted about the country looking for work or plunder. The government did what it could to make men of means hire them, but it also adopted increasingly severe measures against their wandering, their thieving, their roistering, and indeed their very existence. Whom the workhouses and prisons could not swallow the gallows would have to, or perhaps the army. When England had military expeditions to conduct abroad, every parish packed off its most unwanted inhabitants to the almost certain death that awaited them from the diseases of the camp.

As the mass of idle rogues and beggars grew and increasingly threatened the peace of England, the efforts to cope with them increasingly threatened the liberties of Englishmen. Englishmen

From Edmund S. Morgan, "Slavery and Freedom: The American Paradox," *Journal of American History* 59 (June 1972): 14-29. Reprinted by permission. Footnotes omitted.

prided themselves on a "gentle government," a government that had been releasing its subjects from old forms of bondage and endowing them with new liberties, making the "rights of Englishmen" a phrase to conjure with. But there was nothing gentle about the government's treatment of the poor; and as more Englishmen became poor, other Englishmen had less to be proud of. Thoughtful men could see an obvious solution: get the surplus Englishmen out of England. Send them to the New World, where there were limitless opportunities for work. There they would redeem themselves, enrich the mother country, and spread English liberty abroad.

The great publicist for this program was Richard Hakluyt. His *Principall Navigations, Voiages and Discoveries of the English nation* was not merely the narrative of voyages by Englishmen around the globe, but a powerful suggestion that the world ought to be English or at least ought to be ruled by Englishmen. Hakluyt's was a dream of empire, but of benevolent empire, in which England would confer the blessings of her own free government on the less fortunate peoples of the world. It is doubtless true that Englishmen, along with other Europeans, were already imbued with prejudice against men of darker complexions than their own. And it is also true that the principal beneficiaries of Hakluyt's empire would be Englishmen. But Hakluyt's dream cannot be dismissed as mere hypocrisy any more than Jefferson's affirmation of human equality can be so dismissed. Hakluyt's compassion for the poor and oppressed was not confined to the English poor, and in Francis Drake's exploits in the Caribbean Hakluyt saw, not a thinly disguised form of piracy, but a model for English liberation of men of all colors who labored under the tyranny of the Spaniard.

Drake had gone ashore at Panama in 1572 and made friends with an extraordinary band of runaway Negro slaves. "Cimarrons" they were called, and they lived a free and hardy life in the wilderness, periodically raiding the Spanish settlements to carry off more of their people. They discovered in Drake a man who hated the Spanish as much as they did and who had the arms and men to mount a stronger attack than they could manage by themselves. Drake wanted Spanish gold, and the Cimarrons wanted Spanish iron for tools. They both wanted Spanish deaths. The alliance was a natural one and apparently untroubled by racial prejudice. Together the English and the Cimarrons robbed the mule train carrying the annual supply of

Peruvian treasure across the isthmus. And before Drake sailed for England with his loot, he arranged for future meetings. When Hakluyt heard of this alliance, he concocted his first colonizing proposal, a scheme for seizing the Straits of Magellan and transporting Cimarrons there, along with surplus Englishmen. The straits would be a strategic strong point for England's world empire, since they controlled the route from Atlantic to Pacific. Despite the severe climate of the place, the Cimarrons and their English friends would all live warmly together, clad in English woolens, "well lodged and by our nation made free from the tyrannous Spanyard, and quietly and courteously governed by our nation."

The scheme for a colony in the Straits of Magellan never worked out, but Hakluyt's vision endured, of liberated natives and surplus Englishmen, courteously governed in English colonies around the world. Sir Walter Raleigh caught the vision. He dreamt of wresting the treasure of the Incas from the Spaniard by allying with the Indians of Guiana and sending Englishmen to live with them, lead them in rebellion against Spain, and govern them in the English manner. Raleigh also dreamt of a similar colony in the country he named Virginia. Hakluyt helped him plan it. And Drake stood ready to supply Negroes and Indians, liberated from Spanish tyranny in the Caribbean, to help the enterprise.

Virginia from the beginning was conceived not only as a haven for England's suffering poor, but as a spearhead of English liberty in an oppressed world. That was the dream; but when it began to materialize at Roanoke Island in 1585, something went wrong. Drake did his part by liberating Spanish Caribbean slaves, and carrying to Roanoke those who wished to join him. But the English settlers whom Raleigh sent there proved unworthy of the role assigned them. By the time Drake arrived they had shown themselves less than courteous to the Indians on whose assistance they depended. The first group of settlers murdered the chief who befriended them, and then gave up and ran for home aboard Drake's returning ships. The second group simply disappeared, presumably killed by the Indians.

What was lost in this famous lost colony was more than the band of colonists who have never been traced. What was also lost and never quite recovered in subsequent ventures was the dream of Englishman and Indian living side by side in peace and liberty. When the English finally planted a permanent colony at Jamestown they came as conquerors, and their government was far from gentle. The Indians willing to endure it were too few in numbers and too broken in spirit to play a significant part in the settlement.

Without their help, Virginia offered a bleak alternative to the workhouse or the gallows for the first English poor who were transported there. During the first two decades of the colony's existence, most of the arriving immigrants found precious little English liberty in Virginia. But by the 1630s the colony seemed to be working out, at least in part, as its first planners had hoped. Impoverished Englishmen were arriving every year in large numbers, engaged to serve the existing planters for a term of years, with the prospect of setting up their own households a few years later. The settlers were spreading up Virginia's great rivers, carving out plantations, living comfortably from their corn fields and from the cattle they ranged in the forests, and at the same time earning perhaps ten or twelve pounds a year per man from the tobacco they planted. A representative legislative assembly secured the traditional liberties of Englishmen and enabled a larger proportion of the population to participate in their own government than had ever been the case in England. The colony even began to look a little like the cosmopolitan haven of liberty that Hakluyt had first envisaged. Men of all countries appeared there: French, Spanish, Dutch, Turkish, Portuguese, and African. Virginia took them in and began to make Englishmen out of them.

It seems clear that most of the Africans, perhaps all of them, came as slaves, a status that had become obsolete in England, while it was becoming the expected condition of Africans outside Africa and of a good many inside. It is equally clear that a substantial number of Virginia's Negroes were free or became free. And all of them, whether servant, slave, or free, enjoyed most of the same rights and duties as other Virginians. There is no evidence during the period before 1660 that they were subjected to a more severe discipline than other servants. They could sue and be sued in court. They did penance in the parish church for having illegitimate children. They earned money of their own, bought and sold and raised cattle of their own. Sometimes they bought their own freedom. In other cases, masters bequeathed them not only freedom but land, cattle, and houses. Northampton, the only county for which full records exist, had at least ten free Negro households by 1668.

As Negroes took their place in the community, they learned English ways, including even the truculence toward authority that has always been associated with the rights of Englishmen. Tony Longo, a free Negro of Northampton, when served a warrant to appear as a witness in court, responded with a scatological opinion of warrants, called the man who served it an idle rascal, and told him to go about his business. The man offered to go with him at any time before a justice of the peace so that his evidence could be recorded. He would go with him at night, tomorrow, the next day, next week, any time. But Longo was busy getting in his corn. He dismissed all pleas with a "Well, well, Ile goe when my Corne is in," and refused to receive the warrant.

The judges understandably found this to be contempt of court; but it was the kind of contempt that free Englishmen often showed to authority, and it was combined with a devotion to work that English moralists were doing their best to inculate more widely in England. As England had absorbed people of every nationality over the centuries and turned them into Englishmen, Virginia's Englishmen were absorbing their own share of foreigners, including Negroes, and seemed to be successfully moulding a New World community on the English model.

But a closer look will show that the situation was not quite so promising as at first it seems. It is well known that Virginia is its first fifteen or twenty years killed off most of the men who went there. It is less well known that it continued to do so. If my estimate of the volume of immigration is anywhere near correct, Virginia must have been a death trap for at least another fifteen years and probably for twenty or twenty-five. In 1625 the population stood at 1,300 or 1,400; in 1640 it was about 8,000. In the fifteen years between those dates at least 15,000 persons must have come to the colony. If so, 15,000 immigrants increased the population by less than 7,000. There is no evidence of a large return migration. It seems probable that the death rate throughout this period was comparable only to that found in Europe during the peak years of a plague. Virginia, in other words, was absorbing England's surplus laborers mainly by killing them. The success of those who survived and rose from servant to planter must be attributed partly to the fact that so few did survive.

After 1640, when the diseases responsible for the high death rate began to decline and the population began a quick rise, it became increasingly difficult for an indigent immigrant to pull himself up in the world. The population probably passed 25,000 by 1662, hardly what Madison would have called a high degree of populousness. Yet the rapid rise brought serious trouble for Virginia. It brought the engrossment of tidewater land in thousands and tens of thousands of acres by speculators, who recognized that the demand would rise. It brought a huge expansion of tobacco production, which helped to depress the price of tobacco and the earnings of the men who planted it. It brought efforts by planters to prolong the terms of servants, since they were now living longer and therefore had a longer expectancy of usefulness.

It would, in fact, be difficult to assess all the consequences of the increased longevity; but for our purposes one development was crucial, and that was the appearance in Virginia of a growing number of freemen who had served their terms but who were now unable to afford land of their own except on the fontiers or in the interior. In years when tobacco prices were especially low or crops especially poor, men who had been just scraping by were obliged to go back to work for their larger neighbors simply in order to stay alive. By 1676 it was estimated that one-fourth of Virginia's freemen were without land of their own. And in the same year Francis Moryson, a member of the governor's council, explained the term "freedmen" as used in Virginia to mean "persons without house and land," implying that this was now the normal condition of servants who had attained freedom.

Some of them resigned themselves to working for wages; others preferred a meager living on dangerous frontier land or a hand-to-mouth existence, roaming from one county to another, renting a bit of land here, squatting on some there, dodging the tax collector, drinking, quarreling, stealing hogs, and enticing servants to run away with them.

The presence of this growing class of poverty-stricken Virginians was not a little frightening to the planters who had made it to the top or who had arrived in the colony already at the top, with ample supplies of servants and capital. They were caught in a dilemma. They wanted the immigrants who kept pouring in every year. Indeed they needed them and prized them the more as they lived longer. But as more and more turned free each year, Virginia seemed to have inherited the problem that she was helping England to solve.

Virginia, complained Nicholas Spencer, secretary of the colony, was "a sinke to drayen England of her filth and scum."

The men who worried the uppercrust looked even more danger-ous in Virginia than they had in England. They were, to begin with, young, because it was young persons that the planters wanted for work in the fields; and the young have always seemed impatient of control by their elders and superiors, if not downright rebellious. They were also predominantly single men. Because the planters did not think women, or at least English women, fit for work in the fields, men outnumbered women among immigrants by three or four to one throughout the century. Consequently most of the freedmen had no wife or family to tame their wilder impulses and serve as hostages to the respectable world.

Finally, what made these wild young men particularly dangerous was that they were armed and had to be armed. Life in Virginia required guns. The plantations were exposed to attack from Indians by land and from privateers and petty-thieving pirates by sea. Whenever England was at war with the French or the Dutch, the settlers had to be ready to defend themselves. In 1667 the Dutch in a single raid captured twenty merchant ships in the James River, to-gether with the English warship that was supposed to be defending them; and in 1673 they captured eleven more. On these occasions Governor William Berkeley gathered the planters in arms and at least prevented the enemy from making a landing. But while he stood off the Dutch he worried about the ragged crew at his back. Of the able-bodied men in the colony he estimated that "at least one third are Single freedmen (whose Labour will hardly maintaine them) or men much in debt, both which wee may reasonably expect upon any Small advantage the Enemy may gaine upon us, wold revolt to them in hopes of bettering their Condicion by Shareing the Plunder of the Country with them."

Berkeley's fears were justified. Three years later, sparked not by a Dutch invasion but by an Indian attack, rebellion swept Virginia. It began almost as Berkeley had predicted, when a group of volunteer Indian fighters turned from a fruitless expedition against the Indians to attack their rulers. Bacon's Rebellion was the largest popular rising in the colonies before the American Revolution. Sooner or later nearly everyone in Virginia got in on it, but it began in the frontier counties of Henrico and New Kent, among men whom the governor and his friends consistently characterized as rabble. As it spread eastward, it turned out that there were rabble everywhere, and Berkeley understandably raised his estimate of their numbers. "How miserable that man is," he exclaimed, "that Governes a People wher six parts of seaven at least are Poore Endebted Discontented and Armed."

Virginia's poor had reason to be envious and angry against the men who owned the land and imported the servants and ran the government. But the rebellion produced no real program of reform, no ideology, not even any revolutionary slogans. It was a search for plunder, not for principles. And when the rebels had redistributed whatever wealth they could lay their hands on, the rebellion subsided almost as quickly as it had begun.

It had been a shattering experience, however, for Virginia's first families. They had seen each other fall in with the rebels in order to save their skins or their possessions or even to share in the plunder. When it was over, they eyed one another distrustfully, on the lookout for any new Bacons in their midst, who might be tempted to lead the still restive rabble on more plundering expeditions. When William Byrd and Laurence Smith proposed to solve the problems of defense against the Indians by establishing semi-independent buffer settlements on the upper reaches of the rivers, in each of which they would engage to keep fifty men in arms, the assembly at first reacted favorably. But it quickly occurred to the governor and council that this would in fact mean gathering a crowd of Virginia's wild bachelors and furnishing them with an abundant supply of arms and ammunition. Byrd had himself led such a crowd in at least one plundering foray during the rebellion. To put him or anyone else in charge of a large and permanent gang of armed men was to invite them to descend again on the people whom they were supposed to be protecting.

The nervousness of those who had property worth plundering continued throughout the century, spurred in 1682 by the tobacco-cutting riots in which men roved about destroying crops in the fields, in the desperate hope of producing a shortage that would raise the price of the leaf. And periodically in nearby Maryland and North Carolina, where the same conditions existed as in Virginia, there were tumults that threatened to spread to Virginia.

As Virginia thus acquired a social problem analogous to England's own, the colony began to deal with it as England had done, by restricting the liberties of those who did not have the proper badge of freedom, namely the property that government was supposed to protect. One way was to extend the terms of service for servants entering the colony without indentures. Formerly they had served until twenty-one; now the age was advanced to twenty-four. There had always been laws requiring them to serve extra time for running away; now the laws added corporal punishment and, in order to make habitual offenders more readily recognizable, specified that their hair be cropped. New laws restricted the movement of servants on the highways and also increased the amount of extra time to be served for running away. In addition to serving two days for every day's absence, the captured runaway was now frequently required to compensate by labor for the loss to the crop that he had failed to tend and for the cost of his apprehension, including rewards paid for his capture. A three week's holiday might result in a year's extra service. If a servant struck his master, he was to serve another year. For killing a hog he had to serve the owner a year and the informer another year. Since the owner of the hog, and the owner of the servant, and the informer were frequently the same man, and since a hog was worth at best less than one-tenth the hire of a servant for a year, the law was very profitable to masters. One Lancaster master was awarded six years' extra service from a servant who killed three of his hogs, worth about thirty shillings.

The effect of these measures was to keep servants for as long as possible from gaining their freedom, especially the kind of servants who were most likely to cause trouble. At the same time the engrossment of land was driving many back to servitude after a brief taste of freedom. Freedmen who engaged to work for wages by so doing became servants again, subject to most of the same restrictions as other servants.

Nevertheless, in spite of all the legal and economic pressures to keep men in service, the ranks of the freedmen grew, and so did poverty and discontent. To prevent the wild bachelors from gaining an influence in the government, the assembly in 1670 limited voting to landholders and householders. But to disfranchise the growing mass of single freemen was not to deprive them of the weapons they had wielded so effectively under Nathaniel Bacon. It is questionable how far Virginia could safely have continued along this course, meeting discontent with repression and manning her plantations with annual importations of servants who would later add to the unruly ranks of the free. To be sure, the men at the bottom might have had both land and liberty, as the settlers of some other colonies did, if Virginia's frontier had been safe from Indians, or if the men at the top had been willing to forego some of their profits and to give up some of the lands they had engrossed. The English government itself made efforts to break up the great holdings that had helped to create the problem. But it is unlikely that the policy-makers in Whitehall would have contended long against the successful.

In any case they did not have to. There was another solution, which allowed Virginia's magnates to keep their lands, yet arrested the discontent and the repression of other Englishmen, a solution which strengthened the rights of Englishmen and nourished that attachment to liberty which came to fruition in the Revolutionary generation of Virginia statesmen. But the solution put an end to the process of turning Africans into Englishmen. The rights of Englishmen were preserved by destroying the rights of Africans.

I do not mean to argue that Virginians deliberately turned to African Negro slavery as a means of preserving and extending the rights of Englishmen. Winthrop Jordan has suggested that slavery came to Virginia as an unthinking decision. We might go further and say that it came without a decision. It came automatically as Virginians bought the cheapest labor they could get. Once Virginia's heavy mortality ceased, an investment in slave labor was much more profitable than an investment in free labor; and the planters bought slaves as rapidly as traders made them available. In the last years of the seventeenth century they bought them in such numbers that slaves probably already constituted a majority or nearly a majority of the labor force by 1700. The demand was so great that traders for a time found a better market in Virginia than in Jamaica or Barbados. But the social benefits of an enslaved labor force, even if not consciously sought or recognized at the time by the men who bought the slaves, were larger than the economic benefits. The increase in the importation of slaves was matched by a decrease in the importation of indentured servants and consequently a decrease in the dangerous number of new freedmen who annually emerged seeking a place in society that they would be unable to achieve.

If Africans had been unavailable, it would probably have proved impossible to devise a way to keep a continuing supply of English immigrants in their place. There was a limit beyond which the abridgment of English liberties would have resulted not merely in rebellion but in protests from England and in the cutting off of the supply of further servants. At the time of Bacon's Rebellion the English commission of investigation had shown more sympathy with the rebels than with the well-to-do planters who had engrossed Virginia's lands. To have attempted the enslavement of English-born laborers would have caused more disorder than it cured. But to keep as slaves black men who arrived in that condition *was* possible and apparently regarded as plain common sense.

The attitude of English officials was well expressed by the attorney who reviewed for the Privy Council the slave codes established in Barbados in 1679. He found the laws of Barbados to be well designed for the good of his majesty's subjects there, for, he said, "although Negros in that Island are punishable in a different and more severe manner than other Subjects are for Offences of the like nature; yet I humbly conceive that the Laws there concerning Negros are reasonable Laws, for by reason of their numbers they become dangerous, and being a brutish sort of People and reckoned as goods and chattels in that Island, it is of necessity or at least convenient to have Laws for the Government of them different from the Laws of England, to prevent the great mischief that otherwise may happen to the Planters and Inhabitants in that Island." In Virginia too it seemed convenient and reasonable to have different laws for black and white. As the number of slaves increased, the assembly passed laws that carried forward with much greater severity the trend already under way in the colony's labor laws. But the new severity was reserved for people without white skin. The laws specifically exonerated the master who accidentally beat his slave to death, but they placed new limitations on his punishment of "Christian white servants."

Virginians worried about the risk of having in their midst a body of men who had every reason to hate them. The fear of a slave insurrection hung over them for nearly two centuries. But the danger from slaves actually proved to be less than that which the colony had faced from its restive and armed freedmen. Slaves had none of the rising expectations that so often produce human discontent. No one had told them that they had rights. They had been nurtured in heathen societies where they had lost their freedom; their children would be nurtured in a Christian society and never know freedom.

Moreover, slaves were less troubled by the sexual imbalance that helped to make Virginia's free laborers so restless. In an enslaved labor force women could be required to make tobacco just as the men did; and they also made children, who in a few years would be an asset to their master. From the beginning, therefore, traders imported women in a much higher ratio to men than was the case among English servants, and the level of discontent was correspondingly reduced. Virginians did not doubt that discontent would remain, but it could be repressed by methods that would not have been considered reasonable, convenient, or even safe, if applied to Englishmen. Slaves could be deprived of opportunities for association and rebellion. They could be kept unarmed and unorganized. They could be subjected to savage punishments by their owners without fear of legal reprisals. And since their color disclosed their probable status, the rest of society could keep close watch on them. It is scarcely surprising that no slave insurrection in American history approached Bacon's Rebellion in its extent or in its success.

Nor is it surprising that Virginia's freedmen never again posed a threat to society. Though in later years slavery was condemned because it was thought to compete with free labor, in the beginning it reduced by so much the number of freedmen who would otherwise have competed with each other. When the annual increment of freedmen fell off, the number that remained could more easily find an independent place in society, especially as the danger of Indian attack diminished and made settlement safer at the heads of the rivers or on the Carolina frontier. There might still remain a number of irredeemable, idle, and unruly freedmen, particularly among the convicts whom England exported to the colonies. But the numbers were small enough, so that they could be dealt with by the old expedient of drafting them for military expeditions. The way was thus made easier for the remaining freedmen to acquire property, maybe acquire a slave or two of their own, and join with their superiors in the enjoyment of those English liberties that differentiated them from their black laborers.

A free society divided between large landholders and small was much less riven by antagonisms than one divided between landholders and landless, masterless men. With the freedman's expectations, sobriety, and status restored, he was no longer a man to be feared. That fact, together with the presence of a growing mass of alien slaves, tended to draw the white settlers closer together and to reduce the importance of the class difference between yeoman farmer and large plantation owner.

The seventeenth century has sometimes been thought of as the day of the yeoman farmer in Virginia; but in many ways a stronger case can be made for the eighteenth century as the time when the yeoman farmer came into his own, because slavery relieved the small man of the pressures that had been reducing him to continued servitude. Such an interpretation conforms to the political development of the colony. During the seventeenth century the royally appointed governor's council, composed of the largest property owners in the colony, had been the most powerful governing body. But as the tide of slavery rose between 1680 and 1720 Virginia moved toward a government in which the yeoman farmer had a larger share. In spite of the rise of Virginia's great families on the black tide, the power of the council declined; and the elective House of Burgesses became the dominant organ of government. Its members nurtured a closer relationship with their yeoman constituency than had earlier been the case. And in its chambers Virginians developed the ideas they so fervently asserted in the Revolution: ideas about taxation, representation, and the rights of Englishmen, and ideas about the prerogatives and powers and sacred calling of the independent, propertyholding yeoman farmer—commonwealth ideas.

In the eighteenth century, because they were no longer threatened by a dangerous free laboring class, Virginians could afford these ideas, whereas in Berkeley's time they could not. Berkeley himself was obsessed with the experience of the English civil wars and the danger of rebellion. He despised and feared the New Englanders for their association with the Puritans who had made England, however briefly, a commonwealth. He was proud that Virginia, unlike New England, had no free schools and no printing press, because books and schools bred heresy and sedition. He must have taken satisfaction in the fact that when his people did rebel against him under Bacon, they generated no republican ideas, no philosophy of rebellion or of human rights. Yet a century later, without benefit of rebellions, Virginians had learned republican lessons, had introduced schools and printing presses, and were as ready as New Englanders to recite the aphorisms of the commonwealthmen.

It was slavery, I suggest, more than any other single factor, that had made the difference, slavery that enabled Virginia to nourish representative government in a plantation society, slavery that transformed the Virginia of Governor Berkeley to the Virginia of Jefferson, slavery that made the Virginians dare to speak a political language that magnified the rights of freemen, and slavery, therefore, that brought Virginians into the same commonwealth political tradition with New Englanders. The very institution that was to divide North and South after the Revolution may have made possible their union in a republican government. . . .

Peter H. Wood

MOUNTING ANXIETY AMONG WHITES

Like Morgan, Peter H. Wood believes that late-seventeenth- and eighteenth-century events played a crucial part in establishing the basic patterns of American slavery. In his study of colonial South Carolina, Wood analyzes the reaction of whites to the growing number of slaves. His analysis reveals the complex relationship between economic interests and social attitudes; slavery became a structure of social control as well as an economic system. Professor Wood, who teaches at Duke University, won the Beveridge Award of the American Historical Association for the best book on the history of the United States, Canada, or Latin America for his 1974 publication, The Black Majority: Negroes in Colonial South Carolina from 1670 through the Stono Rebellion, *from which the following selection is taken.*

I

For Europeans, fears and fantasies based on skin color had predated the entire process of overseas colonization.[1] The formation of a

From *Black Majority: Negroes in Colonial South Carolina from 1670 through the Stono Rebellion,* by Peter H. Wood, pp. 218–37. Reprinted by permission of Alfred A. Knopf, Inc.

[1] Jordan, *White Over Black,* Chapter I.

settlement such as that in South Carolina in no way automatically intensified these fears. Far from being augmented and elaborated in the new colony, certain European anxieties may have dissipated before the realistic demands of life on a thoroughly interracial frontier. But in the face of a distinct majority of blacks, the apprehensions felt by white colonists gradually deepened. Concern stemmed first from a simple awareness of numbers, but it spread out to encompass a variety of ambiguities concerning the identity of the colony and the tenuous position of the Europeans who were ostensibly its masters.

Not even straightforward population awareness came easily, for numbers, after all, are a highly subjective matter. Even after the systematic enumeration of slaves had begun, it was hard for Europeans to come to terms directly with the demographic situation which was so thoroughly apparent around them. The way local population figures were analyzed and altered suggests the dimensions of this uneasiness. The number of blacks, first of all, was simply exaggerated. And not only newcomers struck by the contrast with Europe but also residents of long standing misrepresented conditions. Samuel Wragg, the owner of land in St. George's Parish and elsewhere and a magnate in South Carolina commerce for nearly two decades, testified before the Commissioners for Trade and Plantations in 1726 that "that country formerly had but very few negroes, but now they employ near 40,000," fully twice the number actually enslaved. Though 1726 was the first year in which black arrivals approached 1,000, Wragg minimized his own role in Carolina's African trade by claiming that "they now *usually* import 1,000 per annum."[2] Several years later John Peter Purry wrongly estimated "above 40,000 Negroes."[3] And in 1734, as annual slave imports were passing 2,000 for the first time, Capt. Von Reck could claim "there are imported generally 3,000 fresh Negroes every Year."[4]

A further confusion arose from the tendency to measure white male adults against the entire black population. This statistic took on increasing importance for European colonists as they felt themselves

---

[2] Hearing before the Board of Trade, May 4, 1726, in *Journal of the Commissioners for Trade and Plantations* (London, 1928), pp. 251–54, italics added. Cf. Wood, "Black Majority," p. 369 *n.* For a useful cautionary statement on these matters, see Curtin, *Atlantic Slave Trade,* Chapter I.

[3] Purry, "A Description of the Province of South Carolina, . . . 1731," rpt. in Force, *Tracts,* II, 6.

[4] "Extracts of Mr. Von Reck's Journal," in Force, *Tracts,* IV, 9.

physically threatened by the number of Africans, and numerous population estimates after 1720, contrasting men on the muster rolls with all adults and children in the slave quarters, reflect the emerging concept of white manhood opposing a preponderant race. This explains why Von Reck stated in 1734 that "There are five Negroes to one White."[5] It also helps make understandable (although not correct) the assertion of a European in 1737 that "In Charleston and that neighborhood there are calculated to be always 20 blacks . . . to one white man,"[6] as well as the claim of another visitor five years later that "the heathen slaves are so numerous here that it is estimated that there are fifteen for every white man."[7]

Even after framing the disproportion in its starkest form, white colonists faced the added realization that the slave population was being augmented annually while their own numbers scarcely rose. Indeed, an Anglican minister noted in 1725, "we have some reason to believe that we rather decrease than increase in the small number of Christian white inhabitants." He went on to explain candidly, "As matters stand with us we make use of a wile for our present security to make the Indians and negros a check upon each other lest by their vastly superior numbers we should be crushed by one or the other."[8] Slaves, who had generally been taken as an asset in the thinly settled proprietary colony, were now viewed in part by whites as a liability. First of all, the presence of an enslaved majority anxious for liberation increased the chances of invasions by foreign powers and reduced the colony's ability to resist such attacks. And moreover, quite apart from the inducement which the slaves provided to foreign enemies, they constituted a rebellious threat in their own right.

Two weeks after South Carolina became a crown colony in 1720, a document drawn at Whitehall described the settlement as being in "great disorder," pointing out that "the Inhabitants are exposed to

[5] Ibid.

[6] Samuel Dyssli to friends in Switzerland, Dec. 3, 1737, *SCHGM*, XXII (1922), 90.

[7] *Muhlenberg*, I, 58. On a later visit to Charlestown, Sept. 8, 1774, this prominent minister recorded (II, 567) "At first it strikes one as strange to see so many Negro slaves, for here, it is said, there are twenty blacks for every white man."

[8] Richard Ludlam to David Humphreys, Goose Creek, March 22, 1725, quoted in Klingberg, *Appraisal*, p. 47. Ludlam continued: "This I imagine one cause that intimidates the planters from being willing that their sensible slaves should be converted to Christianity lest as they allege they should make such an ill use of meeting to do their duty to God as to take the opportunity at such times of seizing and destroying their owners."

incursions of the Barbarous Indians" and "the Encroachments of their European Neighbours," and adding that "ye whole Province was lately in danger of being massacred by their Own Slaves, who are too numerous in proportion to ye White Men there."[9] The white colonists, observed Sir Alexander Cuming in 1730 after six months in the province, "are in danger of the Blacks Riseing up against them, who are Six times the Number of the Whites [that is, white adult males]." Cuming blamed this state of affairs upon "the Mutinous Disposition of their Masters," almost all of whom conceded the colony "to be in a miserable Condition but being divided in their Measures and particular Interests No two of them can agree in any common Measure for their Relief."[10] Four years later, Von Reck's report contained this ominous appraisal:

> There are computed to be 30,000 Negroes in this Province, all of them Slaves, and their Posterity for ever: They work six Days in the Week for their Masters without pay, and are allowed to work on Sundays for themselves. . . . Being thus used, lays amongst them a Foundation of Discontent; and they are generally thought to watch an Opportunity of revolting against their Masters, as they have lately done in the Island of St. John and of St. Thomas, belonging to the Danes and Sweeds; and it is the Apprehension of these and other Inconveniences, that has induced the Honourable Trustees of Georgia, to prohibit the Importation and Use of Negroes within their Colony.[11]

II

As Capt. Von Reck's report makes clear, scraps of news from abroad regarding perils inherent within the slave system were closely watched by Europeans in Carolina. Incidents from the slave trade itself offered repeated evidence of the desperate ends to which captive people might be driven, and white Carolinians took a wary interest in the frequent stories of reversals on the Guinea Coast. The fate of the *Clare,* as reported in London and Boston, must have been a subject of common gossip along Charlestown piers in 1729:

[9] Lords Commissioners for Trade and Plantations to their Excellencies the Lords Justices, Aug. 30, 1720, BPRO Trans., VIII, 99–100. Compare the statement by Benjamin Martyn, Chapter V, note 85, above.

[10] "The humble Memorial of Sir Alexander Cuming Bart to his Grace the Duke of Newcastle," received July 11, 1730, BPRO Trans., XIV, 225.

[11] "Extracts of Mr. Von Reck's Journal," in Force, *Tracts,* IV, 9.

We have an account from Guinea by Way of Antigua, that the Clare
Galley, *Capt. Murrell, having compleated her Number of Negroes had
taken her Departure from the Coast of Guinea for South Carolina; but
was not got 10 Leagues on her Way, before the Negroes rose and making
themselves Masters of the Gunpowder and Fire Arms, the Captain and
Ships Crew took to their Long Boat, and got shore near Cape Coast
Castle. The Negroes ran the Ship on Shore within a few Leagues of the
said Castle, and made their escape.*[12]

. . . The items which struck closest to home, however, were those
from the nearby Caribbean. The revolts in the Virgin Islands in 1734,
as Von Reck had noted, were carefully followed by white Carolinians.
In early March the *Gazette* relayed the news that the slaves on St.
John's "had intirely massacred all the white People on that Island,
consisting of about 200 Families, and were very inhuman in the
Execution of their Murders." The next issue carried a story that white
landing parties from St. Kitts and St. Thomas had attacked the rebels
"with such vigour, that in less than one hour they cut them all to
pieces, some were taken Prisoners, and afterwards hang'd and quarter'd as they deserved, and not one of 'em escaped." But in fact the
suppression was by no means so thorough, and not until nine
months later did the *Gazette* report that French and Indians trained
in slave hunting had finally been imported from Martinique to track
down the resisters. Dozens of the Negroes committed suicide to
escape torture, and it was recounted that "one of the Rebels was so
hardy, that he would not go in with the rest, but was resolved to kill
some body before he was taken, upon which a Company went out
and shot him, so an End was put to the melancholly Scene." Meanwhile, the word came of an attempted rising in St. Kitts, "by setting
Six Houses on Fire," and a similar effort must have occurred several
years later, for Robert Pringle wrote to a friend on St. Kitts in 1739
that he was "much Concern'd to hear . . . of your being alarm'd for

---

[12] *Boston News-Letter,* Sept. 25, 1729. This item is in Donnan, *Documents,* IV, 274, with
the comment by the editor that "There is nothing unusual about this disaster to the
Clare save the wide publicity which it seems to have received." Note that the incident
reflects a prior knowledge of guns and gunpowder among the slaves, as does an item
from the *SCG,* July 14, 1733: "The Robert, Capt. Hamilton, was lately blown up by the
Negroes on the Coast of Guinea." For a general discussion of such insurgency, see
Darold D. Wax, "Negro Resistance to the Early American Slave Trade," *JNH,* LI (1966),
1–15.

fear of an Insurrection of the Negroes but hope their wicked Designs will prove abortive & turn to their own Confusion."[13]

The most dramatic stories of Caribbean upheaval during the 1730s, however, proceeded from Jamaica, and the *Gazette* chronicled the violence there as fully as possible. Word came via Rhode Island in 1732 that a Jamaican militia company had seized "a large Negro Town, . . . had killed and taken above 40 Negroes, and expected Recruits every Day to secure the Town for the English Inhabitants."[14] In May 1734 the *Gazette* quoted the letter of a white Jamaican saying that "Our rebellious Negroes are so numerous that they attack us everywhere, and are not afraid of our greatest Force. About ten Days ago," the source continued, "they attacked near 100 Men most Soldiers, carried away their Arms, Provisions, and what plunder they pleased; most of our people fled; we can get no body to stand before them."[15]

The following January, Carolina readers were informed that in the fall a British man-of-war had been dispatched from Gibraltar "to quell the Rebellious Negroes in Jamaica" where martial law was in effect. The *South Carolina Gazette*, which printed only several columns of news per week, continued to feature intermittent dispatches. In September it reported that a force of more than seventeen hundred was pursuing the rebels and roads were being cut through the island to speed their suppression, but the following month word came from Jamaica "that it is as bad there with the rebellious Negroes as ever, being there runs every Day over to them 3 for every one that is taken."[16] With fascination and horror, slaveholders in the

---

[13] *SCG*, March 2, 1734; March 9, 1734; Dec. 21, 1734; May 11, 1734; Robert Pringle to Francis Guichard, Feb. 5, 1739, Pringle Letterbook.
[14] *SCG*, Nov. 1, 1732. For details of race relations in Jamaica between 1729 and 1739, including the war between the Maroons and the English, see George Metcalf, *Royal Government and Political Conflict in Jamaica, 1729–1783* (London, 1965), Chapter II.
[15] *SCG*, May 18, 1734. The issue of Sept. 7, 1734, carried other letters from Kingston written about the same time. One correspondent related: "We are at present more apprehensive of a Civil than a Foreign War, the rebellious Negroes that are settled in the Mountains having been very troublesome of late, and are now become more numerous by . . . those that are daily running away from several of the Adjacent Settlements to join them; they have lately made Incursions into some of the Neighbouring Plantations, and done considerable Damage; and it is feared, if some effectual Means are not taken to reduce them they may in a Little Time render themselves stronger than the Force that can be sent against them."
[16] *SCG*, Jan. 18, 1735; July 12, 1735; Sept. 20, 1735; Oct. 11, 1735.

southern colonies followed these dispatches on the Maroon War through to the final treaty in 1738.

For Carolina, with its rapidly increasing African trade, there were dire implications, and even in Virginia, where the free populace would never become a minority, the repercussions of high slave imports were becoming the subject of growing concern. In 1736 Virginia's William Byrd wrote the Earl of Egmont congratulating him on the prohibition of slavery in Georgia and urging an end to the slave trade, Byrd described at length the ambivalence which made mainland planters feel increasingly foolish and furious, and numerous South Carolina slaveowners, scanning reports from the Caribbean at this time, must have shared his anxious thoughts.

> *They import so many Negroes hither, that I fear this Colony will some time or other be confirmed by the Name of New Guinea. I am sensible of many bad consequences of multiplying these Ethiopians amongst us. They blow up the pride, and ruin the Industry of our White People, who seeing a Rank of poor Creatures below them, detest work for fear it should make them look like Slaves. . . .*
>
> *Another unhappy Effect of Many Negros is the necessity of being severe. Numbers make them insolent, and their foul Means must do what fair will not. We have however nothing like the Inhumanity here that is practiced in the Islands, and God forbid we ever shoud. But these base Tempers require to be rid with a tort Rein, or they will be apt to throw their Rider. Yet even this is terrible to a good naturd Man, who must submit to be either a Fool or a Fury. And this will be more our unhappy case, the more Negros are increast amongst us.*
>
> *But these private mischiefs are nothing if compared to the publick danger. We have already at least 10,000 Men of these descendants of Ham fit to bear Arms, and their Numbers increase every day as well by birth as Importation. And in case there shoud arise a Man of desperate courage amongst us, exasperated by a desperate fortune, he might with more advantage than Cataline kindle a Servile War. Such a man might be dreadfully mischeivous before any opposition could be formed against him, and tinge our Rivers as wide as they are with blood.*[17]

[17] Col. William Byrd to Earl of Egmont, July 12, 1736, printed in Donnan, *Documents,* IV, 131–32.

III

The dilemma posed by events in the West Indies had particular acuteness for whites in South Carolina. Their province, after all, was something of an anomaly to both the mainland and Caribbean colonial worlds, as is suggested by the fact that wills and travel accounts still referred to "Carolina in the West Indies" upon occasion.[18] While these Carolinians admired the numerical strength and economic diversity of Europeans farther north, they shunned the well-known commercial subservience of the provision colonies; and although they envied the luxurious life-style of associates in the sugar islands, they were newly fearful of the risks it entailed. By the early 1730s they could feel both horns of the dilemma sharply, for no sooner had rice been removed from the empire's list of enumerated commodities in 1730 and the way cleared for South Carolina's triumph as a staple colony than word from the Caribbean raised fresh concern about the dangers of plantation life: should white Carolinians view the trouble in the West Indies as a windfall to speed their ascendancy, or as an omen to warn against destruction? . . .

For more than a decade the white minority in South Carolina would wrestle with ways to obtain the best of both worlds, keeping the price of rice up and the percentage of slaves down. One of the most ingenious plans for combining the advantages of a staple colony with those of a provision colony was that offered to readers of the *Gazette* by "Agricola" the following winter. He dispensed with the recurrent idea of crop diversification by remarking "how improbable 'tis that a Planter, who has engaged his Crop for Negroes, (which is, perhaps, the Case of too many of us) should venture on new, and uncertain Projects." He also dismissed well-intentioned efforts to mechanize rice production with mills and dams on the simple grounds that there were too few artificers to maintain them. Instead, "Agricola" urged intensification designed to reduce the quantity and improve the quality of rice. According to his argument:

> *if in lieu of five Acres to a Hand, our Planter were obliged to plant no more than two; it is reasonable to presume, that in a short Time, the Produce of the two Acres, would yield as much at Market, as the Produce of the five. And I would fain know, whether a Man could not find what to do with the rest of his Negroe's Time? Yes certainly. He would apply it to*

---

[18] *SCHGM*, IV (1903), 235. . . .

the Improvement of his Cattle, and preparing Beef, and Pork for the Islands; and our old Rice Fields would then be of singular Use for Pasturage: The Situation of our Country would enable us to be the earliest of all the Northern Colonies at Market, & of course, to engross all that valuable Trade: The surplus Time also would, without inconveniency, enable us to endeavour to cultivate all other useful Manufactures.[19]

Rice planters already realized, as did tobacco growers in Virginia, that to decrease acreage per slave was almost impossible in an economy where land was cheap and labor scarce. But there seemed another means by which the colony might have its cake and eat it too: if forced migration from Africa could be offset by voluntary immigration from Europe, then white colonists could reap the benefits of plantation agriculture without being dangerously outnumbered or limited to a single crop. A memorial filed in 1720, apparently by English merchants trading with South Carolina, had contained suggestions as to "What may be done to retrieve the desolation of Carolina, to strengthen that frontier of our colonies on the continent & to encrease its inhabitants & trade." One recommendation was the enactment and enforcement of a law by which the number of slaves was limited to ten per white man and their distribution was carefully recorded, "whereby ye negros may be prevented from rising."[20]

In line with this argument, the colonial Assembly made repeated efforts to impose a limit upon the ratio of slaves to whites, and in 1727 it passed "An Act for the better Securing this Province from Negro Insurrections, & for Encouraging of Poor People by Employing them in Plantations." Gov. Johnson noted in several of his letters to England at the end of the decade, "Nothing is so much wanted in Carolina as White Inhabitants," and in 1735 the legislature determined to put the income from the duty on Africans directly into subsidies for importing poor Protestants,[21] but slaveowning assemblymen were still less than total in their commitment to offsetting black labor with white. In 1738, during debate over a Negro bill, a clause giving planters three months to comply with the requirement for the presence of one white man to every ten slaves was voted down, as was a proposal that the regulation "should be read in the Churches throughout the several Parishes."[22]

[19] *SCG*, Feb. 3, 1733.
[20] BPRO Trans., VIII, 228.
[21] BPRO Trans. XII, 231; BPRO Trans., XIII, 425 (cf. BPRO Trans., XIV, 237); *Statutes*, III, 409.
[22] *SCCHJ, 1737–1738*, p. 429. It was finally agreed that the measure should be read

IV

Even though official encouragement was sporadic, there did exist a steady flow of poor white immigrants. Their numbers were by no means adequate to offset the heavy importation of Negroes, but shiploads of servants arriving from Europe were occasionally advertised in the *Gazette*, and surviving vestry books show a marked increase in concern over indigent Europeans.[23] According to one description of their lot from 1738: "Only in and around the towns are houses to be found, but in the country only shacks or shanties made of boards and covered with brush, in which the people stay." Most newcomers were said to subsist on cakes made from Indian corn and baked over a fire (a diet more familiar to Africans and Indians than Europeans), and the very poor, claimed the account, "get nothing all the year round for their sustenance but potatoes, which they dig out of the ground themselves. With these alone they have to keep themselves alive, and they see neither bread, meat, or anything else."[24]

Conditions facing this immigrant class were comparable to those faced by the first white settlers, but unlike their predecessors they found themselves at the bottom of an existing social order—or almost. Officials shared William Byrd's misgivings that the presence of bondsmen below the whites in this hierarchy would lead to laziness, but there was also concern that even the most industrious newcomers would not be able to compete with slaves for jobs. The unfree workers, who were involved in almost every colonial activity, earned low wages—lower when employed illegally—and were not directly responsible (it was argued) for maintaining themselves or their families.[25] White slaveowners therefore found themselves confronted

---

before every militia company twice each year. Several days later word came from Jamaica that an act had been passed there "For Obliging every owner to keep a White for every 30 Negroes &ᶜ or pay £3-5-0 a Quarter Deficiency." BPRO Trans., XIX, 37.

[23] *SCG*, Sept. 30, 1732. Several early vestry books have been published; others are available in typescript in the SCL. Benjamin Joseph Klebaner, "Public Poor Relief in Charleston, 1800–1860," *SCHGM*, LV (1954), 210, points out that in 1734 the St. Philip's Parish Vestry rented a house for the purpose of giving paupers "proper attendance," and two years later the parish obtained authorization for erecting a substantial workhouse which would absorb paupers, vagrants, and common beggars. Cf. BPRO Trans., XIV, 86–87; *SCHGM*, XXI (1924), 193–94.

[24] Trachsler, "Brief Description of a Journey," p. 103.

[25] The Clerk of the Market protested in 1741 that his daily fee of seven shillings "was not Negroes' Hire; and sure then not a living for any white Man of the lowest rank in Life." *SCCHJ, 1741–1742,* p. 21.

with trying to curb a variety of Negro economic activities (from which they themselves usually gained), or else risking a rise in the parish poor rolls and a decline in the arrival of European immigrants.

Tension between black and white workers, a recurrent theme in America's later history, increased with the number of whites, and the hard-earned predominance of the Negro majority in parts of the colony's varied labor force was called into question. When debate began on a new Negro bill in 1737 it was proposed that no Charlestown slaves "be permitted to buy or sell or to be employed for Hire as Porters, Carters or Fishermen." This was amended to allow that "the Negroes be at Liberty to fish and ply as Porters and Carters under Lycense from the Commissioners of the Work House."[26] The owners of slaves sent out as carters and porters paid a weekly sum for the privilege, and every Negro fisherman was charged £5 per annum for a license. Each received a numbered badge for identification, and the fees were used in support of the town watch.[27]

At the same time pressure mounted against the participation of slaves in a variety of skilled crafts. The Negro Act of 1735 imposed a fine of £50 upon any master who allowed slaves to maintain any "houses of entertainment or trade," whether in their own names or under his protection, and two years later a protest was issued against the "too common Practice" of barbers, many of whom were Negroes, shaving customers on Sundays.[28] During the reappraisals which followed in the wake of the Stono Uprising, a "Committee appointed to consider the most effectual Measures to bring into this Province white Persons to increase our Strength and Security" reported to the Assembly "that a great Number of Negroes are brought up to and daily employed in mechanic Trades both in Town and Country." The committee recommended a statute "prohibiting the bringing up [of] Negroes and other Slaves to mechanic Trades in which white Persons usually are employed,"[29] but a formal prohibition was not enacted until 1755 and appears never to have been totally enforced.[30] . . .

---

[26] _SCCHJ, 1737–1738_, p. 364.

[27] _Ibid._, pp. 365, 428. For mention of the brass badges traditionally worn by Negroes allowed to work out, see the memoirs of D. E. Huger Smith in Alice R. Huger Smith, _Carolina Rice Plantation_, pp. 94–95.

[28] _Statutes_, VII, 396; _SCG_, Nov. 5, 1737.

[29] _SCCHJ, 1742–1743_, pp. 345–46.

[30] _SCG_, Supplement, May 8, 1755. An industrial census of Charlestown in 1848 shows

V

One specific result of these economic pressures is worth noting separately. Where blacks and whites had previously shared most activities, distinguished only by the fact that the latter gave the commands and took the proceeds, workers were now occasionally set apart by race. At the same time that Negroes were being forced away from certain skilled trades, they were receiving more exclusive custody of the society's most menial tasks. Jobs which were in various ways taxing or offensive became, as Byrd had feared, "unfit" for white labor. As slaves assumed the entirety of the onerous business of rice production, they were also made to take on other oppressive chores as well.

The collection and disposal of refuse, to cite one example, was increasingly delegated to slaves. An early request of the first royal governor in 1721 was that "all necessary Houses, draines, and Sinks . . . be kept clean and [free] from noisome smells." And in 1734 "the Want of a Scavenger, and proper Regulations for keeping clear the Streets of Charles-Town" was presented as a grievance to the Grand Jury, with particular note being taken of the fact that the sewer ditch which ran across Church Street and through Mrs. Bettison's garden was generally stopped up, "whereby the way to and from the Church is often almost unpassable." Subsequently, government committee issued a report suggesting the division of the city into four districts, in each of which an elected official could assess every household for at least one slave above the age of nine. Every three months, or whenever a white citizen filed a legal complaint about offensive dung hills in the streets, the official would send out word via the corporal of militia or the parish constable that on a set day these men and women were "to meet at the Court House by Beat of Drum at six oClock in the Morning." Each Negro was to bring "a Box, Basket, Spade or Shovel," and it was hoped that their unpleasant labors would keep the town healthy, clean, and "beautified."[31]

---

that Negroes outnumbered whites in more than one-third of the forty-nine occupations listed. Blacks were a majority in the following categories on the list: "Carpenters and joiners, Masons and stone cutters, Painters and plasterers, Wharf builders, Tailors and cap makers, Barbers and hairdressers, Bakers, Coopers, Ship carpenters and joiners, Other mechanics and journeymen, Coachmen, Draymen, Wherfingers, stevedores and porters, Apprentices, Domestic servants, Laborers, Fishermen." Phillips, "The Slave Labor Problem," p. 435.

[31] SCUHJ, 1721, mfm BMP/D 487, SCDAH; *SCHGM*, XXV (1924), 194; "Report on Ways

As in any society, many of the lowest jobs were also the most laborious. Besides the actual production of rice and naval stores (and later indigo), all of the hauling and loading of these commodities was done by Negroes, as was the building of roads and the cutting of canal passages. Black porters, carters, and stevedores on land were matched by hundreds of black oarsmen on the water. Even the boats which taxied persons to and from ships in the harbor were manned by slaves.[32] While all of these tasks were essential, others exploited Negro strength in far more dubious ways. When sailors were being pressed into service against pirates in 1718, it was four slaves who executed the press-master's orders for a month.[33] In later years Negroes were encouraged to take part in the apprehension of white sailors who deserted their ships, and owners were promised compensation from the Public Treasury "if any Slave shall be killed or maimed in apprehending such fugitive Seamen."[34] Slaves themselves were often put to work on local privateers, and occasionally while at sea, captains allowed or even forced slaves to beat European crewmen.[35]

The use of Negroes as roughnecks was even more common on land. A statute of 1712, reiterated in 1714 and 1722, made it a crime for slaves to strike a white except in defense of their masters, "Provided always, that such striking, conflict or maiming, be not by command of . . . their master, mistress, or owners of their families, or of their goods."[36] This proviso was made necessary by the fact that it was common practice for insolvent slaveholders to urge their Negroes to resist seizure in payment of debts. This was generally a place where the interests of owner and slaves coincided, and the job of the provost marshal was made almost untenable as a result. After 1713 the provost marshal was empowered to summon indebted planters to Charlestown, but in 1726, at a time when few slaveowners

---

and Means to cleanse and keep clean the several Streets in Charles Town . . . ," March 5, 1737, *SCCHJ, 1736–1737,* p. 288.

[32] "Life of Equiano," p. 96.

[33] *SCCHJ, 1725,* p. 59.

[34] *SCCHJ, 1742–1743,* pp. 228, 230, 284.

[35] SCUHJ, June 22, 1722, mfm BMP/D 487, SCDAH; *SCG,* Nov. 6, 1740; Admiralty Court Records on mfm in SCDAH. See "Harvey & others vs. Ebsworthy," Aug. 1738 (reel 2, pp. 176–78), in which the captain of the *Sea Flower* was charged by his crewmen with having encouraged the slaves on board to beat a white shipmate; also "The King vs. Joesph Harrison," June 1758 (reel 3, pp. 45–52), in which a black linguist aboard the snow *Rainbow* was allowed revenge upon white crewmen.

[36] *Statutes,* VII, 359; cf. 366, 377.

were solvent, the Assembly forced a return to the older system of *capias*, whereby this official had to go and personally lay hold of slaves or other property belonging to the debtor. Thomas Lowndes, who had been granted the post the previous year, reported that an officer hazarded his life in making seizures outside Charlestown and often had slaves "rescued" from him while returning. He claimed that frequently "the Negroes are let loose upon him, and he . . . whipped or drawn through a ditch," and all this without legal recourse since it can never be proven "that it was by their Masters order tho' every one knows it could not be done without it."[37]

The allegiance of the Assembly at this time can be seen by the fact that when one provost marshal sought to use a group of Negroes in his own right to force a debtor to prison, he was promptly removed from office.[38] And yet at the same time whites who were private citizens seem to have been condoned in using slave muscle not only to keep the government at bay but also to settle private scores as well.[39] To a few slaves such brutal activities may have afforded an outlet for aggressions and perhaps a certain notoriety. But nothing could offset the broader degradation which came with the forced acceptance of the society's most tedious, harsh, and squalid tasks.

Numerous laws reflected indirectly, and also furthered, this process of economic and social subjugation. The prohibition of the use of firearms by slaves, for example, and severe constraints upon their movements curtailed innocuous as well as subversive ambitions. Even clothes became a matter of legislation: the Negro Act of 1735 took special note of the many Negroes who wore "clothes much above the condition of slaves, for the procuring whereof they use sinister and evil methods." The easiest way to remove the incentive for earning or taking money with which to purchase good clothes was to prohibit such apparel altogether. The law, therefore, pre-

---

[37] BPRO Trans., XV, 72–73, 309.

[38] *SCCHJ, 1726–1727*, p. 24.

[39] *SCG*, July 24, 1736: "We are inform'd that a certain Gentleman in the Country having some business in Town left one of his reputed Friends at his House to take care of his Spouse and to manage his Affairs in his absence. The Gentleman at his return hearing by one of his Negroes that his Friend has used a little too much Familiarity with his Wife, immediately took a loaden Pistol and went to meet his Friend in the Fields, who avoiding the blow, fell to wrestling with him, but the Gentleman calling his Negroes to assistance, cut off his Friends Ears, and for fear of loosing the Use of his Wind pipe is gone to Cape Fear."

scribed the materials suitable for slave clothing, allowing only the cheapest fabrics: "negro cloth, duffelds, course kearsies, osnabrigs, blue linnen, checked linen," and also "course garlix or callicoes, checked cottons or scotch plaids," if these last were not valued at more than ten shillings per yard. Any slave wearing a garment of some finer, different, or more valuable material could have it stripped away. This dress code was intended (as were those enacted earlier among Englishmen in the northern colonies) to impose and emphasize social stratification, to enforce the maintenance of social distance through the emblem of apparel. One sure indication that the law had deeper significance for whites than simply preventing slaves from stealing expensive clothes is the fact that when the question was put in debate as to whether Negroes should be allowed to wear the cast-off clothes of their masters and mistresses, it carried in the negative.[40]

An even more serious measure of involuntary separation and forced inferiority concerns the rationing of food. Inevitably, as wealth built up among the whites, their general fare became more expensive and diversified, while the diet of slaves remained cheaper and less varied. Moreover, this widening distinction, like that in clothing, was given official sanction during the 1730s and 1740s. In public accounts, food for Negroes was budgeted separately at half to three-quarters the rate allowed for whites, and it was becoming accepted doctrine among freemen that slaves needed—and got— smaller quantities of cheaper foodstuffs with minimal allotments of meat. On a six-month military venture against the Spanish in 1740 it was projected that one thousand white foot soldiers would each consume seven pounds of beef, fourteen quarts of rice, and an equal amount of corn each week, while the weekly food allotment for eight hundred "Pioneers" was put at half a piece of beef and twelve quarts of corn per man.[41]

Legal authorities were even worse than military authorities with respect to rations. In 1741 the official at a trial submitted to the Assembly two bills, "one for 10 Days' Diet of 50 white Persons, the other for as many Days Diet of the same Number of Negroes," and

[40] *Statutes,* VII, 396; *SCCHJ, 1734–1735,* p. 145.
[41] *SCCHJ, 1739–1740,* p. 175. In the previous century in Barbados, slaves enrolled in the militia who performed commendably under fire earned the right to receive a white servant's allowance of food from their masters. Harlow, *Barbados,* pp. 209–11.

the Committee on Accounts appraised them at £100 and £20, respectively.[42] The annual budget submitted by the provost marshal for 1743 suggested a rate of one shilling, three pence for each white person's daily ration ("allowing one Pound of Bread and one Pound of Flesh all wholesome Provisions") and only nine pence for the rations of Negroes in his custody. This latter figure was the only one which the Assembly questioned among hundreds of diverse fees, and after several hours of debate they reduced the daily allotment of food for Negroes to a value of six pence.[43] As yet, little is known about the exact implications of pervasive and long-term differences in the nutrition available to the African and European populations in America.

VI

Increased discrimination regarding food and clothing was matched by deepening white anxiety over the even more basic issue of physical intimacy. As the ratio of white men to women became more balanced with time, one motive for sexual relations between freemen and slaves diminished,[44] and as the size of the Negro population grew, the impetus among Europeans for white offspring increased.[45] From the minority's point of view, every baby born to European parents "improved" the dangerous racial imbalance, while each child with a white father and a black mother increased the ranks of the slaves and served as a reminder of the Europeans' precarious social and genetic position. Mulattoes, editorialized the *Gazette*, "are seldom well belov'd either by the Whites or the Blacks."[46] But their presence, however limited, could hardly be denied. "The whites mix with the blacks and the blacks with the whites," commented a Euro-

---

[42] *SCCHJ, 1739–1741*, p. 493 (see also pp. 184–85, 284). The committee responded to another bill, submitted by the same official two years later, "that eighteen Pence per Day for Negroes and five Shillings per Day for white Men will be a sufficient Allowance," *SCCHJ, 1742–1744*, p. 377 (see also pp. 138, 367, 370).

[43] *SCCHJ, 1742–1744*, pp. 148, 196. Cf. *SCCHJ, 1736–1739*, p. 511.

[44] See Jordan, *White Over Black*, p. 175.

[45] The *SCG* made pointed allusions to notable instances of European longevity or fertility and encouraged large families with such notes as the following, from the third issue (Jan. 22, 1732): "We are told, there are several Weddings upon the Anvil, we therefore take the Freedom to advise the young Sparks that are concern'd, to strike, whilst the Iron's hot, and we doubt not, but in time, we shall be a numerous, and flourishing People."

[46] *SCG*, March 22, 1735. The full passage is reprinted in Jordan, *White Over Black*, p. 170.

pean in 1737, "and if a white man has a child by a black woman, nothing is done to him. . . . It also occurs that the English marry . . . black women, often also Indian women."[47] Six years later the presentments of the Grand Jury in Charlestown included the following grievance: "We present THE TOO COMMON PRACTICE OF CRIMINAL CONVERSATION with NEGRO and the other SLAVE WENCHES IN THIS PROVINCE, as an Enormity and Evil of general Ill-Consequence."[48]

Twice during the 1730s full-scale debates erupted in the public press concerning this sensitive issue. The use of poetry and the attempts at cleverness cannot disguise the underlying anxieties in either case. Early in 1732 the *Gazette* ran a brief poem entitled "The Cameleon Lover" which suggested half-whimsically that whites with a taste for black lovers, being "Stain'd with the Tincture of the Sooty Sin," might well "imbibe the Blackness of their Charmer's Skin."[49] This harmless threat prompted a much longer and more serious prose piece from "Albus" (a double-edged pseudonym invoking the Latin words for "white" and "English"), who described miscegenation as an *"Epidemical Disease"* less natural and more odious than the smallpox distemper then infecting the colony.[50] The gist of his arguments and the degree of his indignation presaged a long history of tirades on this matter, but for the moment the last word was given to "Sable," who promptly provided a sympathetic verse entitled "Cameleon's Defence."[51]

In 1736 male settlers in Georgetown tried to induce white women from elsewhere in the colony to join them, but the death of several upon arrival discouraged others, and the bachelors turned to a motley shipment of sixty women from Bermuda.[52] These newcomers were said to be healthier, but apparently few in Georgetown could

---

[47] Samuel Dyssli to friends in Switzerland, Dec. 3, 1737, *SCHGM,* XXIII (1922), 90. During the same year an Anglican missionary in Prince Frederick's Parish northwest of Georgetown baptized "one *Negroe* Woman, and six of her Children *Mulattoes;* she herself and her three elder Children could read well, and repeat the Church-Catechism; and two of the remaining three could repeat the Creed and the Lord's-Prayer." Quoted in Klingberg, *Appraisal,* p. 85.

[48] *SCG,* March 28, 1743. A slave woman advertised several months earlier as being capable of "almost any Work required either in publick or private House" was given the halfhearted endorsement of being "neither a Theif, Whore, or Drunkard." *SCG,* Dec. 27, 1742. It can be guessed that prostitution was among those onerous tasks mentioned above to which an increasing number of Negroes found themselves consigned.

[49] *SCG,* March 11, 1732.

[50] *SCG,* March 18, 1732.

[51] Ibid.

[52] *SCG,* July 10, 1736.

afford to pay the cost of their transport, upon which the women's importer placed a bitter notice in the *Gazette*. He suggested to single men, "that if they are in a Strait for Women, to wait for the next Shipping from the Coast of Guinny. Those African Ladies," the author continued caustically, "are of a strong robust Constitution; not easily jaded out, able to serve them by Night as well as Day. When they are Sick, they are not costly, when dead, their funeral charges are but *viz* an old Matt, one Bottle Rum, and a lb. Sugar."[53]

The following week a correspondent was prompted to argue defensively that "our Country-Women are full as capable for Service either night or day as any African Ladies whatsoever, unless their native Constitution is much alter'd," and an anonymous warning accompanied the letter:

> *Certain young Men of this Town are desired to frequent less with their black Lovers the open Lots and the Chandler's House on the Green between old Church-street and King's Street, there being something intended to coole their Courage and to expose them; but they have no need to be idle, since of their own Colour are lately arrived so many buxom Ladies, who are tender-hearted and no doubt will comply easily with their request on small rewards, to cure their Itch and Courage. N.B. Be careful of Fire.[54]*

This veiled threat was quickly parried in the next issue by a bit of doggerel which asked, *"Kiss black or white, why need it trouble you?"*[55] And there the exchange ended for the time being.

The white anxieties which underlay such interchanges found their most profound and succinct psychological expression in the fantasy of rape. Negroes were threatening to compete too successfully economically; they were shouldering an awesome proportion of the colony's physical labor; they were gradually asserting their power through sheer force of numbers. It is no surprise that the weekly paper of the Europeans, seeing nothing newsworthy in the ravishments of Negro women by whites, which could not have been an unknown occurrence, seized upon stories of rapes committed by slaves in distant provinces. During its first year the *Gazette* published an italicized item about the scheduled execution of a Negro man convicted of raping a white woman on the Massachusetts frontier. In

---

[53] *SCG*, July 17, 1736.
[54] *SCG*, July 24, 1736.
[55] *SCG*, July 31, 1736.

October 1734 a similar offense, also in Massachusetts, was reported in considerable detail, and two months later readers were informed that the suspect had subsequently "set the Prison on fire, and . . . made his Escape, but was taken again."[56] The following year an issue which contained news of the rebellion in Jamaica and of the efforts of several slaves to poison a white family in New England also carried a story from Philadelphia about a Negro who was "whip'd round the Town at the Cart's Tail, 63 Lashes, for attempting to ravish a white Child about 12 Years of Age."[57]

Such mounting preoccupation with ravishment reflected not only the personal fears of white readers, but also the collective anxieties of the white minority as well. Individual rape if committed by a black man was suggestive of social overthrow, just as broad upheaval had implications of personal rape. And occasionally these two elements were brought into close conjunction in local lore, much as they were in the tale of the Sabine women, which had inspired ancient Romans and which horrified the English colonists. One story which found its way into the *London Magazine* in 1757 described how each leader of a South Carolina slave plot in 1730 had confessed, before execution, "whose wife, daughter, or sister he had fixed on for his future bedfellow."[58] There was an actual conspiracy in August 1730 for which only limited evidence has been found. It is clear, however, that the incident made a lasting impression, for almost the same account was given to a Hessian officer who served in Charlestown during the Revolutionary War. Although the listener got the year wrong (1736), he eagerly recorded the more lurid details. The black conspirators, according to these white recollections of the incident, had intended to massacre the entire European population, sparing only those women who could be enslaved or used to gratify their lusts.[59]

[56] *SCG*, Nov. 11, 1732; Oct. 26, 1734; Dec. 21, 1734.

[57] *SCG*, Sept. 20, 1735. It was not surprising for a Baptist minister from South Carolina, traveling to Virginia several decades later, to take special note of such incidents in his diary; as in his entry of Dec. 1, 1769, or of Jan. 16, 1770: "This Town is called New London and is about 120 Miles from Richmond . . .—a negroe lately executed here for ravishing a white young woman." Journal of Oliver Hart, SCL.

[58] *London Magazine*, XXVI (1757), 330–31. A contemporary account of this plot said nothing about such confessions. *Boston News-Letter*, Oct. 22, 1730. See Aptheker, *Slave Revolts*, pp. 180–81.

[59] "The Diary of Captain Johann Hinrichs," in Bernard A. Uhlendorf, trans. and ed., *The Siege of Charleston (Univeristy of Michigan Publications, History and Political Science*, vol. XII, Ann Arbor, 1938), p. 323. This vision was by no means confined to South Carolina, and upon occasion rumors from other colonies no doubt became entwined

The increasing white obsession with physical violation, therefore, must be taken as an integral part of the white minority's wider struggle for social control. The degree of shared interest and un- avoidable intimacy which had held the two races in uneasy coexis- tence during the proprietary period was breaking down. Slaves were becoming a more numerous and distinctive group, and their very real efforts toward social and economic self-assertion prompted the anx- ious white minority to fantasies of ravishment and to concrete mea- sures of containment. . . .

---

with local stories. The Stephen Bordley Letterbook, 1738–40, Md. Hist. Soc., Baltimore, contains a letter written in Annapolis, Jan. 30, 1739 or 1740. (Historians are not clear on the date: see Aptheker, *Slave Revolts*, p. 192n.; Land, *Bases of the Plantation Society*, p. 228.) Bordley claimed that a plot which had been brewing among slaves there for eight months involved destroying "their several families Negro women and all except for the young white women only whom they intended to keep for their wives."

It is said, before the Appointment of any day for the execution of the design a negroe woman lying abed in a quarter overheard several of the negroe fellows talking in their country language, concerning this very affair, and she accordingly told her mistress of it the next morning, but could not gain relief; foolish woman! that sooner than give herself the trouble of looking into the affair would run the hazard of having her throat cutt; but perhaps she had a mind for a black husband.

Gary B. Nash

THE MIXING OF PEOPLES

In this selection Gary B. Nash of the University of California, Los Angeles fully explores a theme that Wood touched on—the sexual relationships be- tween races. Nash compares Whites' attitudes toward physical intimacy with Indians and Blacks as a way of measuring acculturation and assimilation. He finds that eighteenth-century public opinion shifted against interracial mixing evan as miscegenation continued. White masters sought to preserve absolute social control over their black slaves, while simultaneously acting out their sexual fantasies. Nash's study combined with the works of Morgan and Wood reflect the growing belief among historians that developments in the colonial period made slavery a fixture in American society.

From Gary B. Nash, *Red, White, and Black: The Peoples of Early America*, © 1974, pp. 276–97. Reprinted by permission of Prentice-Hall, Englewood Cliffs, N.J. Footnotes omitted.

While Indians, Africans, and Europeans, each embracing a diversity of people, were working out their destinies in a complicated setting of tribal and imperial rivalry, economic growth, population change, and social and political transformation, they were also interacting with each other at the most intimate and personal levels. This sexual and social mixing of individuals of different genetic stocks, usually called miscegenation, is in itself of little interest unless one is concerned with pseudoscientific attempts to specify the relative size of various "racial" groups in a society, an exercise usually conducted with propagandistic and political purposes in mind. Miscegenation is, however, important in another way. By measuring the extent of it we can develop insights into the process of acculturation and assimilation—the mixing of cultural elements and the absorption of one culture into another. Miscegenation is usually an important element in both these processes.

Most thinking on the subject of miscegenation in North America starts with the arresting notion that Europeans on this continent simply did not intermix with Africans and Indians with anywhere near the same frequency as in colonial Latin American societies. Nor did Africans and Indians mix to the same degree. Latin America is known as the area of the world where the most extensive intermingling of the races in human history has taken place; and North America, where Europeans, Indians, and Africans also converged during roughly the same period of time, is noted for the general absence of any such genetic intermixture. . . .

Two explanations are commonly advanced to explain this. The first is that before the European rediscovery of the New World the Spanish and Portuguese had far greater experience in interacting with people of different cultures, particularly with darkskinned people, than did the English. Through centuries of war and trade with the Berbers, Moors, and other peoples of the Middle East and North Africa, Iberian culture had already absorbed new cultural and genetic elements and developed flexible attitudes about the mixing of peoples in sexual congress. The English, by contrast, had largely remained within their island fortress, sheltered from other cultures and therefore predisposed toward viewing interracial contacts with suspicion and even alarm.

A corollary to this argument is that, once in the New World, the permissive attitudes of the Catholic church toward non-Christian people, the Roman system of law, which preserved a place of dignity and semiautonomy for the slave, and the paternalistic attitudes of the authoritarian Iberian governments combined to make racial intermixture acceptable and therefore common in the areas of the world where Spain and Portugal were confronting Indians and Africans in large numbers. By contrast, it is argued that English Protestantism was unusually rigid in considering admittance of "savage" people to the covenant of the faith; English law had nothing to say on the subject of enslavement, leaving colonists free to elaborate the most rigid institutions to contain their bound laborers; and the English government was uninterested in exercising very much authority in its colonies, especially in the matter of the treatment of subordinate non-English groups. Given these differences in prior experience, in institutions and attitudes, and in governmental policy, it was therefore not surprising that the history of interracial mixing should be so different in the colonies of Spain and Portugal and the colonies of England.

Such arguments have lost much of their explanatory force in recent years as historians have looked more carefully at the social and demographic conditions underlying the history of cultural interaction in various parts of the New World. Although material and ideological factors are admitted by almost all historians to be interrelated, the differences in the degree and nature of interracial mixing in North and South America now seem to be fundamentally related to conditions encountered in the New World rather than attitudes developed in the Old World. The availability of white women; the ratio of Europeans, Africans, and Indians in a given area; the extent to which Indians could be pressed into forced labor systems; and the need to employ non-Europeans in positions of importance—all of these seem to have had a role in shaping the pattern of intercultural mixing. Thus it is no surprise to discover that in areas where European women were in short supply white men put aside whatever racial prejudices they might have brought to the New World and consorted with women of another race. Their alternatives were sexual abstinence, homosexuality, or bestiality. All three attracted some males; but the vast majority of men seem to have preferred heterosexual relations with women of a different cultural group. Nor should we be surprised to find that where Indians or Africans were relatively numerous, intermixture was far more common than where they were relatively scarce. In New England, where Indians were only sparsely settled and had been devastated by epidemics in the early years of European settlement, little red-white mixing occurred. In Mexico, where Spanish men were engulfed by the densely settled Indians, a great deal of mixing occurred throughout the colonial period.

Such common-sense explanations are overly simplistic, of course, and must be subjected to far more detailed study. Only in the area of black-white relations has enough research been undertaken to allow for firm generalizations. Indian-white relations remain largely unstudied. Since this is the work of the next generation of scholars only tentative suggestions can be offered in these areas.

Indian-European Contact

Because contact between Indians and Europeans preceded all other contacts and may have had some influence on what later occurred, it is best to begin with them. In New England, and later in the Mid-Atlantic colonies of New York, New Jersey, Pennsylvania, and Delaware, miscegenation between Europeans and Indians was extremely limited. Englishmen had emigrated to these parts of the emerging English empire with their families, or, if they were single men, found a sufficient number of single women to satisfy their needs for marriage partners. Parity between the sexes was established very quickly and continued throughout the colonial period, except following periods of war when women sometimes outnumbered men by a small margin. Reinforcing this demographic situation was a strong cultural factor. Emigration by family insured the rerooting of an entire cultural superstructure to which miscegenation was highly threatening, especially given the view, almost universal among whites, that their culture was far superior to that of red and black "savages."

The second demographic factor operating was the relatively small number of Indians in these areas and the relative inaccessibility of those who escaped epidemics or the periodic conflict which rapidly reduced the coastal Indian societies during the initial period of contact. Intercultural marriage was a rarity. A number of fur traders operating on the frontier took Indian wives and almost all of them had frequent sexual contact with Indian women. But the one notable case of intermarriage in the settled regions involved William Johnson, the northern superintendent of Indian affairs, who took a

Mohawk wife. Later knighted for his military exploits, Johnson gained great influence with the Mohawk, who renamed him Warraghiyagey, meaning "man who undertakes great things." This high tribute was conferred in large part because Johnson had deviated so radically from the white norm in accepting Mohawk customs and learning their language, as few white men cared to do. Johnson was not born or raised in the colonies and few cared to follow the example of even a high imperial official when it came to matrimony so long as there were plenty of European women in the Northern colonies. It was said that Johnson's precedent-shattering marriage, noteworthy enough to attract the attention of the London newspapers, led to eighteen other red-white unions, but even so the number is insignificant.

Farther south in the Chesapeake colonies a different demographic pattern prevailed in the first few decades. With few exceptions, white women were unavailable in Virginia until about 1620. Yet white men do not seem to have had much recourse to Indian women. This could be explained either by the conscious decision of the Powhatan-affiliated tribes to prevent their women from mixing with the European intruders, who seemed hostile from the outset, or by an English aversion to Indian women strong enough to overcome heterosexual desires. Several early eighteenth-century Virginia commentators believed the latter to have been the case. They were advocating inter-marriage with Indians even at this late date and advising that if such a "modern policy" had been followed from the outset, the costly hostilities of the early years might have been avoided. William Byrd, no stranger to the pleasures of the flesh with women of different skin colors, claimed the English were imbued with a "false delicacy" in the early years and thus could not bring themselves to sleep with Indian women. Byrd believed that the Chesapeake tribes had been offended by this rejection and could never "perswade themselves that the English were heartily their Friends, so long as they disdained to intermarry with them." Robert Beverley, author of *The History and Present State of Virginia,* took a similar view, regretting that intermarriage had never occurred and convinced that the Indians had been eager for it.

The limited evidence bearing on this question does not support such views however. A large part of the predominantly male Virginia colony was composed of representatives of the English lower class, including many who had military experience in Ireland, the Spanish

Netherlands, and other parts of the world. Squeamishness was not notable in their makeup and their later willingness to consort with African women suggests that the real cause of infrequent sexual contact with Indian women is to be found in Indian rather than European desires. The English did not establish themselves as conquerors in the early years, as had the Spanish and Portuguese, and therefore the Chesapeake tribes were under no constraints to yield up their women. Indian women were not denied to Virginians who stole away from oppressive conditions in their own community to live among Powhatan's people, and their numbers became large enough to bring about laws imposing severe penalties on such renegade behavior. But the one case of intermarriage within the white community involved vows taken between John Rolfe and Pocahontas. That the marriage was political, regardless of whatever love the two may have felt for each other, has already been pointed out. Some historians have claimed that the King's council, by deliberating whether Rolfe had not committed high treason in marrying an Indian princess, discouraged any further intermarriage. But the charge under consideration was high treason, for marrying the daughter of a quasi-enemy, and the fact is that Pocahontas and Rolfe were feted in London wherever they went, including the royal court. By the early eighteenth century the Board of Trade was pushing an official policy of intermarriage in the American colonies, a clear indication that moral scruples were not offended in England by thoughts of the commingling of red and white blood.

After the first few decades of English settlement on the Chesapeake, the imbalance of white males and females was redressed. Moreover, by the end of the second Indian war in 1644 the native population in the tidewater area was only a small fraction of the white population and by the conclusion of Bacon's Rebellion in 1675 only a few Indians remained within the areas of white settlement. That Governor Spotswood could claim in 1717 that the "inclinations of our people are not the same with those of [the French] Nation" regarding intermarriage, as evidenced by the fact that not one such marriage was known in Virginia at that time, cannot be taken as evidence that racial prejudice prohibited such partnerships. Neither the need nor the opportunity for Indian-white marriages remained. That French "inclinations" in New France were different is not so much a reflection on variations in national character as on differential needs. And even along the St. Lawrence, where Frenchmen commonly took Indian wives and mistresses, it was admitted that European women were preferred. But Indian women remained far preferable to no women at all.

The only English area in which demographic characteristics even roughly paralleled those in the Spanish and Portuguese colonies was the Southeast—the Carolinas and Georgia. It was here in the early years that white women were relatively unavailable but Indian women could easily be found. The result was a considerable contact between Englishmen and Indian women. Conspicuously absent from the records are any indications of "squeamishness" when it came to intercultural sexual liaisons. Instead, contemporary accounts and records are filled with references to unembarrassed sexual relations between the two peoples. This was especially true of the fur traders who operated in the interior regions and would not give up the satisfactions of Indian "She-Bed-Fellows," as the early eighteenth-century commentator John Lawson called them. Women were specifically designated by the Indian tribes as "Trading Girls," according to Lawson, and were given special haircuts to denote that their role was to satisfy the traders while getting money "by their Natural Parts." Only these women were available to white men, however, for Indian males, wrote Lawson, "are desirous (if possible) to keep their Wives to themselves, as well as those in other Parts of the World."

While traders consorted with Indian women in the interior, white Carolinians confronted Indian women sold into slavery in the coastal settlements. After the Yamasee War of 1715, in which slave raiding figured as an important cause, the enslavement of Indians in Carolina diminished. But during the first half-century of the colony's history, the large number of children of Indian mothers and white fathers in Charleston testified to the extensive miscegenation practiced there. White men outnumbered white women in South Carolina by more than 13 to 9 as late as 1708 and womanless men were not reluctant to avail themselves of Indian women. In Georgia no less a figure than Thomas Bosomworth, chaplain of Oglethorpe's utopian colony, found it respectable to marry a Creek woman in the early years of settlement and many others followed his example. Both John McDonald and Alexander Cameron, Deputy Indian Commissioners to the Cherokees in the late colonial period, married Cherokee women and the postrevolutionary Cherokee leaders, Sequoyah and George Lowrey, were both born of interracial marriages during this era.

Interracial mixing between Indians and Europeans, then, was limited more by demographic considerations than by prior attitudes. It is also clear in the miscegenation laws passed by all the colonies during the colonial period that attitudes differed toward black-skinned Africans and tawny-skinned Indians. Miscegenation laws were aimed almost exclusively at white-black mating. Only North Carolina and Virginia forbade marriage between Indians and whites (though Massachusetts debated such a law) and no colonies applied special penalties for red-white fornication as they often did for cases involving blacks and whites. In fact, many transplanted Europeans, applying their own standards of beauty, described Indian women as beautiful, whereas no such descriptions can be found of African women. Indian women, wrote Robert Beverley in 1705, were "generally Beautiful, possessing uncommon delicacy of Shape and Features, and wanting no Charm but that of a fair complexion." Many other colonial commentators spoke in a similar vein.

The general lack of red-white sexual intermingling forecast the overall failure of the two cultures to assimilate. The amalgamation of Indians and whites never proceeded very far in eighteenth-century America because Indians were seldom eager to trade their culture for one which they found inferior and because the colonists found the Indians useful only as trappers of furs, consumers of European trade goods, and military allies. All these functions were best performed outside the white communities. This is in striking contrast to the Latin American colonies where the lack of white women and the subjugation of Indian laborers had brought the two peoples into close contact and thus created a large mestizo population. Even the most conservative estimates of the mestizo population show that it had reached 25 percent of the population in early nineteenth-century Spanish America and many of these individuals rose to the position of artisan, foreman on the encomiendas, militiaman, and even collector of tithes and taxes. But in colonial America the half-Indian, half-white person, usually the product of a liaison between a white fur trader and an Indian woman, remained in almost all cases within Indian society. A number of the male offspring became fur traders themselves or intermediaries between English and Indian society.

Others, such as Joseph Brant of the Mohawks and Alexander McGil-
livray of the Creeks, became noted leaders of Indian resistance in the
second half of the eighteenth century. Although historians have not
yet systematically studied the American mestizo, who revealingly was
called by the derogatory term "half-breed," there are some indications that these persons, whom white colonists recognized only as
Indians, were the most alienated of all people from white society.
One Virginian gave explicit expression to this in 1757 when he wrote
that traders who consorted with Indian "squaws" left their offspring
"like bulls or bears to be provided for at random by their mothers.
. . . As might be expected," he pointed out, "some of these
bastards have been the leading men or war captains that have done
us so much mischief."

The one case in which transculturation between Indians and
Europeans did occur involved the Indianization of whites rather than
the Europeanization of Indians. Throughout the colonial period,
much to the horror of the guardians of white culture, colonists in
eastern North American ran away to Indian settlements, or, when
they were captured in war and had lived with a tribe for a few years,
frequently showed great reluctance to return to white society. This
"reversion to savagery," as those who insisted on the superiority of
white culture regarded it, has attracted the attention of American
novelists since the late eighteenth century. For white colonists, of
course, the prospect of their own people preferring the Indian way of
life to their own was a disturbing anomaly. "None can imagine what
it is to be captivated, and enslaved to such atheistical, proud, wild,
cruel, barbarous, brutish (in one word) diabolical creatures as these,
the worst of the heathen," wrote a seventeenth-century Puritan.

But in spite of such fantasy characterizations, colonists were obliged to live with the notion that many of their own kind found Indian
society more fulfilling to their needs than Anglo-American culture. To
make matters worse, virtually no Indians took the reverse route,
choosing to remain in white society after exposure to it. Hector St.
Jean Crevecoeur, the famous Frenchman who lived in America for
more than a decade in the late colonial period, wrote in his celebrated *Letters from an American Farmer:*

> *By what power does it come to pass, that children who have been
> adopted when young among these people, can never be prevailed on to*

readopt European manners? Many an anxious parent I have seen after the last war [Seven Years War], who at the return of peace, went to the Indian villages where they knew their children had been carried in captivity; when to their inexpressible sorrow, they found them so perfectly Indianised, that many knew them no longer, and those whose more advanced ages permitted them to recollect their fathers and mothers, absolutely refused to follow them, and ran to their adopted parents for protection against the effusions of love their unhappy real parents lavished on them! Incredible as this may appear, I have heard it asserted in a thousand instances, among persons of credit. . . . There must be in their social bond," Crevecoeur speculated, *"something singularly captivating, and far superior to anything to be boasted of among us; for thousands of Europeans are Indians, and we have no examples of even one of those Aborigines having from choice become Europeans.*

Crevecoeur's testimony, an elaboration of a phenomenon earlier observed by Cadwallader Colden, governor of New York, and Benjamin Franklin, has been amply corroborated by historical research, leaving little doubt that this transculturation operated basically in only one direction and that it became extremely difficult to convince "white Indians" to return to their native culture once they had experienced Indian life. The reason for this provides a piercing insight into the differences between the two cultures. Even before the arrival of Europeans, Indian cultures had customarily adopted into their society as full-fledged members any persons captured in war. On some occasions a captive was even taken into a particular family to replace a lost child or other relative. This integration of newcomers into the kinship system and into the community at large, without judgmental comparisons of the superiority of the captor culture, made it easy for the captured "outsider" to make a rapid personal adjustment. A white child taken into Indian society was treated on equal terms and prepared for any role open to others of his or her age. That a number of whites and Negroes who had fled to Indian communities or had been captured by them became chiefs is the most dramatic evidence of the nearly complete receptiveness of Indian cultures to "outsiders."

White society contrasted sharply in this regard. Though a number of Indian children were adopted into white families, the general pattern was to socially isolate the newcomer. "It was not that the Indian could not be raised 'up' to the level of civilization," writes one student of the subject, "but rather, the lack of an equivalent desire on the part of whites to welcome and assimilate the Indian, and the absence of any established cultural means that would mediate the transition from one culture to the other in a manner that was psychologically sound." Even Christianized Indians trained in white schools, such as the Mohegan Samson Occum, were expected to return to Indian society rather than occupy a place of dignity in white culture. Indians were always regarded as aliens and were rarely allowed to live within white society except on its periphery. The colonists, operating from their small communities and surrounded by a culture they chose to regard as not only inferior but as "barbaric" and "savage," "erected a defensive wall of heightened consciousness of superiority" in order to keep out those who seemed so threatening. This inability to develop the mentality or social mechanisms for incorporating Indians into their midst betrayed a sense of personal and cultural insecurity among a people who never tired of proclaiming the superiority of their way of life.

White-Black Intermixture

The extent of white-black intermixture in colonial America is a more complicated phenomenon because whites and blacks were always in close proximity, both in areas where white women were plentiful and in areas where they were scarce. This proximity led to widespread sexual contact, although it rarely involved intermarriage. At first glance, one might imagine that the rarity of racial intermarriage stemmed from a deep-seated white aversion to blackness itself, but if this was the case it would be impossible to explain what almost every observer of eighteenth-century society claimed to see—that "the country swarms with mulatto bastards," in the words of one Virginian. Though such comments do nothing to define miscegenation with statistical precision, eighteenth-century censuses help to clarify the point. In Maryland in 1755 a special census showed that 8 percent of the Negroes in the colony were mulatto. A generation later in Rhode Island the census of 1783 revealed that 16.5 percent of the colony's 2,806 Negroes were of mixed blood. A register of slaves for Chester County, Pennsylvania, in 1780 listed 20 percent of the Negroes as mulattoes. In all three areas white women were almost as numerous as white men, indicating that even when white women were available, white men frequently had sexual relations with black women.

That these contacts were not even more extensive can be explained primarily by the fact that in the period when white women were in short supply, black women were also unavailable. Slaves did not begin to enter the English colonies in significant numbers until the end of the seventeenth century and by that time the number of white women in all but the infant colony of South Carolina nearly equalled the number of white men. In the Southern plantations in 1720, the slave population was about 50,000; not more than about 10,000 of these could have been black women. At the same time some 70,000 adult white colonists inhabited the Southern colonies of whom almost half were women. This is in stark contrast to the situation in Portuguese Brazil, Spanish Peru, or even the English islands in the West Indies. In all of these zones of contact European women were relatively unavailable for much longer periods of time.

It is the example of the English Caribbean colonies that provides the clinching evidence for the case against prior attitudes determining the nature and degree of racial intermixture. With white women not present in roughly equal numbers with white men until the second century of settlement, black women were unhesitantly exploited to fill the gap. Even married white plantation owners "keep a Mulatto or Black Girl in the house or at lodgings for certain purposes," reported one traveler, and a famous eighteenth-century historian of the English sugar islands colorfully pronounced that "He who should presume to shew any displeasure against such a thing as simple fornication, would for his pains be accounted a simple blockhead; since not one in twenty can be persuaded, that there is either sin; or shame in cohabiting with his slave."

In the mainland colonies, however, interracial sex brought private pleasure but public condemnation. But this was mainly an eighteenth- rather than a seventeenth-century development. Historians have worked assiduously to show that Africans in North America were being separated from whites shortly after their arrival in the second decade of the seventeenth century. But not until 1662, when Virginia passed a law imposing a fine for fornication between white and black partners that was twice the usual amount, did an unambiguous law appear on the books that expressed public distaste for racial intermixture. Interracial marriage was banned in Virginia in 1691, in Massachusetts in 1705, in Maryland in 1715, and thereafter in Delaware, Pennsylvania, North and South Carolina, and Georgia.

The key change in the eighteenth century was not a marked increase or decrease in miscegenation, reflecting changes in private urges, but a shifting of public attitudes toward it. "By the turn of the century," writes Winthrop Jordan, "it was clear in many continental colonies that the English settlers felt genuine revulsion for interracial sexual union, at least in principle." The grand jury in Charleston, South Carolina, for example, inveighed against "The Too Common Practice of Criminal Conversation with Negro and other Slave Wenches in this Province" in 1743. Similar comments can be found in all of the colonies. But with the black population growing rapidly and slavery becoming a basic institution in colonial society, lawmakers were discovering that while they could not manage biology they could at least keep the legitimate offspring of the dominant group purebred by laws prohibiting interracial marriage.

In a society where slavery was touching the lives of a great proportion of the inhabitants, it was becoming necessary to contain the black population in a tight web of authority and to reassert again and again the dominance of whites. One way of accomplishing this was to emphasize the heathen or "savage" condition of the slave, which justified slavery on the one hand and made sexual contact publicly impermissible on the other. In a variety of public statements and in laws, the offspring of white-black copulation were being described as "spurious" or "mongrel." That the mulatto was given no higher standing than the pureblood black, and that he was in law regarded as fully black, not only contrasted starkly with the situation of the mulatto in almost every other part of the New World but was profoundly revelatory of the frame of mind that was overtaking eighteenth-century Americans. Black women were not needed by white males in a demographic sense. But sexual relations with them went on and on. Desire could not be legislated out of the white psyche and if the laws and public pronouncements did not correspond with private urges, there was little harm done so long as the domination of whites was preserved by disowning children of mixed racial inheritance.

As the eighteenth century wore on, racial attitudes towards Indians and Afro-Americans began to diverge sharply. This divergence was closely tied to striking differences in the nature and degree of sexual contact that characterized red-white and black-white relationships. White attitudes toward the black man cannot be dissociated from the fact that sexual relations, especially between white men and black women, were frequent and usually coercive throughout the eighteenth century. White men might ban interracial marriage as a way of stating with legal finality that the Negro, even when free, was not the equal of the white man. But white power was also served by sexually exploiting black women outside of marriage—a way of acting out the concept of white domination. Racial intermingling, so long as it involved free white men and slave black women, was a way of intimately and brutally proclaiming the superior rights and strength of white society.

Contact of this character had no parallel in the case of the Indian woman. When she was accessible, for example, to fur traders, she was not in the hapless position of a slave woman, nearly defenseless to resist the advances of a master with power of life and death over her. If an Indian woman chose to submit to a white man, it was usually on mutually agreeable terms. Furthermore, it was widely known that Indian men rarely molested female prisoners. In these differences we can find the source and meaning of a fear which has preoccupied white America for three hundred years—the fear of the black male lusting after the white woman. This vision of the "black rapist," so enduring in contemporary attitudes and literature, runs through the accounts of slave uprisings which occurred in the eighteenth and nineteenth centuries. In large part this fear of black men, who are seen rising not in quest of their freedom but in pursuit of white women, seems to stem from feelings of guilt originating in the sexual exploitation of black women and an associated fear of the black avenger, presumably filled with anger and poised to retaliate against those who first enslaved him and then plundered his women. This element of sexual fear is only rarely expressed in the literature concerning the Indian. Since little guilt could have been aroused by the occasional and noncoercive contacts with Indian women, white men, when they encountered hostile Indian males, rarely pictured them as sexual avengers. In the eighteenth century the Indian was almost never caricatured as the frenzied rapist, lurking in the bush or stalking white women. Indeed, the Indian was sometimes viewed as a peculiarly asexual creature; this in turn created a confused image in the white mind of a hostile, and yet sexually passive, "savage." His hostility was not doubted; but the hostile Indian, it was commonly regarded, was a man with knife in hand, bent on obtaining the scalp of the white encroacher. It was imagined, however, that hostile black men had focused on a different part of the anatomy in their quest for revenge.

The most striking fact about miscegenation in pre-Revolutionary America is that it did not result in widespread acculturation or assimilation, at least in comparison to other New World societies. . . .

In the North American colonies . . . assimilation was rejected by Englishmen, who had strong objections not to sexual relations with black-skinned women but to conferring status on blacks by accepting such intermingling as legitimate or by admitting its product to white society. Though skin color came to assume importance through generations of association with slavery, white colonists developed few qualms about intimate contact with black women. But raising the social status of those who labored at the bottom of society and who were defined as abysmally inferior was a matter of serious concern. It was resolved by insuring that [the] mulatto would not occupy a position midway between white and black. Any black blood classified a person as black; and to be black was almost always to be a slave. The "mulatto escape hatch" that Carl Degler has described in Latin American society did not exist in British North America, for there was relatively little need to call upon Negroes or mulattoes for important, status-conferring services and the extremely well-rooted institution of the white family, an outgrowth of a family pattern of settlement and a generous supply of white women, gave special reasons for excluding the living evidence of a sexual congress that threatened the purity of white culture.

In the American colonies, then, the need was for plantation labor and the urge was for occasional sex partners with whom one could act out all one's sexual fantasies, since black women were defined as lascivious by nature. By prohibiting racial intermarriage, winking at interracial sex, and defining all mixed offspring as black, white society found the ideal answer to its labor needs, its extracurricular and inadmissible sexual desires, its compulsion to maintain its culture purebred, and the problem of maintaining, at least in theory, absolute social control.

That this system of sexual politics was linked not so much to the national prejudices of Englishmen as to the historical circumstances of English settlement in North America becomes clearer by looking at the status of the mulatto in English Jamaica. By the mid-eighteenth century more than 90 percent of the Jamaica population was black, and white men greatly outnumbered white women. Such distorted demographic features called for a system in which black women would be available without scruple to white men and where mulatto offspring would rise to places of importance in the island society. This is precisely what happened. Miscegenation occurred on a massive scale and by 1733 the practice of conferring privileges and property on mulattoes was written into law. The Jamaican example, writes Degler, "strongly suggests that under certain circumstances even the quite different cultural attitudes of Englishmen could be changed, and in a direction remarkably like that taken by the Portuguese in Brazil. . . ."

In the final analysis the mixture of peoples in eighteenth-century America was the combined product of demographic ratios and the historical circumstances of English settlement. By 1770 there were some 2.3 million persons living east of the Allegheny Mountains but of these, 1.7 million were white, 0.5 million were black, and only 0.1 million or less were red. Such a preponderance of whites stood in stark contrast to almost every other part of the New World where Europeans had settled and, all other factors aside, would have guaranteed a fairly low level of miscegenation. Where people of different colors did live in close proximity, interracial contact occurred to a considerable extent. That interracial liaisons were not socially legitimized, as in other European colonies, reflected not only a difference in settlement patterns but the special concern for the preservation of "civilized society" in English North America, centering around the family. Whatever prior attitudes may have been among the Portuguese in Brazil, the French in Canada, or the English in the West Indies, these colonists represented a small minority of the population in their New World environments and, short of defeating their own purposes, could hardly have adopted the kind of strict ethnocentric social attitudes and laws that the English legislated in their North American colonies, where they stood forth as such an overwhelming part of the total population.

To be sure, what is most surprising is the degree of crossing of color lines that occurred within a society where the dominant group was making such strenuous claims for keeping its bloodstream pure. The gap between public pronouncements, as expressed in laws prohibiting miscegenation, and actual social practice, as visible in the large mixed blood population, can only be explained in terms of the white desire to maintain rigid social control while at the same time indulging in sexual gratification, which partners with different skin color heightened rather than threatened.

Leon F. Litwack

SLAVERY TO FREEDOM

In the following excerpt from North of Slavery: The Negro in the Free States, 1790–1860, *Professor Litwack describes the pattern of emancipation and abolition which swept the Northern states in the Revolutionary era. This movement against slavery illustrates the real, if limited, impact of Revolutionary ideology on a long-established social institution. Yet even though slavery was abolished in the North, the racial attitudes which were part of it persisted; while in the South, abolition sentiment faltered, unable to match the pressure generated for the perpetuation of such a broadly based social and economic system. As a result, although Northern emancipation made slavery an exclusively Southern phenomenon, most Americans continued to believe in white superiority and black inferiority. Professor Litwack teaches at the University of California, Berkeley.*

On the eve of the War of Independence, American Negro slavery knew no sectional boundaries. Every colony recognized it and sharply defined the legal position of free and enslaved blacks. The Declaration of Independence boldly asserted the natural rights of man but made no mention of slavery; the Constitution subsequently sanctioned and protected the institution without naming it. By that time, however, the Revolution had worked some important changes. Human bondage, it seemed certain, would henceforth assume a sectional character, for the North had sentenced it to a slow death. By 1800, some 36,505 northern Negroes still remained in bondage, most of them in New York and New Jersey, but almost every northern state

Reprinted from *North of Slavery,* by Leon F. Litwack, by permission of The University of Chicago Press, pp. 3–16. Copyright 1961 by the University of Chicago. Footnotes omitted.

had either abolished slavery outright or had provided for its gradual extinction.*

State statutes, constitutions, and court decisions recorded the methods of northern abolition but said little about the motives. Why did northern slaveholders surrender, with little apparent opposition or compensation, a valuable investment in human property? Perhaps, some have argued, it was not that valuable. In the complex economy and uncongenial climate of the North, slave labor presumably proved to be unprofitable; savage Africans lacked the mental capacity to learn anything more than how to tend a single crop. Climate and geography thus prompted the employing class to turn to the more profitable use of free white laborers, thereby dooming slavery. "The winter here was always unfavourable to the African constitution," one New Englander explained. "For this reason, white labourers were preferable to blacks."

Although commonly accepted, the economic explanation for northern abolition has not been adequately demonstrated. Plantation capitalism did not root itself in the North; the economy of that region came to be based largely on commerce, manufacturing, and small-scale agriculture. But this did not necessarily preclude the profitable use of slave labor. On the contrary, evidence suggests that the scarcity and expense of free white labor prompted ambitious northerners to make a profitable use of slaves and that these Negro bondsmen could and did perform successfully a variety of tasks—agricultural and mechanical, skilled and unskilled—in a diversified economy. On farms, slaves assisted in the production of foodstuffs and dairy products and in sheep and stock raising; in the cities, they worked in various skilled trades—as bakers, carpenters, cabinetmakers, sawyers, blacksmiths, printers, tailors, and coopers—and perhaps most prominently in the maritime industry.

Wherever utilized, slave labor was still cheap labor. Free labor, on the other hand, involved additional expense. In comparing the economic value of the two groups, John Adams admitted that his personal abhorrence of slavery had cost him "thousands of dollars for the labor and subsistence of free men, which I might have saved by

*Slavery was abolished by the constitutions of Vermont (1777), Ohio (1802), Illinois (1818), and Indiana (1816); by a judicial decision in Massachusetts (1783); by constitutional interpretation in New Hampshire; and by gradual-abolition acts in Pennsylvania (1780), Rhode Island (1784), Connecticut (1784 and 1797), New York (1799 and 1817), and New Jersey (1804).

the purchase of Negroes at times when they were very cheap." Moreover, some northern slaveholders appeared unconvinced that abolition would rid them of an economic encumbrance. Vigorously opposing a proposed duty on the importation of Negroes, a group of Pennsylvania merchants cited the scarcity of laborers and artisans and argued that additional slaves would reduce "the exorbitant price of Labour, and, in all probability, bring our Staple Commoditys to their usual prices." Despite public abolition sentiment, a Massachusetts physician recalled in 1795, it took legal action to force many slaveholders to part with their human chattel. Such reluctance would seem to suggest that slaves at least performed some useful and profitable services.

If slave labor was indeed unprofitable, not only did some masters reluctantly give up their property, but white workers protested often and bitterly against the Negro's competitive position. By the end of the seventeenth century, for example, workers in New York City had already complained that Negro labor had "soe much impoverisht them, that they Cannot by their Labours gett a Competency for the Maintenance of themselves and Family's." In 1737, the lieutenant governor of New York asked the Assembly to consider the justifiable complaints of "honest and industrious tradesmen" that skilled slave labor had reduced them to unemployment and poverty. Twenty years later, when Lieutenant Governor James Delancey proposed a poll tax on slaves, he argued that this would attract more white laborers and occasion little local resistance. "[T]he price of labor is now become so high," he explained, "and hence the owners of slaves reap such advantage, that they cannot reasonably complain of a tax on them." In Massachusetts, John Adams recalled, the opposition of white labor assured the extinction of slavery, for it "would no longer suffer the rich to employ these sable rivals so much to their injury." Had slavery not been abolished, Adams observed, the white laborers would simply have removed the Negro by force. In any case, their hostility had already rendered the institution unprofitable. "Their scoffs and insults, their continual insinuations, filled the negroes with discontent, made them lazy, idle, proud, vicious, and at length wholly useless to their masters, to such a degree that the abolition of slavery became a measure of economy."

If contemporary explanations have any validity, the liquidation of slavery in the North should not be considered simply on the grounds of profits and losses, climate, or geography. Abolition sentiment generally ignored these factors and chose instead to emphasize one particular theme: that the same principles used to justify the American Revolution, particularly John Locke's natural-rights philosophy, also condemned and doomed Negro slavery. Such an institution could not be reconciled with colonial efforts to resist English tyranny; indeed, its existence embarrassed the American cause. "To contend for liberty," John Jay wrote, "and to deny that blessing to others involves an inconsistency not to be excused." Until America ridded herself of human bondage, "her prayers to Heaven for liberty will be impious."

During the Revolution, official pronouncements reiterated the incompatibility of slavery and the struggle for independence. In Pennsylvania, for example, the Executive Council suggested to the Assembly in 1778 that the further importation of slaves be prohibited as a first step toward eventual abolition. Such a move, the Council pointed out, would not only be humane and just but would raise American prestige among the Europeans, "who are astonished to see a people eager for Liberty holding Negroes in Bondage." One year later, the Council contended that slavery disgraced a people supposedly fighting for liberty and urged a plan for gradual abolition. In 1780, the state legislature incorporated these sentiments in the preamble to a gradual-abolition act. Inasmuch as Americans had gone to war to obtain their freedom, the legislature asserted, such a blessing should be shared with those who had been and were being subjected to a similar state of bondage. In neighboring New Jersey, the governor urged the legislature in 1778 to provide for gradual abolition on the grounds that slavery conflicted with the principles of Christianity and was especially "odious and disgraceful" for a people professing to idolize liberty.

Perhaps the most radical extension of the Revolutionary ideology to Negro rights was made in New York. In 1785, the New York legislature passed a gradual-abolition act. The Council of Revision, however, rejected the bill because of a clause which prohibited Negroes from exercising the franchise. Contending that the freedmen should be granted full citizenship, the Council found this clause contrary to basic liberties and "repugnant to the principle on which the United States justify their separation from Great Britain," for it "supposes that those may rightfully be charged with the burdens of government, who have no representative share in imposing them." If free Negroes failed to secure the vote, the Council warned, a time might come when they would be numerous, wealthy, and powerful, and they might then turn against a constitution which deprived them of their just rights. The legislature failed to override the Council's veto and delayed gradual abolition for another fourteen years.

Massachusetts, where resistance to British authority had been the most dramatic and far-reaching, perhaps reflected most clearly the troublesome conflict between the Revolutionary ideals and slavery. Few public pronouncements had been made on the subject of Negro bondage, Dr. Jeremy Belknap of Boston recalled, "till we began to feel the weight of oppression from 'our mother country' as Britain was then called. The inconsistency of pleading for our own rights and liberties, whilst we encouraged the subjugation of others, was very apparent; and from that time, both slavery and the slave-trade began to be discountenanced." Early in the Revolutionary struggle, James Otis struck at both colonial and Negro bondage. Although *The Rights of the British Colonies Asserted and Proved* has had more enduring fame as a forceful statement of the colonial constitutional position, that same tract applied John Locke's natural-rights philosophy not only to the current troubles with England but also to Negro slavery. "It is a clear truth," Otis wrote, "that those who every day barter away other mens [sic] liberty, will soon care little for their own."

As the colonial crisis became more intense and headed for a showdown, many New Englanders felt even more conscious of the inconsistency of opposing English tyranny and practicing slavery. "It always appeared a most iniquitous scheme to me," Abigail Adams wrote her husband in 1774, "to fight ourselves for what we are daily robbing and plundering from those who have as good a right to freedom as we have." Massachusetts town meetings began to couple their protests against royal and Parliamentary usurpation with pleas that slavery be abolished. Two months after the Declaration of Independence, the state house of representatives climaxed this growing sentiment by resolving that human bondage violated the natural rights of man and was "utterly inconsistent with the avowed principles in which this and other States have carried on their struggle for liberty." Meanwhile, several Massachusetts towns did not wait for legislative or judicial action but simply voted to have no slaves in

their midst and to bear any expense that might arise from the emancipated Negroes' old age, infirmities, or inability to support themselves. By the end of 1776, one observer wrote, public opinion had
virtually extirpated slavery.

In Massachusetts, unlike Pennsylvania, New Jersey, and New York,
court action legally ended slavery. Prior to 1783, several slaves collected money among themselves and successfully sued for their
freedom. Some even secured compensation for their services. John
Adams, who represented several bondsmen in such cases, recalled
that he "never knew a jury, by a verdict, to determine a negro to be a
slave. They always found them free." Those arguments most commonly used to obtain a Negro's freedom, Adams stated, were based
on "the rights of mankind, which was the fashionable word at that
time." Successful court action encouraged the voluntary liberation of
other slaves. To avoid court litigation, some slaves simply took the
new constitution at its word when it affirmed the freedom and
equality of all men, and either asked for and received their release or
took it without consent.

Against this favorable background, the Massachusetts Supreme
Court dealt Negro slavery a final blow. Quork Walker, a Negro slave,
claimed his freedom on the basis of his master's verbal promise.
Although this would ordinarily have been insufficient evidence to
release him from bondage, Walker's attorneys found other grounds,
the most important of which stressed the natural rights of man, the
newly adopted Massachusetts Declaration of Rights, and the need for
a more consistent stand against tyranny. "Can we expect to triumph
over G. Britain," counsel Levi Lincoln asked, "to get free ourselves
until we let those go free under us?" Chief Justice William Cushing's
subsequent charge to the jury reiterated much of this argument.
Regardless of previous practices, he declared, the American people
had demonstrated a greater devotion to the natural rights of man
"and to that natural, innate desire of Liberty, with which Heaven
(without regard to color, complexion, or shape of noses, features)
has inspired all the human race." The new constitution, Cushing
concluded, made this quite clear; consequently, "the idea of slavery
is inconsistent with our own conduct and Constitution." This decision, handed down in 1783, ended slavery in the Puritan Commonwealth.

Exploiting the abolition sentiment aroused by the Revolution,

Negro slaves and their white allies sought to dramatize the conflict between colonial principles and practices. Obviously aware of the symbolic value of the War of Independence for the cause of emancipation, Negro petitioners claimed a natural, a God-given, right to freedom and asserted "that Every Principle from which America has Acted in the Cours of their unhappy Dificultes with Great Briton Pleads Stronger than A thousand arguments in favours of your petioners." In the New London *Gazette*, "a Negro" made this point even more forcefully:

> Is not all oppression vile?
> When you attempt your freedom to defend,
> Is reason yours, and partially your friend?
> Be not deceiv'd—for reason pleads for all
> Who by invasion and oppression fall.
> I live a slave, and am inslav'd by those
> Who yet pretend with reason to oppose
> All schemes oppressive; and the gods invoke
> To curse with thunders the invaders yoke.
> O mighty God! let conscience seize the mind
> Of Inconsistent men, who wish to find
> A partial god to vindicate their cause,
> And plead their freedom, while they break its laws.

If such theoretical or poetic appeals did not suffice, an estimated five thousand Negroes—most of them northerners—fought with white men for American independence. Despite colonial laws excluding Negroes from the militia and an early hesitancy to enlist them in the war, military expediency finally broke down these barriers and prompted the Continental Congress and most of the states to enlist slaves and free Negroes. Between 1775 and 1781, Negro soldiers participated in virtually every major military action. In return for their military services, most states either freed them upon enlistment or at the end of hostilities.

In several states, religious organizations played an active and sometimes decisive role in the work of emancipation. After all, the pulpit was still a most influential and authoritative position from which to mold public opinion. Colonial parishioners had long been indoctrinated with the ideas of John Locke and their implications for the struggle with the mother country. Consistency and moral rectitude demanded, many churchmen insisted, that the laws of God and Nature also be directed at the glaring sin of human slavery. Otherwise the Revolutionary struggle had little significance. "Would we enjoy liberty?" a Massachusetts minister asked in 1774. "Then we must grant it to others. For shame, let us either cease to enslave our fellow men, or else let us cease to complain of those, that would enslave us." Quoting directly from the Scriptures, one churchman deplored the inconsistency of colonial practices and professions: "Happy is he saith the apostle Paul that condemneth not himself in that thing which he alloweth."

Most conspicuous among the antislavery religious groups were the Quakers. Abolition sentiment in Pennsylvania, for example, resulted largely from early and persistent Quaker opposition to slavery as inconsistent with the true spirit of Christianity. In 1758, the Philadelphia Yearly Meeting voted to exclude anyone who bought or sold slaves from participation in the meetings and affairs of the church; in 1774, it increased the penalty to disownment, and two years later it directed its members to "testify their disunion" with any member who resisted a last entreaty to free his slaves. The Quaker anti-slavery stand was not limited to any one state, however. Following the lead of Pennsylvania, yearly meetings in New England, New York, Baltimore, Virginia, and North Carolina soon adopted similar condemnations of slaveholding. After completing their work of emancipation, Quakers shifted their attention to improving the educational and economic level of the free Negro population.

Quakers also participated actively in the organization, leadership, and activities of the Pennsylvania Society for the Abolition of Slavery. Organized in 1775, the Society first directed its efforts toward securing an abolition law in Pennsylvania and protecting the free Negro from being kidnaped and sold into slavery. The victims of kidnaping were usually ignorant of legal remedies or unable to secure competent legal assistance. After a successful campaign for adequate protective legislation, the Society helped to enforce the new laws through the organization of committees of correspondence and by hiring competent counsel to secure the conviction of offenders. Although the Society suspended its work during the war, individual members continued to be active. Reorganized in 1787 as the Pennsylvania Society for Promoting the Abolition of Slavery, the Relief of Free Negroes Unlawfully Held in Bondage, and for Improving the Condition of the African Race, the Society joined the Quakers in granting assistance to freedmen.

In celebrating the abolition of slavery in New York, a Negro leader singled out for particular praise the Quakers and the New York Manumission Society, which he termed "the most powerful lever, or propelling cause." That society had organized in 1785 with John Jay as president and Alexander Hamilton as vice-president, thus reflecting the strong Federalist interest in abolition. As early as 1777, Jay had felt that Revolutionary consistency required the abolition of Negro bondage; twenty-two years later, as governor, Jay signed a bill providing for the gradual emancipation of New York's twenty-one thousand slaves. Having fulfilled its major goal, the Manumission Society concerned itself with enforcing and liberalizing the provisions of the abolition act and also joined with the Pennsylvania Society to secure improved anti-kidnaping laws and educational facilities for free Negroes.

By 1830, whether by legislative, judicial, or constitutional action, Negro slavery had been virtually abolished in the North. Only 3,568 Negroes remained in bondage, and more than two-thirds of these resided in New Jersey. Although the Revolutionary ideology had also penetrated the South, particularly Virginia, emancipation had made little headway there. Powerful social and economic factors, the most obvious being Eli Whitney's cotton gin, made slavery the cheapest and most productive form of labor in the South. During the Revolution, some southerners had indeed joined with their northern compatriots to deplore the inconsistency of slavery and the struggle for liberty, but the postwar years brought only disappointment and finally complete disillusionment. After congratulating New England on its successful elimination of bondage, one Virginia judge sadly confessed in 1795 that deep-rooted white prejudices, the fear of large numbers of free Negroes, the impossibility of assimilating them into white society, and the need for a large and cheap servile labor force had combined to frustrate and defeat any plan for gradual abolition. "If, in Massachusetts," he wrote, "where the numbers are comparatively small, this prejudice be discernable, how much stronger may it be imagined in this country, where every white man felt himself born to tyrannize, where the blacks were regarded as of no more importance than the brute cattle, where the laws rendered even venial offences criminal in them, where every species of degradation towards them was exercised on all occasions, and where even their lives were exposed to the ferocity of the masters." By the turn of the century, human bondage had become a "peculiar institution." Freedom did not suddenly confer citizenship on the Negro. Emancipation, although enthusiastically welcomed by the northern slave, had its limitations. Until the post-Civil War era, in fact, most northern whites would maintain a careful distinction between granting Negroes legal protection—a theoretical right to life, liberty, and property—and political and social equality. No statute or court decision could immediately erase from the public mind, North or South, that long and firmly held conviction that the African race was inferior and therefore incapable of being assimilated politically, socially, and most certainly physically with the dominant and superior white society. Despite the absence of slavery in the North, one observer remarked, "chains of a stronger kind still manacled their limbs, from which no legislative act could free them; a mental and moral subordination and inferiority, to which tyrant custom has here subjected all the sons and daughters of Africa."

Kenneth M. Stampp

CHATTELS PERSONAL

In the nineteenth century the laws pertaining to slavery and race relations underwent a variety of changes, so that the distinction between slaves and free black people was undermined in the South. Ironically, it appears that as racism became more pronounced, the legal codes were providing increased recognition of the humanity of slaves. This selection from Stampp's classic study The Peculiar Institution *illustrates the ambiguity and tension of race relations as they were reflected in law. Professor Stampp is Morrison Professor of History at the University of California, Berkeley.*

In Alabama's legal code of 1852 two clauses, standing in significant juxtaposition, recognized the dual character of the slave.[1]

From *The Peculiar Institution,* by Kenneth M. Stampp, pp. 192–235. Copyright © 1956 by Kenneth M. Stampp. Reprinted by permission of Alfred A. Knopf, Inc.

[1] Extracts from the slave codes presented in this chapter were taken from the legal

The first clause confirmed his status as property—the right of the owner to his "time, labor and services" and to his obedient compliance with all lawful commands. Slavery thus being established by law, masters relied upon the state to use its power against white men who "tampered" with their bondsmen, and against bondsmen they could not subdue. Courts, police, and militia were indispensable parts of the machinery of control.

The second clause acknowledged the slave's status as a person. The law required that masters be humane to their slaves, furnish them adequate food and clothing, and provide care for them during sickness and in old age. In short, the state endowed masters with obligations as well as rights and assumed some responsibility for the welfare of the bondsmen.

But legislators and magistrates were caught in a dilemma whenever they found that the slave's status as property was incompatible with his status as a person. Individual masters struggled with this dilemma in different ways, some conceding much to the dictates of humanity, others demanding the utmost return from their investment. Olmsted explained the problem succinctly: "It is difficult to handle simply as property, a creature possessing human passions and human feelings, . . . while, on the other hand, the absolute necessity of dealing with property as a thing, greatly embarrasses a man in any attempt to treat it as a person."[2]

After adopting Draconian codes in the early eighteenth century, the various legislatures in some respects gradually humanized them, while the courts tempered their application, but there was no way to resolve the contradiction implicit in the very term "human property." Both legislators and judges frequently appeared erratic in dealing with bondsmen as both *things* and *persons.* Alabama's code defined the property status of the slave before acknowledging his human status, and throughout the ante-bellum South the cold language of statutes and judicial decisions made it evident that, legally, the slave was less a person than a thing.

The fact that southern slavery was, in the main, Negro slavery gave an advantage to those who wished to preserve it. If he ran away, the Negro slave with his distinctive skin color could not so

---

codes or revised statutes of the southern states. See also Hurd, *Law of Freedom and Bondage*, and the various studies of slavery in individual states.

[2] Olmsted, *Back Country*, p. 64.

easily escape detection as could a white indentured servant. Moreover, all Negroes were brought to America in bondage, and legislatures soon adopted the principle of *partus sequitur ventrem*— the child inherits the condition of the mother. Therefore, the English common-law presumption in favor of freedom did not apply to Negroes; in all the slave states (except Delaware) the presumption was that people with black skins were slaves unless they could prove that they were free. Any strange Negro found in a southern community without "freedom papers" was arrested as a fugitive.

But southern slavery was not *exclusively* Negro slavery. The status of a child of mixed Negro and white ancestry depended upon the status of the mother. The offspring of a Negro slave father and a free white mother was free. The offspring of a free white father and a Negro, mulatto, quadroon, or octoroon slave mother was a slave. In fact, the Texas Supreme Court once ruled that the child of a slave mother was a slave no matter how remote the Negro ancestry.[3] Hence some slaves were whites by any rational definition as well as by all outward appearances, even though some distant female ancestor may have been a Negro. One Virginia fugitive had a "complexion so nearly white, that . . . a stranger would suppose there was no African blood in him."[4]

Not all southern slaves were Negroes, and not all southern masters were whites. In 1830, more than thirty-six hundred free Negroes or persons of mixed ancestry owned slaves. The great majority of these colored slaveowners had merely purchased husbands, wives, or children and were unable to emancipate them under existing state laws. A few were substantial planters, such as the Negro in King George County, Virginia, who owned seventy-one slaves; another in St. Landry Parish, Louisiana, who owned seventy-five; and two others in Colleton District, South Carolina, who owned eighty-four apiece. Though southern whites overwhelmingly disapproved, only in Delaware and Arkansas did the courts refuse to sanction the ownership of slaves by "free persons of color." The Arkansas Supreme Court held that slavery had its foundation "in an *inferiority of race*," and the bondage of one Negro to another lacked "this solid foundation to rest upon."[5]

[3] Catterall (ed.), *Judicial Cases*, V, p. 295.
[4] Richmond *Enquirer*, February 7, 1837.
[5] Carter G. Woodson, *Free Negro Owners of Slaves in the United States in 1830* (Washington, D.C., 1924); Catterall (ed.), *Judicial Cases*, IV, p. 215; V, p. 257.

Since Negroes were presumed to be slaves and whites were presumed to be free, the southern states found it essential in cases of mixed ancestry to decide who were to be treated as Negroes and who as whites. No state adopted the principle that "a single drop of Negro blood" made a person legally a member of the "inferior race." Each state prescribed the proportion of Negro ancestry which excluded a person from the privileges enjoyed by white men. . . .

Any person with Negro ancestors too remote to cause him to be classified as a mulatto was by law a white man. While such a person could be held as a slave, the burden of proof was placed upon the putative master. In Kentucky, affirmed the Court of Appeals, "it has been well settled, that . . . having less than a fourth of African blood, is *prima facie* evidence of freedom." A Virginia jury having found that a woman suing for her freedom was white, it was incumbent upon her master to prove that she "was descended in the maternal line from a slave. Having not proved it, she and her children must be considered free."[6]

Some slaveholders preferred to use "bright mulattoes" as domestics; a few paid premium prices for light-skinned females to be used as concubines or prostitutes. But most masters saw the inconvenience of owning slaves who were nearly white: the presumption of freedom in their favor, and the greater ease with which they could escape. One former bondsman, a "white man with blue eyes," recalled his master's repeated attempts to sell him, always unsuccessful. A Kentucky slave, "owing to his being almost white, and to the consequent facilities of escape," was adjudged to be worth only "half as much as other slaves of the ordinary color and capacities."[7] Here was convincing evidence of the importance of racial visibility in keeping the Negro in bondage.

* * *

Every slave state had a slave code. Besides establishing the property rights of those who owned human chattels, these codes supported masters in maintaining discipline and provided safeguards for the white community against slave rebellions. In addition, they held slaves, as thinking beings, morally responsible and punishable for misdemeanors and felonies.

---

[6] Catterall (ed.), *Judicial Cases*, I, pp. 121, 330.
[7] Drew, *The Refugee*, pp. 123–32; Catterall (ed.), *Judicial Cases*, I, p. 278.

Fundamentally the slave codes were much alike. Those of the Deep South were somewhat more severe than those of the Upper South, but most of the variations were in minor details. The similarities were due, in part, to the fact that new states patterned their codes after those of the old. South Carolina's code of 1712 was almost a copy of the Barbadian code; Georgia's code of 1770 duplicated South Carolina's code of 1740; and later the Gulf states borrowed heavily from both. In the Upper South, Tennessee virtually adopted North Carolina's code, while Kentucky and Missouri lifted many passages from Virginia's. But the similarities were also due to the fact that slavery, wherever it existed, made necessary certain kinds of regulatory laws. The South Carolina code would probably have been essentially the same if the Barbadian code had never been written.

After a generation of liberalization following the American Revolution, the codes underwent a reverse trend toward increasing restrictions. This trend was clearly evident by the 1820s, when rising slave prices and expansion into the Southwest caused more and more Southeners to accept slavery as a permanent institution. The Nat Turner rebellion and northern abolitionist attacks merely accelerated a trend which had already begun. . . .

At the heart of every code was the requirement that slaves submit to their masters and respect all white men. The Louisiana code of 1806 proclaimed this most lucidly: "The condition of the slave being merely a passive one, his subordination to his master and to all who represent him is not susceptible of modification or restriction . . . he owes to his master, and to all his family, a respect without bounds, and an absolute obedience, and he is consequently to execute all the orders which he receives from him, his said master, or from them." A slave was neither to raise his hand against a white man nor to use insulting or abusive language. Any number of acts, said a North Carolina judge, may consitute "insolence"—it may be merely "a look, the pointing of a finger, a refusal or neglect to step out of the way when a white person is seen to approach. But each of such acts violates the rules of propriety, and if tolerated, would destroy that subordination, upon which our social system rests."[8]

The codes rigidly controlled the slave's movements and his com-

---

[8] Catterall (ed.), *Judicial Cases*, II, p. 168.

munication with others. A slave was not to be "at large" without a pass which he must show to any white man who asked to see it; if he forged a pass or free papers he was guilty of a felony. Except in a few localities, he was prohibited from hiring his own time, finding his own employment, or living by himself. A slave was not to preach, except to his master's own slaves on his master's premises in the presence of whites. A gathering of more than a few slaves (usually five) away from home, unattended by a white, was an "unlawful assembly" regardless of its purpose or orderly decorum.

No person, not even the master, was to teach a slave to read or write, employ him in setting type in a printing office, or give him books or pamphlets. A religious publication asked rhetorically: "Is there any great moral reason why we should incur the tremendous risk of having our wives slaughtered in consequence of our slaves being taught to read incendiary publications?" They did not need to read the Bible to find salvation: "Millions of those now in heaven never owned a bible."[9]

Farms and plantations employing slaves were to be under the supervision of resident white men, and not left to the sole direction of slave foremen. Slaves were not to beat drums, blow horns, or possess guns; periodically their cabins were to be searched for weapons. They were not to administer drugs to whites or practice medicine. "A slave under pretence of practicing medicine," warned a Tennessee judge, "might convey intelligence from one plantation to another, of a contemplated insurrectionary movement; and thus enable the slaves to act in concert."[10]

A slave was not to possess liquor, or purchase it without a written order from his owner. He was not to trade without a permit, or gamble with whites or with other slaves. He was not to raise cotton, swine, horses, mules, or cattle. Allowing a slave to own animals, explained the North Carolina Supreme Court, tended "to make other slaves dissatisfied . . . and thereby excite . . . a spirit of insubordination."[11]

Southern cities and towns supplemented the state codes with additional regulations. Most of them prohibited slaves from being on

[9] *Southern Presbyterian*, quoted in *De Bow's Review*, XVIII (1855), p. 52; *Farmers' Register*, IV (1836), p. 181.
[10] Catterall (ed.), *Judicial Cases*, II, pp. 520–21.
[11] Ibid., II, pp. 240–41.

the streets after curfew or living in dwellings separate from their masters. Richmond required Negroes and mulattoes to step aside when whites passed by, and barred them from riding in carriages except in the capacity of menials. Charleston slaves could not swear, smoke, walk with a cane, assemble at military parades, or make joyful demonstrations. In Washington, North Carolina, the town Commissioners prohibited "all disorderly shouting and dancing, and all disorderly . . . assemblies . . . of slaves and free Negroes in the streets, market and other public places." In Natchez, all "strange slaves" had to leave the city by four o'clock on Sunday afternoon.[12]

Violations of the state and local codes were misdemeanors or felonies subject to punishment by justices, sheriffs, police, and constabulary. Whipping was the most common form of public punishment for less than capital offenses. Except in Louisiana, imprisonment was rare. By mid-nineteenth century branding and mutiliation had declined, though they had not been abolished everywhere. South Carolina did not prohibit branding until 1833, and occasionally thereafter slave felons still had their ears cropped. Mississippi and Alabama continued to enforce the penalty of "burning in the hand" for felonies not capitally punished.[13]

But most slave offenders were simply tied up in the jail or at a whipping post and flogged. Some states in the Upper South limited to thirty-nine the number of stripes that could be administered at any one time, though more could be given in a series of whippings over a period of days or weeks. In the Deep South floggings could legally be more severe. Alabama permitted up to one hundred stripes on the bare back of a slave who forged a pass or engaged in "riots, routs, unlawful assemblies, trespasses, and seditious speeches."

State criminal codes dealt more severely with slaves and free Negroes than with whites. In the first place, they made certain acts felonies when committed by Negroes but not when committed by whites; and in the second place, they assigned heavier penalties to Negroes than whites convicted of the same offense. Every southern state defined a substantial number of felonies carrying capital punishment for slaves and lesser punishments for whites. In addition to murder of any degree, slaves received the death penalty for at-

---

[12] Ibid., II, p. 182; Henry, *Police Control*, p. 48; [Ingraham], *South-West*, II, pp. 72–73; Phillips, *American Negro Slavery*, pp. 497–98.
[13] Henry, *Police Control*, p. 52; Sydnor, *Slavery in Mississippi*, p. 83.

tempted murder, manslaughter, rape and attempted rape upon a white woman, rebellion and attempted rebellion, poisoning, robbery, and arson. A battery upon a white person might also carry a sentence of death under certain circumstances. In Louisiana, a slave who struck his master, a member of the master's family, or the overseer, "so as to cause a contusion, or effusion or shedding of blood," was to suffer death—as was a slave on a third conviction for striking a white.

The codes were quite unmerciful toward whites who interfered with slave discipline. Heavy fines were levied upon persons who unlawfully traded with slaves, sold them liquor without the master's permission, gave them passes, gambled with them, or taught them to read or write. North Carolina made death the penalty for concealing a slave "with the intent and for the purpose of enabling such slave to escape." Aiding or encouraging a bondsman to rebel was the most heinous crime of all. "If a free person," said the Alabama code, "advise or conspire with a slave to . . . make insurrection, . . . he shall be punished with death, whether such rebellion or insurrection be made or not."

Every slave state made it a felony to say or write anything that might lead, directly or indirectly, to discontent or rebellion. In 1837, the Missouri Legislature passed an act "to prohibit the publication, circulation, and promulgation of the abolition doctrines." The Virginia code of 1849 provided a fine and imprisonment for any person who maintained "that owners have not right of property in their slaves." Louisiana made it a capital offense to use "language in any public discourse, from the bar, the bench, the stage, the pulpit, or in any place whatsoever" that might produce "insubordination among the slaves." Most southern states used their police power to prohibit the circulation of "incendiary" material through the United States mail; on numerous occasions local postmasters, public officials, or mobs seized and destroyed antislavery publications.

Southerners justified these seizures on the ground that some slaves were literate in spite of the laws against teaching them to read. A petition to the South Carolina legislature claimed that "the ability to read exists on probably every plantation in the State; and it is utterly impossible for even the *masters* to prevent this—as is apparent from the cases in which servants learn to write by stealth." But whether or not slaves could read, the "corrupting influence" of antislavery propaganda was bound to reach them unless it was suppressed. There seemed to be no choice but to construct an "intellectual blockade" against ideas hostile to slavery if property were to be protected and the peace of society secured. Hence the laws controlled the voices and pens of white men as well as black.[14] . . .

Southern slave codes protected the owners of bondsmen who attempted to abscond by requiring officers to assist in their recapture and by giving all white men power to arrest them. . . .

Occasionally a band of runaways was too formidable to be dispersed by volunteers, and the governor called upon the militia to capture or destroy it. Ordinarily, however, this and other organized police activity was delegated to the slave patrols. A system of patrols, often more or less loosely connected with the militia, existed in every slave state. Virginia empowered each county or corporation court to "appoint, for a term not exceeding three months, one or more patrols" to visit "all negro quarters and other places suspected of having therein unlawful assemblies," and to arrest "such slaves as may stroll from one plantation to another without permission." Alabama compelled every slaveowner under sixty and every nonslaveholder under forty-five to perform patrol duty. The justices of each precinct divided the eligible males into detachments which had to patrol at least one night a week during their terms of service. Everywhere the patrols played a major role in the system of control. . . .

The final clauses in the southern legal codes relating directly to the control of slaves were those governing free Negroes. The laws reflected the general opinion that these people were an anomaly, a living denial "that nature's God intended the African for the *status* of slavery." They "embitter by their presence the happiness of those who remain slaves. They entice them and furnish them with facilities to elope." They were potential allies of the slaves in the event of a rebellion. In 1830, David Walker, a free Negro who moved from North Carolina to Boston, wrote and attempted to circulate in the South a pamphlet which urged the slaves to fight for their freedom. He thus aroused southern legislatures to the menace of the free Negro.[15]

[14] Undated petition from Chester District, South Carolina Slavery Manuscripts Collection; Clement Eaton, *Freedom of Thought in the Old South* (Durham, 1940), passim.
[15] Jackson *Mississippian*, February 26, 1858; Tallahassee *Floridian and Journal*, April 11, 1857; *American Farmer*, XI (1829), p. 167; Johnson, *Ante-Bellum North Carolina*, pp. 515–16.

The trend of antebellum legislation was toward ever more stringent controls. Free Negroes could not move from one state to another, and those who left their own state for any purpose could not return. In South Carolina and the Gulf states Negro seamen were arrested and kept in custody while their vessels were in port. Though free Negroes could make contracts and own property, in most other respects their civil rights were as circumscribed as those of slaves. They were the victims of the white man's fears, of racial prejudice, and of the desire to convince slaves that winning freedom was scarcely worth the effort.

Many Southerners desired the complete expulsion of the free Negroes, or the re-enslavement of those who would not leave. Petitions poured in to the state legislatures demanding laws that would implement one or the other of these policies. In 1849, a petition from Augusta County, Virginia, asked the legislature to make an appropriation for a program of gradual removal; all free Negroes who refused to go to Liberia should be expelled from the state within five years.[16] In 1859, the Arkansas legislature required sheriffs to order the state's handful of free Negroes to leave. Those who remained were to be hired out as slaves for a year, after which those who still remained were to be sold into permanent bondage.

A Texas editor caught the spirit of the extreme proslavery element during the 1850s when he proclaimed that the time was "near at hand for determined action." Southern free Negroes were "destined to be remitted back into slavery," which was their "true condition."[17] In this last antebellum decade most states adopted laws authorizing the "voluntary enslavement" of these people and enabling them to select their own masters. Virginia went a step further and permitted the sale into "absolute slavery" of free Negroes convicted of offenses "punishable by confinement in the penitentiary"; Florida applied the same penalty to those who were "idle" or "dissolute." This problem, some apparently felt, would remain unsolved until all Negroes and "mulattoes" were not only *presumed* to be slaves but were in *fact* slaves.

"A slave," said a Tennessee judge, "is not in the condition of a horse. . . . He has mental capacities, and an immortal principle in

---

[16] Virginia Legislative Petitions.
[17] Austin *Texas State Gazette*, September 12, 1857.

his nature." The laws did not "extinguish his high-born nature nor deprive him of many rights which are inherent in man."[18] All the southern codes recognized the slave as a person for purposes other than holding him accountable for crimes. Many state constitutions required the legislature "to pass such laws as may be necessary to oblige the owners of slaves to treat them with humanity; to provide for them necessary clothing and provisions; [and] to abstain from all injuries to them, extending to life or limb."

The legislatures responded with laws extending some protection to the persons of slaves. Masters who refused to feed and clothe slaves properly might be fined; in several states the court might order them to be sold, the proceeds going to the dispossessed owners. Those who abandoned or neglected insane, aged, or infirm slaves were also liable to fines. In Virginia the overseers of the poor were required to care for such slaves and to charge their masters.

Now and then a master was tried and convicted for the violation of one of these laws. . . . But prosecutions were infrequent. Since a slave could neither file a complaint nor give evidence against his master, action depended upon the willingness of whites to testify in the slave's behalf. This happened only under unusual circumstances.

Some of the codes regulated the hours of labor. As early as 1740, South Carolina limited the working day to fifteen hours from March to September and fourteen hours from September to March. All the codes forbade field labor on Sunday. In Virginia, a master who worked his slaves on Sunday, "except in household or other work of necessity or charity," was to be fined two dollars for each offense. It was permissible, however, to let slaves labor on the Sabbath for wages; and the North Carolina Supreme Court ruled that it was not an indictable offense to give them Sunday tasks as a punishment.[19] With rare exceptions, masters who were so inclined violated these laws with impunity.

The early colonial codes had assessed only light penalties, or none at all, for killing a slave. South Carolina, "to restrain and prevent barbarity being exercised toward slaves," provided, in 1740, that a white who willfully murdered a slave was to be punished by a fine of seven hundred pounds or imprisonment at hard labor for seven years. Killing a slave in "sudden heat or passion" or by "undue

[18] Catterall (ed.), *Judicial Cases*, II, p. 530.
[19] Ibid., II, p. 107.

correction" carried a fine of three hundred and fifty pounds. In Georgia prior to 1770, and in North Carolina prior to 1775, taking a slave's life was not a felony.

After the American Revolution there was a drastic change of policy. Virginia, in 1788, and North Carolina, in 1791, defined the malicious killing of a slave as murder subject to the same penalty imposed upon the murderer of a freeman. In 1817, North Carolina applied this principle to persons convicted of manslaughter. Georgia's Constitution of 1798 contained a clause that was copied, in substance, into the constitutions of several states in the Southwest: "Any person who shall maliciously dismember or deprive a slave of life shall suffer such punishment as would be inflicted in case the like offence had been committed on a free white person."

Eventually all the southern states adopted laws of this kind. . . .

By the 1850s, most of the codes had made cruelty a public offense even when not resulting in death. . . .

But these laws invariably had significant qualifications. For example, the accidental death of a slave while receiving "moderate correction" was not homicide. Killing a slave in the act of rebellion or when resisting legal arrest was always "justifiable homicide." South Carolina permitted a white person to "apprehend and moderately correct" a slave who was at large without a pass and refused to submit to examination; "and if any such slave shall assault and strike such white person, such slave may be lawfully killed." The South Carolina law against cruelty concluded with a nullifying clause: "nothing herein contained shall be so construed as to prevent the owner or person having charge of any slave from inflicting on such slave such punishment as may be necessary for the good government of the same." Southern courts, by their interpretations of the laws, in effect added further qualifications. Thus the North Carolina Supreme Court ruled that a homicide upon a slave did not require as much provocation as a homicide upon a white to make it justifiable.

Under most circumstances a slave was powerless to defend himself from an assault by a white man. According to the Tennessee Supreme Court, severe chastisement by the master did not justify resistance. If a master exercised his right to punish, "with or without cause, [and] the slave resist and slay him, it is murder . . . because the law cannot recognize the violence of the master as a legitimate cause of provocation." According to the Georgia Supreme Court, even if the owner should "exceed the bounds of reason . . . in his chastisement, the slave must submit . . . unless the attack . . . be calculated to produce death."[20] . . .

In a few notable cases the courts enforced the laws against the killing of slaves. A North Carolinian was sentenced to death for the murder of his own female chattel. Over a period of months he had "beat her with clubs, iron chains, and other deadly weapons, time after time; burnt her; inflicted stripes . . . which literally excoriated her whole body." The court held him "justly answerable" for her death, though he did not "specially design it.". . .

Decisions such as these were exceptional. Only a handful of whites suffered capital punishment for murdering slaves, and they were usually persons who had committed the offense upon slaves not their own. When a master was convicted, it was generally for a lesser crime, such as killing in "sudden heat or passion" or by "undue correction." And a convicted killer, whether or not the master, rarely received as heavy a penalty as he would have for a homicide upon a white.

Actually, the great majority of whites who, by a reasonable interpretation of the law, were guilty of feloniously killing slaves escaped without any punishment at all. Of those who were indicted, most were either acquitted or never brought to trial. For several reasons this was almost inevitable.

One major reason was that neither slaves nor free Negroes could testify against whites. There were, as one Southerner observed, "a thousand incidents of plantation life concealed from public view," witnessed only by slaves, which the law could not reach. One of slavery's "most vulnerable points," a defender of the institution agreed, was the "helpless position of the slave" when his master was "placed in opposition to him." His "mouth being closed as a witness," he had to depend upon whites to testify in his behalf.[21]

But here was the second major obstacle in the way of convictions: white witnesses were reluctant to testify against white offenders. Most white men were obsessed with the terrible urgency of racial solidarity, with the fear that the whole complex mechanism of control

---

[20] Ibid., II, pp. 549–50; III, pp. 35–36.
[21] Henry, *Police Control*, p. 79; Thomas R. R. Cobb, *An Inquiry into the Law of Negro Slavery in the United States of America* (Philadelphia, 1858), pp. 97–98.

would break down if the master's discretion in governing slaves were questioned. It took a particularly shocking atrocity to break through this barrier—to enable a white man to win the approval of his neighbors for giving evidence against another white. A North Carolinian knew of "a number" of instances in which "nobody in the neighborhood had any doubt that the death of the slave was caused by the severity of his treatment," but no guilty party was indicted or brought to trial. Frederick Douglass cited the case of a Maryland woman who murdered a slave with a piece of firewood. A warrant was issued for her arrest, but it was never served.[22]

There was still a third obstacle. Even when whites agreed to testify, there remained the problem of getting a white jury to convict. . . . The foreman of a South Carolina jury declared frankly that he "would not convict the defendant, or any other white person, of murdering a slave."[23] This was the feeling of most jurymen. . . .

The fate of a slave who was the principal, rather than the victim, of an alleged misdemeanor or felony was highly uncertain. The state codes established regular judicial procedures for the trial of slaves accused of public offenses, but probably most minor offenses, such as petit larceny, were disposed of without resort to the courts. For instance, when an Alabama slave was caught stealing from a neighboring plantation, the proprietor agreed not to prosecute if the overseer punished the slave himself. The state Supreme Court sanctioned the informal settlement of such cases. Even though an offense was "criminally punishable," said the court, so far as the public was concerned it was better to have the punishment "admeasured by a domestic tribunal."[24]

Nevertheless, many bondsmen who violated the law were given public trials. In colonial days they were always arraigned before special "Negro courts," which were usually less concerned about the formalities of traditional English justice than about speedy verdicts and certain punishments. A slave accused of a capital offense, according to the South Carolina code of 1740, was to be tried "in the most summary and expeditious maner"; on conviction he was to

[22] Bassett, *Slavery in North Carolina*, pp. 91–92; Douglass, *My Bondage*, pp. 125–26.
[23] Davis (ed.), *Diary of Bennet H. Barrow*, p. 148; Gavin Diary, entries for November 4, 16, 1857; Catterall (ed.), *Judicial Cases*, II, p. 343.
[24] Catterall (ed.), *Judicial Cases*, III, pp. 158–59.

suffer death by such means as would be "most effectual to deter others from offending in the like maner." Justice in the "Negro courts" was at best capricious.

For misdemeanors, and in some states for crimes not punished capitally, the summary processes of "Negro courts" survived until the abolition of slavery. . . .

In the nineteenth century, most states gave slaves jury trials in the regular courts when accused of capital crimes; some went further and gave them this privilege when accused of any felony. The Missouri Constitution of 1820 and the Texas Constitution of 1845 provided that in criminal cases slaves were to have an impartial trial by jury. On conviction, a Missouri slave was to suffer "the same degree of punishment, and no other, that would be inflicted on a free white person for a like offense." North Carolina slaves accused of capital offenses were tried in the superior courts, and the law required the trials to be conducted as the trials of freemen. In Alabama, they were tried before the circuit court of the county, "in the mode provided by law for the trial of white persons," except that two-thirds of the jurors had to be slaveholders. In Georgia, capital crimes continued to be tried before three justices until 1850, when the superior courts were given jurisdiction.

A few states never granted jury trial or abandoned the informal courts and summary procedures even in capital cases. . . .

Many Southerners trained in the law recognized the possibilities for miscarriages of justice in the "Negro courts." A South Carolina judge called these courts "the worst system that could be devised." In his message to the legislature, in 1833, Governor Robert Y. Hayne acknowledged that reform was "imperiously called for." "Capital offenses committed by slaves, involving the nicest questions of the law, are often tried by courts composed of persons ignorant of the law." . . . However, criticism such as this produced few reforms.

In practice, the quality of justice slaves received from juries and regular courts was not consistently better than the justice they received from "Negro courts." When tension was great and the passions of white men were running high, a slave found it as difficult to get a fair trial before a jury in one of the superior courts of North Carolina or Alabama as he did before the justices in one of the informal courts of South Carolina or Virginia. Nowhere, regardless of constitutional or statutory requirements, was the trial of a bondsman apt to be like the trial of a freeman. Though counsel was guaranteed, though jurors might be challenged, though Negroes could testify in cases involving members of their own race, the trial of a slave was never the trial of a man by his peers. Rather, it was the trial of a man with inferior rights by his superiors—of a man who was property as well as a person. Inevitably, most justices, judges, and jurors permitted questions of discipline and control to obscure considerations of even justice.

A slave accused of committing violence upon another slave, rather than upon a white, had a better chance for a fair trial. Here the deeper issues of discipline and racial subordination were not involved, and the court could hear the case calmly and decide it on its merits. Moreover, the penalty on conviction was usually relatively light. Slaves were capitally punished for the murder of other slaves almost as rarely as whites were capitally punished for the murder of slaves. . . .

The southern codes did not prescribe lighter penalties for slaves who murdered other slaves than for slaves who murdered whites. The theory of the law was that one offense was as serious as the other. But the white men who applied the law usually thought otherwise.

* * *

"A free African population is a curse to any country," the Chancellor of the South Carolina Court of Appeals once flatly affirmed. "This race, . . . in a state of freedom, and in the midst of a civilized community, are a dead weight to the progress of improvement." Free Negroes became "pilferers and maurauders," "consumers, without being producers . . . governed mainly by the instincts of animal nature."[25] Racial attitudes such as these, the fear of free Negroes as a social menace, and respect for the rights of property caused the southern states to adopt constitutional prohibitions against the legislative emancipation of slaves without the consent of their owners.

But the state constitutions put few obstacles in the way of masters who wished to manumit their own slaves. In the border states of Delaware, Maryland (until 1860), Kentucky, and Missouri, the sole legislative restrictions were that creditors' claims must be respected

[25] Catterall (ed.), *Judicial Cases*, II, p. 442.

and that a manumitted slave must not become a burden to the public because of age or infirmity. Virginia added the further condition that a manumitted slave was not to remain in the state for more than a year "without lawful permission." A county or corporation court might grant this permission if it had evidence that the freedman was "of good character, sober, peaceable, orderly and industrious." In North Carolina an emancipated slave had to leave the state within ninety days, unless a superior court made an exception because of "meritorious service." In Tennessee a slave freed after 1831 had to be sent beyond her borders immediately; after 1854 he had to be sent to the west coast of Africa.

In the Deep South the trend was toward increasingly severe legislative restrictions. In Louisiana (for many years the most liberal of these states) an act of 1807 limited the privilege of manumission to slaves who were at least thirty years old and who had not been guilty of bad conduct during the previous four years. In 1830, Louisiana required emancipated slaves to leave the state within thirty days; after 1852, they had to leave the United States within twelve months. Five years later, Louisiana entirely prohibited private emancipations within the state.

The remaining states of the lower South had outlawed private emancipations early in the nineteenth century, except when granted by a special act of the legislature as a reward for "meritorious service." . . . The South Carolina legislature purchased the freedom of two slaves and granted them annual pensions of fifty dollars for betraying insurrection plots. The Louisiana legislature emancipated a slave and gave him a reward of five hundred dollars for the same "meritorious service."[26] . . .

Several states in the Deep South . . . prohibited emancipation by last will and testament. South Carolina acted as early as 1841, when it voided all deeds and wills designed to free slaves before or after removal from the state. Mississippi, Georgia, Arkansas, and Alabama adopted similar laws during the next two decades.

Occasionally a testator attempted to circumvent the statutes against emancipation, but almost invariably the court invalidated his will. . . .

[26] Catterall (ed.), *Judicial Cases*, III, p. 21; Henry, *Police Control*, pp. 17–18; Taylor, "Negro Slavery in Louisiana," pp. 203–204. In 1860, Maryland also prohibited private emancipations within the state.

The truth was, of course, that *living* masters in all the southern states—even in those which prohibited manumission by last will and testament—always had the right to remove their slaves to a free state and there release them from bondage. Though no slave state could deprive them of this right, few made use of it.

Moreover, only a handful of slaveholders wrote wills providing for manumissions in states where this continued to be legal. An even smaller number would have done so in the Deep South had the privilege remained open to them. In no slave state, early or late in the antebellum period, were the total yearly emancipations more than a small fraction of the natural increase of the slave population. For example, in 1859, only three thousand slaves were emancipated throughout the entire South. At that time both Virginia and Kentucky permitted manumissions by deed or will. Yet Virginia, with a slave population of a half-million, freed only two hundred and seventy-seven; Kentucky, with a slave population of nearly a quarter-million, freed only one hundred and seventy-six.

Clearly, if the decline of slavery were to await the voluntary acts of individuals, the time of its demise was still in the distant future. The failure of voluntary emancipation was evident long before the 1830s when, according to Judge Lumpkin, "the blind zealots of the North" began their "unwarrantable interference."[27] James H. Hammond got at the crux of the matter when he asked whether any people in history had ever voluntarily surrendered two billion dollars worth of property. . . .

[27] Catterall (ed.), *Judicial Cases*, III, pp. 1–2.

Eugene D. Genovese

IN THE NAME OF HUMANITY
AND THE CAUSE OF REFORM

In this selection from Roll, Jordan, Roll: The World the Slaves Made, *Professor Eugene D. Genovese of the University of Rochester explains the paradox that Stampp encountered. He agrees with Stampp that the period between 1831 and 1861 was one of reaction with respect to restrictions on the slaves' access to freedom, but he argues that at the same time the slaves' lot improved with respect to the material conditions of life. The slaveowners hoped to perpetuate their institution by making it possible for the slaves to accept their fate. Genovese, who believes slavery to have been a system of class power in racial form, interprets this development as a typical manifestation of a ruling class's desire to protect its position.*

Since the great object of social reform is to prevent a fundamental change in class relations, sensible reformers must fight on two fronts within the ruling class. They must fight against those reactionaries who cannot understand the need for secondary, although not necessarily trivial, change in order to prevent deeper change; and they must fight against cheerful fools who think that change is intrinsically wonderful and who therefore cannot distinguish between the safe and the dangerous. Since reactionaries will insist that any change, no matter how slight, will set in motion forces of dissolution and since nothing will convince them other than the experience they fear to obtain, reformers face a formidable task; it becomes the more so as the enthusiasts for change demonstrate blindness toward the reality of the danger. The reactionary argument has a truth of its own, which curiously betrays respect for the personalities of those whom reckless reformers too easily view as mere objects of their schemes—a respect which flows from an awareness that lower-class beneficiaries of change may choose to seize a good deal more than they have been offered, once they have been offered anything at all. And it is no answer that force alone cannot keep people in subjugation, for as G. G. Coulton has remarked, "The gospel of the useless-

From *Roll, Jordan, Roll: The World the Slaves Made,* by Eugene D. Genovese, pp. 49–58. Reprinted by permission of Pantheon Books, a Division of Random House, Inc.

ness of persecution is true only if we look forward to a far longer time than the vast majority of men take into their calculations."[1]

The history of the South from the Revolution to secession constitutes a glorious story of wise self-reformation at once conservative in its preservation of the social order and liberal in its flexible response to altered conditions—glorious, that is, from the point of view of the master class. Step by step, those changes which would strengthen the regime took effect and those which might have opened the floodgates did not. Those who deserve credit for the achievement met the one great challenge they faced: they had to convince a skeptical slaveholding class that the humanization of slave life would strengthen rather than weaken the regime. They controlled the press, stocked the state legislatures with safe men, and compromised the churches.[2] Only occasionally did troublemakers have to be killed. Since the usefulness of violent measures stems primarily from their threat, which calls forth a reaction when carried out too often and too far, the slaveholders preferred restraint.[3] But the slaveholders did use a combination of measures to crush the antislavery movement in the South; they thereby freed themselves to civilize their society according to their own lights. They removed the dangers reform so often entails. The death of southern liberalism, as Ulrich Bonnell Phillips called it, marked the birth of a new effort to ameliorate the conditions of slave life.[4] Phillips shared with most of those who have criticized him the doubtful assumption that southern reform should

[1] G. G. Coulton, *Medieval Panorama: The English Scene from Conquest to Reformation* (Cambridge, 1944), p. 705.

[2] On the role of the churches as a proslavery force for humanization of plantation practice, see esp. Caleb Perry Patterson, *The Negro in Tennessee, 1790–1865* (New York, 1968), p. 117; William S. Jenkins, *Pro-slavery Thought in the Old South* (Chapel Hill, N.C., 1935), pp. 210–11; Willie Greier, "North Carolina Baptists and the Negro, 1727–1877," unpubl. M.A. thesis, University of North Carolina, 1944; Ralph Thomas Parkinson, "The Religious Instruction of Slaves, 1820–1860," unpubl. M.A. thesis, University of North Carolina, 1948, esp. pp. 20–22. For the recollections of the Rev. A. M. Moore, ex-slave from Harrison County, Texas, on the increase of black preachers and the relaxation of opposition to black religious meetings, see Rawick, ed., *Texas Narr.,* V (3), 119.

[3] For accounts of the steady suppression of dissent and the effective if limited use of violence, see Charles S. Sydnor, *The Development of Southern Sectionalism* (Baton Rouge, La., 1948), and Eaton, *Freedom-of-Thought Struggle.*

[4] Ulrich Bonnell Phillips, "Conservatism and Progress in the Cotton Belt," *The Slave Economy of the Old South: Selected Essays in Economic and Social History* (ed. Eugene D. Genovese; Baton Rouge, La., 1968). Phillips here presents the argument that slavery would have been reformed out of existence if the abolitionists had left the South alone.

be identified with moves toward emancipation. Even his leading critics have thought so, the great difference being that he blamed the demise of reform on the northern abolitionists and thought that their defeat would have resurrected it, whereas they have blamed the demise on southern intransigence and have doubted that it could ever have been resurrected while the old regime lasted. But the kind of structural reform that pointed toward emancipation represented only one tendency within the reform movement as a whole, and its defeat increasingly became the *sine qua non* for the ultimately successful opposite tendency, which sought to make reform serve the slavery interest.

Hence the paradox. Historians have correctly viewed the period from 1831 to 1861 as one of reaction. Yet they have also correctly viewed it as one in which the treatment of slaves became progressively better. Both views have been correct in that they refer to different aspects of a single process. The condition of the slaves worsened with respect to access to freedom and the promise of eventual emancipation; it got better with respect to material conditions of life. The same men who fought for the one more often than not fought for the other. Their position made perfect sense: Make the South safe for slaveholders by confirming the blacks in perpetual slavery and by making it possible for them to accept their fate.

The constitutions of the slave states left room for manumissions, but the laws made them increasingly difficult. Virginia's attitude hardened after a flurry of liberalism during the Revolutionary era. By the end of 1793 the legislature had banned free-Negro immigration, and by 1806 it had declared that a freedman must leave the state within a year or suffer re-enslavement. South Carolina maintained a passive attitude until 1800, when it raised bars; in 1841 it moved to seal the escape route altogether. Even states like Tennessee followed the same path. By the late antebellum period every slave state had tightened its procedures so as to confirm blacks in slavery and to dash hopes for personal and collective emancipation.[5]

Thus, the steady progress of anti-emancipation sentiment went

---

[5] In general see Stampp, *Peculiar Institution*, pp. 232–34; also Tate, *Negro in Eighteenth-Century Williamsburg*, p. 175; McColley, *Slavery and Jeffersonian Virginia*, p. 72; John H. Russell, *The Free Negro in Virginia, 1619–1865* (Baltimore, 1913), p. 52; Henry, *Police Control of the Slave*, pp. 168–74; C. P. Patterson, *Negro in Tennessee*, p. 17.

hand-in-hand with demands for amelioration and greater humanity. A petition from citizens of Hanover County to the General Assembly of Virginia, dated January 30, 1831, stated the position plainly:

> *Slaves while kept in subjection are submissive and easily controlled, but let any number of them be indulged with the hope of freedom, one must have but little knowledge of their nature, who is to be informed that they reject restraint and become almost wholly unmanageable. It is by the expectation of liberty, and by that alone, that they can be rendered a dangerous population. So long as we are true to ourselves there can be nothing to fear.*[6]

In 1854, the *Richmond Examiner* explained: "True philanthropy to the Negro begins, like charity, at home; and if Southern men would act as if the canopy of heaven were inscribed with a covenant, in letters of fire, that *the Negro is here, and here forever; is our property, and ours forever* . . . they would accomplish more good for the race in five years than they boast the institution itself to have accomplished in two centuries. . . ."[7]

Dissenters continued to speak out in favor of a more liberal policy, but they usually argued that slavery needed a safety valve, not that emancipation ought to be encouraged widely. Some, like Judge O'Neall of South Carolina, may have held broader views than they generally expressed, but even they generally stayed within the while consensus. Others, like William Gilmore Simms, took unambiguous proslavery ground and yet favored reform as being wise and safe. These voices, however distinguished, grew fainter over time, for they could not easily argue with those who, like Edward Pollard of Virginia, pointed out that if emancipation were a suitable reward for meritorious service, then the idea that slavery benefitted the blacks had to be wrong.[8]

---

[6] Quoted in J. H. Johnston, *Race Relations and Miscegenation,* p. 148.

[7] Quoted in Du Bois, *Black Reconstruction,* p. 5. For an interesting illustration of the humanitarian impulse within a wider acceptance of slavery see Norman Dain, *Disordered Minds: The First Century of Eastern State Hospital in Williamsburg, Virginia, 1776–1866* (Charlottesville, Va., 1971), p. 112, an account of John Minson Galt, head of the Eastern State [Mental] Hospital in Williamsburg, Va., who worked for consideration of the plight of mentally disturbed blacks but emphatically defended slavery and the idea of black inferiority.

[8] See Donald J. Senese, "The Free Negro and the South Carolina Courts, 1790–1860," *SCHM,* LXVIII (July, 1967), 140–53, esp. p. 148; Simms in E. N. Elliott, ed., *Cotton Is King and Pro-slavery Arguments,* pp. 238–39; Lester B. Baltimore, "Southern Nationalists and Southern Nationalism, 1850–1870," unpubl. Ph.D. dissertation, Univer-

The great reaction of 1831–1861 cannot be made the responsibility of abolitionist criticism, as it has been by apologists for the old regime; nor can it be laid to Nat Turner, although this contention has much more force. Abolitionism itself had taken on a shriller tone because the dream of slow and peaceful emancipation had been evaporating. If Mr. Jefferson and his brilliant entourage in Virginia had not succeeded even in getting the matter discussed seriously, what hopes were left? South Carolina and Georgia had always been intransigent, and the derived demand for Virginia's slaves effected by the westward cotton movement sealed the fate of the forces in the Upper South that continued to hope for emancipation. The Virginia debates, which opened the period of reaction, represented the last attempt of forces that had long been in retreat.[9] Once the devil of emancipation had been exorcised, the South could reform itself. The nature and limits of that reform reveal much about the society that was coming to maturity.

No feature of the slave law stirred so many misgivings as the lack of protection for family life. Even that pillar of the slaveholders' regime, Robert Toombs, squirmed badly and joined his fellow Georgian, Alexander Stephens, in calling for reform. But the timidity of the call from the usually firm, blunt planter-politician spoke as loud as his criticism. "We are reproached," he said, "that the marriage relation is neither recognized nor protected by law. This reproach is not wholly unjust, this is an evil not yet remedied by law, but marriage is not inconsistent with the institution of slavery as it exists among us, and the objection therefore lies rather to an incident than to the essence of the system."[10]

Leading proslavery intellectuals like George Frederick Holmes, Henry Hughes, and George Fitzhugh and leading jurists like John Belton O'Neall joined in advocating laws to recognize slave mar-

---

sity of Missouri, 1968. The Catholic slaveholding countries undoubtedly had a more favorable attitude toward manumission, although the extent of the actual practice remains in dispute. But for the most part, slavery in those countries existed within or side-by-side with a seigneurial social system, so that release from slavery did not necessarily alter the more fundamental social relationships, and the less virulent racism allowed for a more open policy.

[9] See McColley, *Slavery and Jeffersonian Virginia,* esp. pp. 90, 115–16; Joseph Clarke Robert, *The Road from Monticello* (Durham, N.C., 1941); W. D. Jordan, *White over Black,* p. 368.

[10] Quoted by Ulrich Bonnell Phillips, *The Life of Robert Toombs* (New York, 1913), p. 161; also p. 166.

riages. As late as 1855 a group of North Carolinians made a major effort to humanize the slave code especially with respect to marriage and literacy, but got nowhere. Their proposals concerning protection of family life evoked more praise than censure across the South, but most of all they evoked silence. The slaveholders understood that such reforms threatened the economic viability of the capital and labor markets. No other issue so clearly exposed the hybrid nature of the regime; so clearly pitted economic interest against paternalism and defined the limits beyond which the one could not reinforce the other.

The long-run prospects for this reform did not look bright, although increasing discussion of compromise proposals suggested some possibilities. Some reformers, as well as thoughtful planters like Samuel Walker of Louisiana, were beginning to work out ideas for legislation to entail the estates of the bankrupt or deceased so as to keep family units together.[11] The fate of such ideas, had the Confederacy won, must remain a matter of conjecture, but the discernible uneasiness of the slaveholders did have the effect of making the separation of families more odious. Such moral pressure alone could not have reduced the evil to the level of Toombs's "incident," for had such ever become the case, that same public opinion, noticeably writhing over the issue, would surely have become ready for a direct attack. The problem and the contradiction it called forth therefore remained—and so did the agony.

What of the material conditions of slave life? Slaveholders claimed, and some slaves acknowledged, that conditions were improving as the nineteenth century progressed and the frontier receded. The most skeptical travelers agreed.[12] During the 1830s and

---

[11] Walker Diary, July 25, 1857 (p. 33); *DBR*, XIX (Aug., 1855), 130; "Exemption of Slaves from Sale Under Execution," *SC*, XI (Oct., 1853), 309; Bremer, *Homes of the New World*, I, 277; II, 488; Allan Nevins, *The Emergence of Lincoln* (2 vols.; New York, 1950), II, 161–62; J. B. Sellers, *Slavery in Alabama*, pp. 169, 191; Sydnor, *Slavery in Mississippi*, p. 64; Wallace B. Turner, "Kentucky Slavery in the Last Ante Bellum Decade," *KHSR*, LVIII (Oct., 1960), 298.

[12] See Joseph Sturge, *A Visit to the United States of America in 1841* (London, 1842), p. 61, and Stirling, *Letters from the Slave States*, p. 285, both of whom report conversations with slaves. Also Bremer, *Homes of the New World*, II, 434; Lyell, *Second Visit*, I, 209, 216–17; Olmsted, *Seaboard*, p. 97, and *Back Country*, p. 81; A Farmer of Lower Virginia, "Slavery in Virginia," *FR*, IV (July, 1836), 180; H.C., "On the Management of Negroes," *SA*, VII (July, 1834), 367–70; "Religious Instruction of Negroes," *Quarterly Review of the Methodist Episcopal Church, South*, I (July, 1847), 319–38; Bonner, *Georgia Agriculture*, p. 203.

1840s Louisiana and Texas suffered from a reputation, probably deserved, for hard driving. Adeline Cunningham, who had been a slave in Texas, recalled, "Dey was rough people and dey treat ev'ry body rough."[13] But even in Texas conditions improved markedly during the 1850s as communities became more stable and as rising slave prices compelled greater attention to reproduction. The sugar plantations of Louisiana, for all their reputation as hellholes, usually provided better care than the small farms, for they were solvent and did not have to skimp on food and clothing. By the 1850s word had traveled back to slaves in Virginia that the more favorable economic conditions of the Southwest meant more comfort.[14]

The idea that slave holders in the Upper South treated their slaves much better than did those in the Lower South arose during the eighteenth century. The slaveholders of eighteenth-century Virginia acquired a good reputation for humanity toward their slaves, at least relative to the slaveholders of South Carolina, about whom Forrest McDonald has written: "The South Carolina planters' callous disregard for human life and suffering was probably unmatched anywhere west of the Dnieper."[15] South Carolina's black population reproduced itself adequately during the early decades of the eighteenth century but suffered a negative rate of natural increase after the big importations from Africa that followed 1720. The treatment of slaves grew increasingly harsh between 1720 and the Stono rising of 1739, which compelled the slaveholders to reflect on their policies. Thereafter, fear of insurrection accomplished what appeals to humanity had not, and conditions gradually improved.[16]

The living conditions of slaves in South Carolina were considera-

[13] Rawick, ed., *Texas Narr.,* IV (1), 26; Martineau, *Society in America,* II, 172; G. W. Featherstonhaugh, *Excursion Through the Slave States* (New York, 1968 [1844]), p. 125.
[14] J. G. Taylor, *Negro Slavery in Louisiana,* p. 46; Sitterson, *Sugar Country,* pp. 90, 436; Lyell, *Second Visit,* II, 125; "Sugar and Slavery in Louisiana," *SC,* V (April, 1847), 55; Earl W. Fornell, "The Abduction of Free Negroes and Slaves in Texas," *SHQ,* LX (Jan., 1957), 379.
[15] Forrest McDonald, *E Pluribus Unum: The Formation of the American Republic, 1776–1790* (Boston, 1965), p. 65. Also McColley, *Slavery and Jeffersonian Virginia,* p. 6; "Travelers' Impressions of Slavery in America from 1750 to 1800," *JNH,* I (Oct., 1916), 404–33; "James Madison's Attitude Toward the Negro," *JNH,* VI (Jan., 1921), 77–78; W. E. B. Du Bois, *The Suppression of the African Slave-Trade to the United States of America, 1638–1820* (New York, 1969 [1898]), pp. 12, 152.
[16] See the forthcoming study by Peter H. Wood, *Black Majority*; also M. Eugene Sirmans, *Colonial South Carolina: A Political History, 1663–1763* (Chapel Hill, N.C., 1966), pp. 108, 209.

bly better at the end of the eighteenth century than they had been at the beginning, nor did the temporary reopening of the African slave trade reverse the gradual amelioration. The regime had settled by then, and the rich coastal areas had developed stable communities in which the expectations of the highly productive slaves in the rice and Sea Island cotton districts could not easily be tampered with. Besides, the planters, knowing that the slave trade would close definitely in 1808, had to look to the future.[17] During the nineteenth century the difference in treatment between the Upper and Lower South became steadily less noteworthy.[18]

During the late antebellum period J. H. Hammond of South Carolina accused the abolitionists of compelling a reversal in the trend toward amelioration. Their agitation, he argued, was resulting in a withdrawal of privileges, which "is painful to us."[19] But his remarks, dubious in any case, applied to matters other than such material conditions as food, clothing, shelter, or even punishment. Harriet Martineau asserted that the abolitionist attacks had, on the contrary, resulted in a decided improvement in the treatment of slaves. Ezekiel Birdseye, an abolitionist in East Tennessee, concurred in her judgment, as did John Flournoy, the rabidly negrophobic antislavery eccentric, who fumed that the slaves in Georgia were receiving more consideration than the poor whites.[20] A. T. Goodloe in effect conceded the point in a harsh attack on his fellow slaveholders, who, he said, were ruining the blacks in an ill-considered attempt to ward off abolitionist criticism. N. D. Guerry of Alabama denounced Goodloe's inhumane tone and insisted that the discernible improvement in treatment had long been overdue. "The days of

---

[17] David Duncan Wallace, *The Life of Henry Laurens* (New York, 1915), pp. 66–67; G. G. Johnson, *Social History of the Sea Islands*, p. 34; Josiah Smith, Jr., to George Austin, Jan. 31, 1774, in the Smith Papers; Heyward, *Seed from Madagascar*, p. 75; Jeffrey R. Brackett, *The Negro in Maryland* (Baltimore, 1889), p. 124.

[18] In general see Eaton, *Growth of Southern Civilization*, p. 81. Also Ingraham, *South-West*, II, 183; Major Amos Stoddard, *Sketches, Historical and Descriptive, of Louisiana* (New York, 1832), p. 332; J. W. DuBose, "Recollections of the Plantation," *AHQ*, I (Spring, 1930), 71; Frank F. Steel to Anna Steel, Dec. 15, 1859.

[19] See Hammond's "Letter to Thomas Clarkson," in E. N. Elliott, ed., *Cotton Is King and Pro-slavery Arguments*.

[20] Martineau, *Society in America*, II, 151; W. Freeman Galpin, ed., "Letters of an East Tennessee Abolitionist," *East Tennessee Historical Society Publications*, No. 3 (Jan., 1931), pp. 135–49; E. Merton Coulter, *John Jacobus Flournoy: Champion of the Common Man in the Ante-bellum South* (Savannah, Ga., 1942), p. 47.

fogyism in the management of Negroes," he snapped, "have gone, the time for brute force is past. . . ."[21]

The campaign to improve the lot of the slaves predated the abolitionist agitation, as did the campaign to confirm the blacks in perpetual slavery. Abolitionism and the southern reaction to it accelerated forces already in motion. As early as the 1820s agricultural journals like Legaré's *Southern Agriculturalist,* published in Charleston, were running a steady stream of articles to encourage better treatment, although other journals—the *Southern Planter,* for example—did not pick up the theme until much later. Some writers frankly placed the discussion in political perspective, but even they demonstrated a wider effort to sharpen their fellow slaveholders' class consciousness by appealing to a sense of moral responsibility. Chancellor Harper set the tone in the 1830s in his militant contribution to the proslavery argument:

> *It is wise, too, in relation to the civilized world around us, to avoid giving occasion to the odium which is so industriously excited against ourselves and our institutions. For this reason, public opinion should, if possibie, bear even more strongly and indignantly than it does at present, on masters who practice any wanton cruelty on their slaves. The miscreant who is guilty of this not only violates the law of God and of humanity, but as far as in him lies, by bringing odium upon, endangers the institutions of his country, and the safety of his countrymen.*[22]

Writing about the same time, an anonymous contributor to the *Southern Agriculturalist* bluntly related the confirmation of the slaves' status to progress in their material comfort: "Is then the condition of the slaves as a caste never to be mitigated? We answer that such mitigation is to be looked for only in the improvement of their masters. That it has already derived much amelioration from this source is a sure harbinger of its future improvement."[23] In 1851, Garnett Andrews warned the Southern Central Agricultural Society of Georgia not to allow unscrupulous masters to use the abolitionist

---

[21] A. T. Goodloe, "Management of Negroes," *SC,* XVIII (April, 1860), 130–31; and N. D. Guerry's reply in XVIII (June, 1860), 176–77.
[22] Chancellor Harper in E. N. Elliott, ed., *Cotton Is King and Pro-Slavery Arguments,* pp. 64–65.
[23] A Reader, "Agricultural Laborers," *SA,* VIII (Jan., 1835), 8; cf. *ACP,* II (Aug., 1854), 253.

agitation to excuse undue severity toward their slaves.[24] In 1860, Dr. John Stainback Wilson condemned those slaveholders who failed to meet their responsibilities toward their slaves. Apparently fearful of being charged with giving aid and comfort to the abolitionists, he added:

> *Duty requires that errors and abuses should be pointed out, with the hope of correction and reformation. This is a duty to the dependent creatures whom God has committed to our charge; it is due to ourselves individually as slaveholders; and it is due to us collectively as a community of slaveholders, deeply, vitally interested in the vindication of our institution before a misguided and gainsaying world. Yes, it is the duty of all slaveowners, of all who are interested either directly, or indirectly, in the perpetuation of the institution, to disclose its abuses . . . with a design of correcting those abuses and thus disarming our enemies.[25]*

Dr. Wilson quoted the Reverend C. F. Sturgis's "Prize Essay on the Duties of Masters to Their Servants" as saying: "As a farmer and a Southerner, I boldly declare that as long as such bad economy is practiced, even in a few cases, it will be impossible to gag the abolitionists. . . ."[26]

The mounting abolitionist critique forced the slaveholders to take a long look at themselves and at others, especially other slaveholders. Proslavery ideologues had difficulty in evaluating Caribbean and South American slavery. They felt the need to defend slavery as a social system in all parts of the world, but wanted to dissociate themselves from the special evils of other regimes and to claim special virtues for their own. As the slaveholders' ideological struggle with the abolitionists sharpened during the 1840s and 1850s, their criticism of the Cuban regime mounted, and they increasingly praised themselves for the excellence of their treatment of their own slaves. In part they coveted Cuba and were trying to create humanitarian grounds for annexation, but they also genuinely recoiled at what they saw and heard there. Cuban slavery, a mild system during the eighteenth century, became a horror story during the nineteenth,

---

[24] Garnett Andrews, in Southern Central Agricultural Society, *Transactions, 1846–1851,* pp. 98–99.
[25] John Stainback Wilson, "The Peculiarities and Diseases of Negroes," *ACPSS,* IV (July, 1860), 319.
[26] Ibid., p. 20; see also *DBR,* III (May, 1847), 421, for a similar theme.

when the sugar boom swept the island.[27] The southern slaveholders
derived particular satisfaction from the favorable comparisons of
their own regime with that of Cuba which were appearing in books
by critical European travelers.[28]

Much of the controversy over "treatment" of slaves turns on a
confusion of meanings. The slaveholders could proclaim their slaves
the best treated in the world and even compare their condition
favorably with that of European workers and peasants, but their
evidence rested entirely on data about the material conditions of life.
They did not talk much about the protection of family life or other
features of cultural autonomy. Nor did they care to discuss access to
freedom and citizenship. Ulrich Bonnell Phillips was probably right in
arguing that American slaves were better treated than Caribbean or
Brazilian, for he too was thinking of material conditions. Stanley M.
Elkins was probably right in saying that American slaves were much
worse treated, for he clearly was thinking of other matters.[29]

The slave regime of the Old South became progressively more
repressive with respect to manumission as it became progressively
more humane with respect to the material conditions of life. In the
specific conditions of southern slavery the one required the other, or
rather, each formed part of a single process of social cohesion. The
slaveholders did not defend their regime by distinguishing among the
several meanings of "treatment," for they would have exposed the
negative side of their practice; nor did the abolitionists usually make
such distinctions in their assaults, for they did not wish to concede
any ground to an enemy perceived as purely evil.[30] Did the white

[27] See the anonymous review of Ariel Abbot's *Letters Written in the Interior of Cuba* in
Southern Review, IV (Aug.–Nov., 1829), 123–36; R. E. Caffrey's report on his trip to
Cuba in *PB,* XV (March 7, 1850), n.p.; Noah B. Cloud, "The Cotton Power, an American
Power," *ACPSS,* II (Nov., 1858), 331; William K. Scarborough, ed., *The Diary of Edmund
Ruffin* (2 vols.; Baton Rouge, La., 1972), March 4, 1859 (I, 290). The best introduction to
the Cuban situation is Franklin W. Knight, *Slave Society in Cuba During the Nineteenth
Century* (Madison, Wis., 1970). For the eighteenth century see Herbert Klein, *Slavery in
the Americas: A Comparative Study of Cuba and Virginia* (Chicago, 1967). Also Deerr,
History of Sugar, II, 359; Aimes, *History of Slavery in Cuba,* pp. 47, 61, 77, 86, 159, 178,
143–44, 254–55, 266; Allan Nevins, *Ordeal of the Union* (2 vols.; New York, 1947), II,
63–64.
[28] See, e.g., Bremer, *Homes of the New World,* II, 309, 437; Stirling, *Letters from the
Slave States,* p. 109.
[29] Stanley M. Elkins, *Slavery: A Problem in American Institutional and Intellectual Life*
(Chicago, 1959), esp. Ch. 2.
[30] For a fuller discussion of the different meanings of "treatment" and their significance, see my "Treatment of Slaves in Different Countries: Problems in the Application of the Comparative Method," *In Red and Black,* Ch. 7.

racism of the slaveholders lead them to value black life so little as to treat slaves like animals? The rhetoric of paternalism aside, the slaveholders knew and said what the abolitionists knew and tried not to say: The South had the only slave system in the New World in which the slaves reproduced themselves. The less than 400,000 Africans imported into the North American British colonies and the United States had become a black population ten times greater by 1860, whereas despite much larger importations by Jamaica, Saint-Domingue, Brazil, and Cuba, these and other slave countries struggled to balance imports against mortality in order to hold their own in population.[31]

The slaveholders sometimes asked: What does racism have to do with the waste of human life? What has race to do with business? Do you not know that the poor whites who worked on the slave ships suffered a significantly higher death rate than did the enslaved Africans themselves?[32] In the South and in the Caribbean the treatment meted out to white indentured servants had rivaled and often exceeded in brutality that meted out to black slaves; brutality to white servants preceded brutality to black slaves. The slaveholders did not treat their slaves with contempt because of racist feeling; they had learned long before to hold the lives of the lower classes cheap.[33] Rich Europeans had always been willing to use up their own lower classes as readily as they would Africans; it was not their fault that their own lower classes had learned how to protect themselves.

The slaveholders did not tell the other side of the story. As the workers and peasants of Europe and America forged weapons of self-defense, the ruling classes increasingly turned to the exploitation of nonwhite labor, and a virulent racism became the indispensable rationalization for their policies. But during the nineteenth century the "treatment" of black labor relative to white in the capitalist world remained a legitimate matter of dispute. . . .

[31] Curtin, *Atlantic Slave Trade.*
[32] See the papers of K. G. Davies and Johannes Posthma in Stanley Engerman and Eugene D. Genovese, eds., *Race and Slavery in the Western Hemisphere: Quantitative Studies* (Princeton, forthcoming).
[33] Richard Dunn, *Sugar and Slaves: The Rise of the Planter Class in the English West Indies, 1624–1713* (Chapel Hill, N.C., 1972); H. O. Patterson, *Sociology of Slavery,* pp. 46–47, 74; J. H. Johnston, *Race Relations and Miscegenation,* p. 184; Frances Trollope, *Domestic Manners of the Americans* (London, 1927), p. 246.

III   THE INTERACTION OF SLAVERY AND SOCIETY

Pan-American Comparisons

Frank Tannenbaum

SLAVE AND CITIZEN

Professor Tannenbaum, who taught for many years at Columbia, was the first scholar to attempt a broad comparison of slavery in North and South America. His book Slave and Citizen: A History of the Negro in the Americas *has attracted a wide audience from the time it initially appeared in 1946. His general thesis—that differences in racial patterns stemmed from cultural rather than economic or demographic circumstances—has remained extremely persuasive to many historians, among them Stanley Elkins and Herbert S. Klein.*

This adventure of the Negro in the New World has been structured differently in the United States than in the other parts of this hemisphere. In spite of his adaptability, his willingness, and his competence, in spite of his complete identification with the mores of the United States, he is excluded and denied. A barrier has been drawn against the Negro. This barrier has never been completely effective, but it has served to deny to him the very things that are of greatest value among us—equality of opportunity for growth and development as a man among men. The shadow of slavery is still cast ahead of us, and we behave toward the Negro as if the imputation of slavery had something of a slave by nature in it. The Emancipation may have legally freed the Negro, but it failed morally to free the white man, and by that failure it denied to the Negro the moral status requisite for effective legal freedom.

But this did not occur in the other parts of this world we call new and free. It did not occur because the very nature of the institution of slavery was developed in a different moral and legal setting, and in turn shaped the political and ethical biases that have manifestly separated the United States from the other parts of the New World in this respect. The separation is a moral one. We have denied ourselves the acceptance of the Negro as a man because we have denied him the moral competence to become one, and in that have challenged the religious, political, and scientific bases upon which our civilization and our scheme of values rest. This separation has a historical basis, and in turn it has molded the varied historical outcome.

The Negro slave arriving in the Iberian Peninsula in the middle of the fifteenth century found a propitious environment.[1] The setting, legal as well as moral, that made this easy transition possible was due to the fact that the people of the Iberian Peninsula were not strangers to slavery. The institution of slavery, which had long since died out in the rest of Western Europe, had here survived for a number of reasons, especially because of the continuing wars with the Moors, which lasted until the very year of the discovery of America.

*   *   *

But the mere survival of slavery in itself is perhaps less important than the persistence of a long tradition of slave law that had come down through the Justianian Code. The great codification of Spanish traditional law, which in itself summarizes the Mediterranean legal *mores* of many centuries, was elaborated by Alfonso the Wise between the years 1263 and 1265. In this code there is inherent belief in the equality of men under the law of nature, and slavery therefore is something against both nature and reason.

*   *   *

---

[1] Elizabeth Donnan, op. cit., Vol. I ("1441–1700," 1930), p. 29: "For as our people did not find them hardened in the belief of the other Moors, and saw how they came in unto the law of Christ with a good will, they made no difference between them and their free servants, born in our own country. But those whom they saw fitted for managing property, they set free and married to women who were natives of the land, making with them a division of their property, as if they had been bestowed on those who married them by the will of their own fathers, and for the merits of their service they were bound to act in a like manner. Yea, and some widows of good family who bought some of these female slaves, either adopted them or left them a portion of their estate by will, so that in the future they married right well, treating them as entirely free. Suffice it that I never saw one of these slaves put in irons like other captives, and scarcely any one who did not turn Christian and was not very gently treated." Quoted from *The Chronicle of the Discovery and Conquesı of Guinea*, by Gomes Eannes de Azurara.

The slave had a body of law, protective of him as a human being, which was already there when the Negro arrived and had been elaborated long before he came upon the scene. And when he did come, the Spaniard may not have known him as a Negro, but the Spanish law and *mores* knew him as a slave and made him the beneficiary of the ancient legal heritage. This law provided, among other matters, for the following:

The slave might marry a free person if the slave status was known to the other party. Slaves could marry against the will of their master if they continued serving him as before. Once married, they could not be sold apart, except under conditions permitting them to live as man and wife. If the slave married a free person with the knowledge of his master, and the master did not announce the fact of the existing slave status, then the slave by that mere fact became free.[2] If married slaves owned by separate masters could not live together because of distance, the church should persuade one or the other to sell his slave. If neither of the masters could be persuaded, the church was to buy one of them so that the married slaves could live together.[3] The children followed the status of their mother, and the child of a free mother remained free even if she later became a slave.[4] In spite of his full powers over his slave, the master might neither kill nor injure him unless authorized by the judge, nor abuse him against reason or nature, nor starve him to death. But if the master did any of these things, the slave could complain to the judge, and if the complaint were verified, the judge must sell him, giving the price to the owner, and the slave might never be returned to the original master.[5] Any Jewish or Moorish slave became free upon turning Christian, and even if the master himself later became a Christian, he recovered no rights over his former slave.[6]

*   *   *

Spanish law, custom, and tradition were transferred to America and came to govern the position of the Negro slave. It is interesting to note that a large body of new law was developed for the treatment

---

[2] *Las Siete Partidas*, Ley I, tit. v, part. 4.
[3] Ibid., Ley II.
[4] Ibid., Ley II, tit. xxi, part. 4.
[5] Ibid., Ley III.
[6] *Las Siete Partidas*, Ley VIII.

of the Indians in America, whereas the Negro's position was covered by isolated *cedulas* dealing with special problems. It was not until 1789 that a formal code dealing with the Negro slave was promulgated.[7] But this new code, as recognized by the preamble itself, is merely a summary of the ancient and traditional law. . . .

This body of law, containing the legal tradition of the Spanish people and also influenced by the Catholic doctrine of the equality of all men in the sight of God, was biased in favor of freedom and opened the gates to manumission when slavery was transferred to the New World. The law in Spanish and Portuguese America facilitated manumission, the tax-gatherer did not oppose it,[8] and the church ranked it among the works singularly agreeable to God. A hundred social devices narrowed the gap between bondage and liberty, encouraged the master to release his slave, and the bondsman to achieve freedom on his own account. From the sixteenth to the nineteenth century, slaves in Brazil, by reimbursing the original purchase price, could compel their masters to free them.[9] In Cuba and in Mexico the price might be fixed at the request of the Negro, and the slave was freed even if he cost "triple of the sum."[10] The right to have his price declared aided the Negro in seeking a new master, and the owner was required to transfer him to another.[11]

*   *   *

In effect, slavery under both law and custom had, for all practical purposes, become a contractual arrangement between the master and his bondsman. There may have been no written contract between the two parties, but the state behaved, in effect, as if such a contract did exist, and used its powers to enforce it. This presumed

[7] *Real Cedula de Su Magestad sobre la Education, Trato, y Occupaciones de los Esclavos, en Todos sus Dominios de Indias, e Islas Filipinas, Baxo las Reglas que Se Expresan.* This law has been reprinted several times, most recently in an article by Raúl Carrancá y Trujillo in *Revista de Historia de America*, Numero 3 (Mexico, September 1938), pp. 50–59.
[8] "In the Cuban market freedom was the only commodity which could be bought untaxed; every negro against whom no one had proved a claim of servitude was deemed free. . . ." William Law Mathieson, op. cit., pp. 37–38.
[9] Sir Harry Johnston, op. cit., p. 89. D. P. Kidder and J. C. Fletcher: *Brazil and the Brazilians* (New York: Childs and Peterson; 1857), p. 133.
[10] Alexander Humboldt: *Political Essay on the Kingdom of New Spain*, translated by John Black (New York: I. Riley; 1811), Vol. I, p. 181.
[11] Richard Henry Dana, Jr.: *To Cuba and Back* (Boston: Tichnor and Fields; 1859), p. 249.

contract was of a strictly limited liability on the part of the slave, and the state, by employing the officially provided protector of slaves, could and did define the financial obligation of the slave to his master in each specific instance as it arose. Slavery had thus from a very early date, at least insofar as the practice was concerned, moved from a "status," or "caste," "by law of nature," or because of "innate inferiority," or because of the "just judgment and provision of holy script," to become a mere matter of an available sum of money for redemption. Slavery had become a matter of financial competence on the part of the slave, and by that fact lost a great part of the degrading imputation that attached to a slavery where it was looked upon as evidence of moral or biological inferiority. Slavery could be wiped out by a fixed purchase price, and therefore the taint of slavery proved neither very deep nor indelible.

In addition to making freedom something obtainable for money, which the slave had the right to acquire and possess, the state made manumission possible for a number of other reasons. A Negro could be freed if unduly punished by his master.[12] He was at liberty to marry a free nonslave (and the master could not legally interfere), and as under the law the children followed the mother, a slave's children born of a free mother were also free.[13] Slaves in Brazil who joined the army to fight in the Paraguayan war were freed by decree on November 6, 1866, and some twenty thousand Negroes were thus liberated.[14] . . .

But significant and varied as were these provisions of the law in the Spanish and Portuguese colonies, they were less important in the long run than the social arrangements and expectancies that prevailed. It was permissible for a slave child in Brazil to be freed at the baptismal font by an offer of twenty milreis,[15] and in Cuba for twenty-five dollars.[16] A female slave could seek a godfather for her baby in some respectable person, hoping that the moral obligation imposed upon the godfather would lead to freeing the child. It was both a meritorious and a pious deed to accept such a responsibility and to fulfill its implicit commitments, and it bestowed distinction

---

[12] Alexander Humboldt: *Political Essay*, op. cit., p. 181.
[13] Henry Koster: *Travels in Brazil* (Philadelphia: M. Carey & Son; 1817), Vol. II, p. 202. Fernando Ortiz, op. cit., p. 337.
[14] Percy Alvin Martin, op. cit., p. 174.
[15] Robert Southey: *History of Brazil* (London, 1819), Part III, p. 784.
[16] William Law Mathieson, op. cit., p. 37.

upon him who accepted them.[17] In the mining regions of Minas Geraes a slave who found a seventeen-and-a-half carat diamond was crowned with a floral wreath, dressed in a white suit, carried on the shoulders of fellow slaves to the presence of his master, and freed and allowed to work for himself.[18] A parent having ten children could claim freedom, whether male or female.

The freeing of one's slaves was an honorific tradition, and men fulfilled it on numerous occasions. Favorite wet nurses were often freed; slaves were manumitted on happy occasions in the family—a birth of a first son, or the marriage of one of the master's children. In fact, the excuses and the occasions were numerous—the passing of an examination in school by the young master, a family festival, a national holiday, and, of course, by will upon the death of the master.[19] A cataloging of the occasions for manumission in such a country as Brazil might almost lead to wonder at the persistence of slavery; but as I have pointed out above, the importations of slaves were large and continuous in Brazil all through the colonial period and late into the nineteenth century.

Opportunities for escape from slavery were further facilitated by the system of labor that prevailed in many places, particularly in cities. Slaves were often encouraged to hire themselves out and bring their masters a fixed part of their wages, keeping the rest. Skilled artisans, masons, carpenters, blacksmiths, wheel-wrights, tailors, and musicians were special gainers from the arrangement.[20] But even ordinary laborers were allowed to organize themselves in gangs, *gente de Ganho*, as they were called.

With all its cruelty, abuse, hardship, and inhumanity, the atmosphere in Brazil and in the Spanish-American countries made for manumission. Even in the rural regions individuals were allowed to sell the products from their own plots, given them to work for themselves, and to save their money toward the day of freedom. In Cuba, one writer notes, the raising of pigs by slaves provided a ready source of the sums accumulated for such a purpose.[21] It should be

[17] Henry Koster, op. cit., p. 195.
[18] John Mawe: *Travels in the Interior of Brazil* (London: Longman, Hurst, Rees, Orme & Brown; 1812), p. 318.
[19] Percy Alvin Martin, op. cit., p. 170.
[20] Fernando Ortiz, op. cit., p. 318.
[21] Rev. Abiel Abbot: *Letters Written in the Interior of Cuba* (Boston: Bowles and Dearborn; 1829), p. 97.

further noticed that, in addition to their Sundays, the Negroes in Brazil had many holidays, amounting all together to eighty-four days a year, which they could use for their own purposes, and for garnering such funds as their immediate skill and opportunities made possible. The purchase of one's freedom was so accepted a tradition among the Negroes that many a Negro bought the freedom of his wife and children while he himself continued laboring as a slave, and among the freed Negroes societies were organized for pooling resources and collecting funds for the freeing of their brethren still in bondage.[22]

These many provisions favoring manumission were strongly influenced by the church. Without interfering with the institution of slavery where the domestic law accepted it, the church early condemned the slave trade and prohibited Catholics from taking part in it. The prohibition was not effective, though it in some measure may have influenced the Spaniards to a rather limited participation in the trade as such. . . .

The presumption against the slave trade was that it forced people into slavery outside the law and against their will. More important in the long run than the condemnation of the slave trade proved the church's insistence that slave and master were equal in the sight of God. Whatever the formal relations between slave and master, they must both recognize their relationship to each other as moral human beings and as brothers in Christ. The master had an obligation to protect the spiritual integrity of the slave, to teach him the Christian religion, to help him achieve the privileges of the sacraments, to guide him into living a good life, and to protect him from mortal sin. The slave had a right to become a Christian, to be baptized, and to be considered a member of the Christian community. . . .

From the very beginning the Catholic churches in America insisted that masters bring their slaves to church to learn the doctrine and participate in the communion. The assembled bishops in Mexico in the year 1555 urged all Spaniards to send the Indians, and especially the Negroes, to church;[23] similarly in Cuba in 1680.[24]

---

[22] Arthur Ramos: *The Negro in Brazil*, translated from the Portuguese by Richard Pattee (Washington, D.C., 1939), p. 70.

[23] *Concilios Provinciales, Primero y Segundo, Mexico, En los Años de 1555 y 1565* (Mexico, 1769), Concilio primero, Cap. III, p. 44.

[24] José Antonio Saco, op. cit., Tomo I, pp. 165–67.

In fact, Negroes were baptized in Angola[25] before leaving for their Atlantic journey to Brazil. Upon arrival they were instructed in the doctrine, and as evidence of their baptism carried about their necks a mark of the royal crown. As a Catholic the slave was married in the church, and the banns were regularly published.[26] It gave the slave's family a moral and religious character unknown in other American slave systems. It became part of the ordinary routine on the slave plantations for the master and slaves to attend church on Sundays, and regularly before retiring at night the slaves gathered before the master's house to receive his blessings.[27] If married by the church, they could not be separated by the master. Religious fraternities sprang up among the slaves. These were often influential and honorific institutions, with regularly elected officers, and funds for the celebration of religious holidays subscribed to by the slaves out of their own meager savings. In Brazil the slaves adopted the Lady of the Rosary as their own special patroness, sometimes painting her black. In a measure these religious fraternities emulated those of the whites, if they did not compete with them, and the slaves found a source of pride in becoming members, and honor in serving one of these religious fraternities as an official.[28]

If the Latin-American environment was favorable to freedom, the British and American were hostile.[29] Legal obstacles were placed in the way of manumission, and it was discouraged in every other manner. The presumption was in favor of slavery.[30] A Negro who could not prove that he was free was presumed to be a runaway slave and was advertised as such; if no claimant appeared, he was

[25] Henry Koster, op. cit., p. 198.
[26] Ibid., p. 202.
[27] Alfred R. Wallace: *A Narrative of Travels on the Amazon and Rio Negro* (London: Reeve & Co.; 1853), p. 92.
[28] Robert Southey, op. cit., p. 784.
[29] There were, briefly speaking, three slave systems in the Western Hemisphere. The British, American, Dutch, and Danish were at one extreme, and the Spanish and Portuguese at the other. In between these two fell the French. The first of these groups is characterized by the fact that they had no effective slave tradition, no slave law, and that their religious institutions were little concerned about the Negro. At the other extreme there were both a slave law and a belief that the spiritual personality of the slave transcended his slave status. In between them the French suffered from the lack of a slave tradition and slave law, but did have the same religious principles as the Spaniards and Portuguese. If one were forced to arrange these systems of slavery in order of severity, the Dutch would seem to stand as the hardest, the Portuguese as the mildest, and the French, in between, as having elements of both.
[30] Willam Law Mathieson, op. cit., pp. 38–40.

sold at public auction for the public benefit.[31] . . . In most of the British colonies heavy taxes had been imposed on manumission, and as late as 1802 a law was passed in the Northern Leeward Islands requiring the owner who would register his slave for manumission to pay five hundred pounds into the public treasury,[32] and this sum had to be provided in his will if it made provision for the liberation of the slave. . . .

In the southern part of the United States the position of the slave was closely similar to that in the British West Indies. What is important to note is the tendency to identify the Negro with the slave. The mere fact of being a Negro was presumptive of a slave status. South Carolina in 1740 (similarly Georgia and Mississippi) provided that "all negroes, Indians (those now free excepted) . . . mulattoes, or mestizos, who are or shall hereafter be in the province, and all their issue and offspring, born or to be born, shall be and they are hereby declared to be and remain forever hereafter absolute slaves and shall follow the condition of the mother."[33] Equally striking is an early law of Maryland, dating from 1663: "All negroes or other slaves within the province, all negroes to be hereafter imported, shall serve *durante vita*"; and their children were to follow the condition of the father. Significantly the same law said: "That whatsoever freeborn women (English) shall intermarry with any slave . . . shall serve the master of such slave during the life of her husband; all the issue of such freeborn women, so married, shall be slave as their fathers were."[34] A free Negro in South Carolina (1740) harboring a runaway slave, or charged "with any criminal matter," upon inability to pay the fine and court charges was to be sold "at public auction."[35] The same state provided that an emancipated Negro set free otherwise than according to the act of 1800 could be seized and kept as a slave by "any person whatsoever."

*   *   *

---

[31] Ibid., pp. 38–40.

[32] Sir Harry Johnston, op. cit., p. 231.

[33] George M. Stroud: *A Sketch of the Laws Relating to Slavery in the Several States of the United States of America* (2nd edition; Philadelphia: H. Longstreth; 1856), pp. 60–61.

[34] Ibid., p. 14.

[35] Ibid., p. 24.

Because the Negroes were brought in as slaves, the black color raised the presumption of slavery, which was generally extended to mulattoes, and in many states this presumption was enunciated by statute, putting on them the onus of proving that they were free. In Virginia and Kentucky one-fourth Negro blood constituted a presumption of slavery, and all children born of slave mothers were slaves.[36]

Under the British West Indian and United States laws the Negro slave could not hope for self-redemption by purchase, and as slavery was assumed to be perpetual, there was only one route to freedom—manumission. But this route, if not entirely blocked, was made difficult by numerous impediments. The bias in favor of keeping the Negro in servitude contrasts with the other slave systems here under consideration, describes the explicit and the implicit test of the two systems, and foreshadows their ultimate outcome. For the attitude toward manumission is the crucial element in slavery; it implies the judgment of the moral status of the slave, and foreshadows his role in case of freedom.

Just as the favoring of manumission is perhaps the most characteristic and significant feature of the Latin-American slave system, so opposition to manumission and denial of opportunities for it are the primary aspect of slavery in the British West Indies and in the United States. The frequency and ease of manumission, more than any other factor, influence the character and ultimate outcome of the two slave systems in this hemisphere. For the ease of manumission bespeaks, even if only implicitly, a friendly attitude toward the person whose freedom is thus made possible and encouraged, just as the systematic obstruction of manumission implies a complete, if unconscious, attitude of hostility to those whose freedom is opposed or denied. And these contrasting attitudes toward manumission work themselves out in a hundred small, perhaps unnoticed, but significant details in the treatment of the Negro, both as a slave and when freed. Either policy reveals the bent of the system, and casts ahead of itself the long-run consequence of immediate practice and attitude.

*   *   *

[36] Thomas R. R. Cobb: *An Inquiry into the Law of Negro Slavery in the United States of America* (Philadelphia and Savannah, 1858), p. 238.

The Georgia constitution safeguards against the charge of murder if the "death should happen by accident in giving such slave moderate correction."[37] In South Carolina the act of 1740 provided that willful murder of a slave should cost the perpetrator "seven hundred pounds current money," and this law, which remained on the statute books till 1821 further provided that if the murder occurred "on sudden heat and passion," it should cost him only £350.[38] But such minor punishments as willfully cutting out the tongue, putting out the eye, castrating, scalding, and similar offenses would, according to the above law, involve the culprit in a cost of merely "one hundred pounds of current money."[39]

Where laws existed protecting the slave against unusual punishment, they were difficult to enforce because he was denied the right to testify in the courts. In the United States, according to Cobb,[40] the rule that slaves could not testify for or against free white persons was enforced without exception; most of the states prohibited such testimony by express statute, others by custom and decision of the courts. In Illinois and Iowa this prohibition extended to free persons of color or emancipated slaves. . . .

The slave had no protector to appeal to, and he could not have his price specified for purposes of redemption and was not allowed to accumulate property to buy his freedom. The slave could acquire no property, and if any property came to him, it would belong to his master;[41] and, being incapable of acquiring property, he could not convey it or give it away. The laws on this point are numerous.

*   *   *

The marriage contract having no validity, none of its consequences followed. While in a state of slavery, marriage, even with the master's consent, produced no civil effect.[42]

There was no custom of freeing the children at the baptismal font for a nominal price, there was nothing known of the moral role of the

---

[37] Art. 4, par. 12, in ibid., p. 61.
[38] Ibid., p. 64.
[39] Ibid., p. 66.
[40] Thomas R. R. Cobb, op. cit., p. 230.
[41] Ibid., p. 238.
[42] Ibid., p. 107.

godfather for the slave child, and the slave family had no status either in law or in public recognition. . . .

Under the law of most of the Southern states, there was no regard for the Negro family, no question of the right of the owner to sell his slaves separately, and no limitation upon separating husband and wife, or child from its mother. That this was so may be seen from the following advertisements:

NEGROES FOR SALE.—*A negro woman, 24 years of age, and her two children, one eight and the other three years old. Said negroes will be sold* SEPARATELY *or together, as desired. The woman is a good seamstress. She will be sold low for cash, or* EXCHANGED FOR GROCERIES.
For terms, apply to MATTHEW BLISS & CO., *1 Front Levee*

[*New Orleans Bee*]

*   *   *

"It is a practice, and an increasing practice in parts of Virginia, to rear slaves for market."[43] And the protagonist of slavery Thomas R. Dew, who became president of William and Mary College in 1836, said with pride that "Virginia is in fact a negro raising state for other states; she produces enough for her own supply, and six thousand for sale. . . . Virginians can raise [them] cheaper than they can buy; in fact, it [raising slaves] is one of their greatest sources of profit."[44]

This business had its implications and consequences. The Negro female was reduced to a breeding animal. "She [a girl about twenty years of age] . . . is very prolific in her generating qualities, and affords a rare opportunity for any person who wishes to raise a family of strong, healthy servants for . . . [his] own use. . . ."[45] The emphasis was upon raising children, for they could be sold at high prices. . . . The demise of the sanctity of marriage had become absolute, and the Negro had lost his moral personality. Legally he was a chattel under the law, and in practice an animal to be bred for the market. The logic of the situation worked itself out in time, but in the process the moral personality of the slave as a human being

[43] Quoted in Frederic C. Bancroft, op. cit., p. 69.
[44] Quoted in ibid., p. 71, from Thomas R. Dew: *Review of the Debate in the Virginia Legislature of 1831 and 1832* (Richmond, 1832).
[45] Quoted by Bancroft, op. cit., p. 74, from the *Charleston Mercury* of May 16, 1838.

became completely obscured. It is no wonder that the right of redemption was seemingly nonexistent and the opportunity for manumission greatly restricted.

The contrast between the United States and British West Indian slave law, on the one hand, and the Spanish and Portuguese, on the other, was further heightened by the different role of the church in the life of the Negro. The slaves in the British West Indies were almost completely denied the privileges of Christianity. The plantation-owners opposed the preaching of the gospel on the grounds that it would interfere with the management of the slaves, make them recalcitrant, and put notions of rebellion and freedom into their minds. The argument that the Christian doctrine would make the slaves more obedient, and therefore more docile, found little response among the planters. More surprising than the attitude of the slave-owners is that of the church itself. It is little exaggeration to say, as does one writer on the West Indies, that "The English Church did not recognize them as baptisable human beings."[46] For in spite of the fact that the Society for the Propagation of the Gospel, organized in 1701, declared through the mouth of Bishop Fleetwood, in 1710, that the three hundred Negroes that it had inherited in Barbados had to be brought into the church, and "that if all the slaves in America and every Island in those seas were to continue infidels forever, yet ours alone must yet be Christian,"[47] the church remained indifferent to its responsibility. . . .

Nor can it be said that the church in the United States was completely unrestricted in preaching the gospel. A series of regulations governing the assembly of Negroes for worship before dawn or after dark seriously interfered with church gatherings; the outright prohibition of Negro preachers or official frowning upon them, the opposition to acquisition of literacy on the part of either slave or freed man, all combined to restrict the development of a Negro church. And the white church proved incompetent to preach the gospel to all the millions of American Negroes. In South Carolina, in 1800, it was prohibited for "any number" of Negroes, mulattoes, or mestizos, even in company with white persons, to meet together for

---

[46] Amos K. Fiske: *The West Indies*, p. 108.
[47] Quoted in the Hon. H. A. Wyndham: *The Atlantic and Slavery*, p. 235.

mental instruction or religious worship "before sunrise or after sunset."[48] Similar laws prevailed in many states.

*   *   *

The contrast, therefore, between the Spanish and Portuguese slave systems on the one hand and that of the British and the United States was very marked, and not merely in their effect upon the slave, but even more significantly upon the place and moral status of the freed man. Under the influence of the law and religion, the social milieu in the Spanish and Portuguese colonies made easy room for the Negroes passing from slavery to freedom. The older Mediterranean tradition of the defense of the slave, combined with the effect of Latin-American experience, had prepared an environment into which the Negro freed from slavery could fit without visible handicap. Slavery itself carried no taint. It was a misfortune that had befallen a human being, and was in itself sufficiently oppressive. The law and religion both frowned upon any attempts to convert this into means of further oppression.

*   *   *

Nothing said above must induce the reader to believe that slavery was anything but cruel. It was often brutal. The difference between the systems lies in the fact that in the Spanish and Portuguese colonies the cruelties and brutalities were against the law, that they were punishable, and that they were perhaps not so frequent as in the British West Indies and the North American colonies. But these abuses had a remedy at law, and the Negro had a means of escape legally, by compulsory sale if the price were offered, and by many other means. More important was the fact that the road was open to freedom, and, once free, the Negro enjoyed, on the whole, a legal status equal to that of any other subject of the King or to that of any other citizen of the state. And if the question of color was an issue, he could purchase "whiteness" for a specific price.

If we now contrast the position of the freed Negro and people of

[48] William Goodell, op. cit., p. 329.

color in the British possessions with those we have just described, it will become evident that whereas freedom in one place meant moral status, in the other it meant almost the opposite. In the British West Indies the achievement of manumission merely involved a release from the obligation to serve a special master. . . .

The position of the manumitted Negro, or even of the mulatto born of a free mother, was not propitious. The legal and social environment was discriminatory and hostile. The English community opposed manumission, feared the growth of free colored people, and reduced those few who had found a route to freedom to as nearly a servile state as possible. In the United States a very similar policy toward freedmen developed. An act of manumission was merely a withdrawal of the rights of the master. It did not confer citizenship upon the freedmen. That power rested with the state.[49] They were not privileged to bear arms, they had to have a guardian to stand in the relation of a patron to them, and in some instances they were denied the right to purchase slaves as property. They tended to be placed on the same footing as slaves in their contact with whites. . . .

The law, the church, and social policy all conspired to prevent the identification of the liberated Negro with the community. He was to be kept as a separate, a lesser, being. In spite of being manumitted, he was not considered a free moral agent.

The different slave systems, originating under varying auspices, had achieved sharply contrasting results. If we may use such a term, the milieu in Latin America was expansive and the attitude pliable. The Negro may have been racially a new element, but slavery was a known and recognized institution—known especially to the law. The law had long since struggled with the subtleties of freedom and servitude and over a period of centuries had created an elaborate code for the slave, and the new Negro slave was automatically endowed with the immunities contained in the ancient prescription. He was no stranger to the law. His obligation and freedoms within the code were both known. In fact, *the element of human personality was not lost in the transition to slavery from Africa to the Spanish or Portuguese dominions.* He remained a person even while he was a slave. He lost his freedom, but he retained his right to become free

---

[49] Thomas R. R. Cobb, op. cit., p. 313.

again and, with that privilege, the essential elements in moral worth that make freedom a possibility. He was never considered a mere chattel, never defined as unanimated property, and never under the law treated as such. His master never enjoyed the powers of life and death over his body, even though abuses existed and cruelties were performed. Even if justice proved to be blind, the blindness was not incurable. The Negro slave under this system had both a juridical and a moral personality, even while he was in bondage.

This legal tradition and juridical framework were strengthened by the Catholic religion and were part of its doctrine and practice. It made him a member of the Christian community. It imposed upon both the slave and the master equal obligations to respect and protect the moral personality of the other, and for practical purposes it admitted the slave to the privileges of the sacraments. In the mundane world it meant that marriage was a sacred union that could not be broken by mere caprice, that the slave had a right to his wife, and that the slave's family was, like other families, a recognized union in a moral universe, not different from that of his master's family. Here, again, the religious prescriptions were perhaps as often violated as obeyed. But both the state and the church combined to maintain the principle of the rule by the exercise of civil and canon law. The church could and did thunder its opposition to the sins committed against the family—against all Christian families, regardless of color and regardless of status. The church, further, in its emphasis upon the moral equality between master and slave, came to favor manumission and to make it a deed laudable in the sight of God.

The legal right to achieve freedom and the religious favoring of manumission, combined with a number of other features peculiarly American, tended to make easy the path to freedom. That it was easy is seen by the large numbers of freedmen everywhere in Latin America during the colonial period and after independence. . . .

Endowing the slave with a moral personality before emancipation, before he achieved a legal equality, made the transition from slavery to freedom easy, and his incorporation into the free community natural. And as there were always large numbers of freedmen and children of freedmen, it never seemed especially dangerous to increase their number. There was never the question that so agitated people both in the West Indies and in the United States—the danger of emancipation, the lack of fitness for freedom. There was never the horrifying spectacle so often evoked in the United States of admitting a morally inferior and therefore, by implication, a biologically inferior people into the body politic on equal terms.

*   *   *

The different ways in which slavery was finally abolished in the two areas illumine the social process of which they were an integral part. In the Latin-American area slavery and freedom were, socially and morally speaking, very close to each other. The passage from slavery to freedom was always possible for the individual, and in practice frequent. There was nothing final or inescapable in the slave status. In fact, the contrary was the case. The social structure was malleable, the gap between slavery and freedom narrow and bridge-able, and almost any slave could hope that either he or his family would pass over from his side of the dividing line to the other. Easy manumission all through the period meant that there were always a large number of people in the community who had formerly been slaves and were now free. This is one of the two crucial differences between the character and the outcome of the slave institution in the Latin-American scene on one hand and in the United States on the other. The second basic difference was to be found in the position of the freedman after manumission. In fact, in Latin America there was for legal and practical purposes no separate class of freedmen. The freedman was a free man.[50] In the Latin-American slave system the easy and continuous change of status implied a process of evolution and a capacity for absorption within the social structure that pre-vented the society from hardening and kept it from becoming di-vided. We are here face to face with an evolutionary social process that did not allow for a horizontal stratification and favored passage vertically from slavery to freedom. There is, in fact, from this point of view, no slave system; there are only individual slaves. There is no slave by nature, no absolute identification of a given group of indi-viduals as slaves, to whom and to whose children the hope of escape from the hardships they are suffering is forever denied.

If in Latin America the abolition of slavery was achieved in every

---

[50] There were exceptions to this general statement that could be cited in so large an area and for a period of over three centuries, but both law and practice were bent in the direction of giving the Negro, once freed, a free man's rights.

case without violence, without bloodshed, and without civil war, it is due to the fact that there was no such fixed horizontal division, no such hardening of form that the pattern could no longer change by internal adaptations. In the Latin-American area the principle of growth and change had always been maintained. In the United States the very opposite had come to pass. For reasons of historical accident and conditioning, the Negro became identified with the slave, and the slave with the eternal pariah for whom there could be no escape. The slave could not ordinarily become a free man, and if chance and good fortune conspired to endow him with freedom, he still remained a Negro, and as a Negro, according to the prevailing belief, he carried all of the imputation of the slave inside him. In fact, the Negro was considered a slave by nature, and he could not escape his natural shortcomings even if he managed to evade their legal consequences. Freedom was made difficult of achievement and considered undesirable both for the Negro and for the white man's community in which the Negro resided. The distinction had been drawn in absolute terms, not merely between the slave and the free man, but between the Negro and the white man. The contrast was between color—the Negro was the slave, and the white man was the free man. Attributes of a sharply different moral character were soon attached to these different elements in the population, and they became incompatible with each other. They might as well, so far as the theory was concerned, have been of a different species, for all of the things denied to the Negro as a slave were permitted to the white man—as a citizen. Our Southern slave-holding community had by law and custom, by belief and practice, developed a static institutional ideal, which it proceeded to endow with a high ethical bias.

Franklin W. Knight

THE LEGAL FRAMEWORK OF CUBAN SLAVERY

Professor Franklin W. Knight of Johns Hopkins University tests Tannen-baum's thesis by examining how Cuban slaveowners interpreted the Spanish slave codes. He concludes that the codes were frequently compromised and that the Spanish officials had little power to enforce them. He implies that Cuban plantation owners, in the midst of the nineteenth-century sugar boom, manipulated the codes to maximize their profits. In Knight's view, economic developments can overwhelm laws and tradition.

Ambivalence and ambiguity have always characterized the attitudes of the white elite groups in every society where slavery played a significant role in the social structure. Such characteristics varied from one place to the other, but they were very pronounced in the American colonial experience owing to the peculiarities of slavery there, and to the changing nature of the societies themselves. For the ideals of the early settlers, either to create the perfect society or to reproduce a microcosm of the metropolis, rapidly faded against the realities of their new physical environment. The new situations offered few parallels with the established patterns of the mother country. And in some cases, most notably in the Caribbean (though not in Cuba), the successive changes of European governments left a mosaic of administrative forms and practices.

Against the realities of frontier conditions, both colonists and central authorities made compromising responses. The colonists, in general, created an ideal form of conduct and attitudes which they assumed to be representative of the metropolis, and to which they paid lip-service. Colonial behavior, nevertheless, freely deviated from the ideal in every way, sometimes to such an extent that it bore no resemblance. For their part, the metropolitan powers attempted in a great variety of ways to reconcile the pecularities of frontier exis-tence with a centralized authority and legislation.

In some British colonies, the laws of England automatically

From Franklin W. Knight, *Slave Society in Cuba during the Nineteenth Century* (Madi-son: University of Wisconsin Press, 1970), pp. 121–36. Reprinted by permission of University of Wisconsin Press. Footnotes omitted.

applied to the colonists. In the legislatures over which the governor presided as the representative of the crown, however, the colonists could formulate laws for their own local communities. The only open restriction upon such legislation was that it had to conform to the royal will. The crown held the powers of veto, and could exercise it to nullify any piece of legislation it thought damaging to any important interests either in England or in the particular colony, and, indeed, did nullify acts of the local legislatures considered to be contrary to the laws of England.

Spanish colonial practices were far more centralized than those of their other European counterparts in the earlier centuries of overseas colonization. Guided to a certain extent by the great Council of the Indies, the Spanish crown dictated all colonial laws. But regardless of the extent to which such laws reflected reports, recommendations, and complaints from the colonies, they could not be equally applicable to all parts of the farflung Spanish empire. Naturally conflicts developed over goals and standards, making "observance and nonobservance . . . a necessary component of the system." This ambiguous local response by the chief colonial administrators was summarized in the famous and graphic phrase *"obedezco pero no cumplo"* (I obey but I do not execute).

Since wide variations between ideal and practice were an accepted part of Spanish colonial life, it would be foolhardy to accept the sets of laws and decrees promulgated in Spain as a conclusive description of "real" conditions in the Indies. And while not denying the substantial contribution that an intensive study of such laws might yield to the study of master-slave relations, John L. Phelan has persuasively demonstrated the limitations of central decrees in some local conditions, even with vigorous and conscientious officials. The appearance of strong centralization within the Spanish empire did not always preclude the operation of local checks and balances.

During the nineteenth century, local planter power often came close to crippling the central authority in Cuba. In 1842 Captain-General Valdés, sensitive to hostile local opposition, refused to publish the law declaring free the slaves who had been introduced illegally since 1820, despite an Anglo-Spanish agreement on that matter. Later, the same problem enveloped the Moret Law of phased abolition which passed the Cortes on July 4, 1870. The Spanish government, under great international pressures to abolish slavery in

Cuba and Puerto Rico, greatly desired that the law be implemented with the least possible delay. In Cuba the governor and captain-general, Antonio Caballero de Rodas, acting on his own initiative—at least in the official context—suspended the implementation of the laws for two years, offering the feeble excuse that the government had not issued the *reglamento* outlining the operation of the law, and that a census had to be taken to determine the slaves who fell under its provisions.

The truth of the situation, however, was that Caballero de Rodas sympathized with the planters, who, contrary to Moret's assertion, had not been consulted prior to the formulation of the law. But, of course, at this time the local Havana plantocracy had already usurped effective political power, and, with a civil war already on his hands, the governor might have realized the difficulties in which he could find himself if he obeyed his superior officers.

In spite of the discrepancy between theory and practice, the slave laws were important as an index of changing conditions and attitudes. Although the principles governing slaves in the New World had their basis in the extremely humane thirteenth-century code of laws, the *Siete partidas*, the Spanish crown found it necessary from time to time to reiterate specific laws, or to issue a complete summary of the laws. In 1680, therefore, the *Recopilación de las leyes de los reynos de las Indias* became the most comprehensive attempt to create order out of the chaos of colonial legislation. Later, as the general proliferation of laws seemed to have got out of hand again, further attempts were made to codify the laws, many of which conflicted with one another.

The change in official attitude towards the slave trade in the later years of the eighteenth century made it necessary to repeat in detail the various decrees governing slavery in the Spanish New World. To this end the crown issued the slave code of 1789. Again, the changed milieu of mid-nineteenth-century Cuba required a special legal pronouncement on slavery.

Elsa Goveia has argued persuasively that the West Indian slave laws could not exist without a favorable climate of opinion. By examining the changes in emphasis over the years, therefore, it is possible to glean quite a lot of information about changes in attitudes and situations in any particular slave society.

The *Siete partidas* was an extremely liberal slave code, without equal among the other European nations. The legal basis for slavery was acknowledged, and the personality of the slave received recognition. The *Siete partidas* emphatically held aloft the idea of liberty: "It is a rule of law that all judges should aid liberty, for the reason that it is a friend of nature, because not only men, but all animals love it." But the public sentiment in the thirteenth century had not yet experienced plantation slavery. Apart from that, the frontier conditions in the New World constituted a unique experience for the Spanish legislators.

The great code of 1680 reflected the changed conditions. The most important considerations were police regulation measures, and attempts to maintain the stratification and racial separation of the colonial society. The biggest problem had been that of runaways, and the fear of Indian-Negro resistance to public order. Free colored people, too, had their lives supervised, and their social station clearly defined. Laws forbade them to wear gold, silk, cloaks, or other kinds of clothing which would make them indistinguishable—in apparel— from the white elite. Free colored people were required to have a patron, even though they had their freedom. An unsuccessful attempt was made to eliminate racial intermixture between Spaniards, Negroes, or Indians. From the outset, of course, religious instruction was a requirement of Spanish slave laws.

The slave code of 1789, besides summarizing all the legal precedents, attempted to introduce ameliorative measures for the slaves. Apart from the usual religious requirements of baptism, daily prayers, religious instruction, and mass, the code freed the slaves from work on holidays, except during the harvest when it was customary to grant permission for them to do so. Masters had to feed their slaves and dress them according to the custom of the country, and in a way which conformed to that of the free workers. The corporal punishment meted out to slaves for misdemeanors on the estate was restricted to twenty-five lashes, preferably administered by the master or overseer. One new feature of this code was the legal restrictions put on the master class; if they failed by obey they could be subject to fines, and, depending on the nature of the contravention, they could even lose their slaves. The royal decree further appointed a protector of slaves to safeguard their rights.

The slave code of 1789 would have been a monumental achievement if it could have been implemented. Unfortunately, contrary to the common opinion—especially as expressed by H. H. Johnston in *The Negro in the New World*—the so-called magnificent code of 1789 was never even read in the colonies. When word leaked out of the new provisions, the colonists became so hostile that the measures were quickly shelved. José Antonio Saco described the nonimplementation in his monumental work on slavery:

> When the royal order of May 31, 1789, was sent out, the vecinos of Havana, as well as those of Santo Domingo, Caracas, and New Orleans, which then belonged to Spain, on the 19th of January 1790, begged the Governor, through their organ, the town councils, not to publish the decree, lest the slaves, interpreting it in a bad light, might revolt. In fact, the Captains-General did not publish it, and when the Council of the Indies consulted Francisco de Saavedra, Ignacio de Urriza and other persons familiar with affairs in America, they all said that it should be suspended, and that in each capital a body of the leading planters, the Bishop, and the Captain-General should propose the laws which ought to govern in that matter. In this way, then, a royal order was nullified, which would have extended the greatest benefit to the slaves of any nation which had them in their colonies.

The 1842 slave code was the result of a series of concurrent pressures on the Spanish government, and came generally as a surprise to the Cuban planters, even though some may have found it convenient. Great Britain, eager that Spain should observe her treaty agreements, was becoming more aggressive about the large-scale illegal traffic in African slaves to Cuba. In Cuba, a state of high tension prevailed. The planters expressed fear that Spain had made a secret deal with Britain to abolish slavery and ruin their property. Minor slave uprisings had led to the belief that a general insurrection was imminent. The slave code was an attempt to diminish the state of suspense. The preamble to the decree declared:

> . . . on dealing with such details, I could not but fix my attention on the fields, interesting in so many aspects, and especially concerning the hands dedicated to the agricultural tasks. To procure the conservation and propagation of such hands through every possible means, to assure the continuation of a humane treatment [un trato humano] without ceasing to maintain them under a severe discipline and unalterable subordination, is the object of our legislation, as it is to work in every way consistent with the true interests of this rich and important part of the monarchy.

. . . The slave code itself, consisting of forty-eight articles, reflected some principles of the unimplemented code of 1789, but more of the code adopted in Puerto Rico in 1826. Its provisions covered five major topics: religion and hispanization; slave welfare and recreation; slaves' rights or benefits; public protection measures; and the administrative procedures for implementing the order.

The first five articles dealt with instruction and moral education of the slaves. The code entreated masters, as a standard practice carried down through the years, to see that their slaves were given religious instruction (even every night after work), baptism, and the sacraments. On Sunday and fiestas, slaves should only work for two hours, except during crop-time, when they should "work as on labor days." Article 5 implied instruction in citizenship—referred to herein as hispanization, since it attempted to create a Spanish social order and propagate Spanish mores:

> *The masters will place the greatest possible attention and diligence in making them* [the slaves] *understand the obedience which they owe to the constituted authorities; the obligation of reverence to the priests, and to respect all white persons; to behave themselves well with the free persons of color; and to live harmoniously with their companions.*

The largest portion of the code pertained to the welfare of the slaves, on matters of food, clothes, health, housing, recreation, and work. Article 6 specified what the slaves should be fed: six to eight plantains, "or their equivalent in ground provisions," eight ounces of meat or codfish, four ounces of rice or flour per day for each slave. It further stated that "the master should give two or three meals per day according to what seems best to him, and what he judges is in the slaves' best interest." Small children whose mothers worked in the fields should be fed milk or porridge until they had teeth to chew harder foods (Article 8).

Slaves should be given two changes of clothing per year, in December and May (Article 7); and little children should be well dressed (Article 11). All infants should be kept in a nursery, under the care of an old Negress (Article 9), but in case of illness, such children should be returned to their mothers who ought to be taken in from the fields, and set on domestic tasks (Article 10). Sick slaves ought not to be freed, but should be attended by their masters (Article 15). Each estate was also required to have a sick bay with medicines and adequate facilities (Articles 27 and 18).

According to the code, the day's labor was set at nine to ten hours of work. In crop-time, however, the day was allowed to be "sixteen hours with two for rest in the days, and six at night to sleep" (Article 12). On Sundays and fiestas, slaves could pursue their own occupation (Article 13); and slaves "over sixty and under seventeen" should not be allowed to work (Article 14).

Visiting and slave dances could be held during daylight hours, under white supervision (Articles 19 and 23). Housing of slaves received detailed consideration (Articles 25, 26, 29). Sleeping quarters for married slaves should be separated from those for single slaves, with "a light to burn all night to see that no mixing took place between the unmarried sexes." No slave should be permitted out at night.

Article 29 stipulated that "masters should prevent illicit relations which foment marriages," but they should not impede marriages involving slaves from another estate, and should permit such couples to get together under the same roof. Article 30 advocated that the master of either slave should purchase the other, or both should sell the married couple to a third party. If the owner of the husband was the purchaser, he should also buy all children under the age of three who belonged to the married slaves.

The articles aimed at public protection sought to prevent the slaves being in a position to conspire, or arm themselves with the intention of fomenting a riot. Articles 16 and 17 sought to have all work implements locked away securely, the master ensuring that the slaves received their tools only in the mornings, and that they returned them in the afternoons. Under no circumstances should any slave be given the keys to the tool room. Neither should any slave leave a hacienda with a tool in his possession (Article 18). Nevertheless, if such a slave were accompanied by a white person, then he might carry a machete on his person. Articles 20, 21, and 22 governed the escape of slaves from the plantations, with the usual provisions that any free person might detain any slave suspected of running away. Return of such slaves should be a mutually gratuitous service among slaveholders. In other cases, masters should pay a reward of four pesos, plus any costs incurred for food and medicines.

Article 24 stipulated that the greatest care should be taken to eliminate excessive drinking by slaves, or intercourse with free colored persons.

One section of the code concerned what may very loosely be termed "slave rights." The most important of these rights was the local custom which had finally been accepted in law, coartación. This practice of coartación was simply the procedure by which a slave and his master definitely fixed the price of the slave so that at no time in the future could the master demand a higher price for the liberty of that slave. It was, in short, a process to remove the value of the slave from the impact of market place considerations or personal whim. It was such a novel legal concept that the word was italicized in the code of 1842. Article 34 established the slaves' right to coartación: "No owner may refuse to *coartar* his slave, provided he is offered fifty pesos toward the price of purchase." Article 35 emphasized the meaning of the Spanish word, "to cut off, or fix": "A *coartado*'s price remains constant, provided he is not sold without his owner's consent," otherwise the sale price would be augmented by various additional taxes and costs. Children of coartado slaves did not enjoy the benefits of their mothers, but could be sold like any other slave (Article 36). Once a coartado had paid fully his agreed price, he could not be denied his liberty (Article 37). Articles 32 and 33 allowed owners to sell any slaves they mistreated, or found continuously difficult. Such owners could determine the price at which they would sell the slave. On the other hand, any slave could petition to have his master sell him.

Besides coartación, the slaves had two other opportunities to get their freedom. Article 38, in a patent reflection of the troubled times, stipulated that any slave reporting any conspiracy, whether of fellow slaves or of free persons, would receive his immediate freedom and a cash reward of five hundred pesos. The money for such rewards was to be obtained from a public fund supported by fines collected from infringement of the slave laws (Article 39). Article 40 allowed slaves to be given their liberty in wills, "or any other legally justified manner, and proceeding from an honest and laudable motive."

Articles 41, 42, and 43 outlined the punishment which could be meted out to slaves in order to discipline them and make them respect white persons. Corporal punishment was limited to twenty-five strokes, to be administered only by the master. Most of the common forms of torture and detention such as "stocks, shackles, chains, clubs, and prisons" were admitted as legal punishment for slaves. . . .

The slave laws of 1842 as represented in the codes were considerably less liberal than the attempted recommendations of 1789. The restrictions on the movements and activities of the slaves, the more detailed regulations for work, and the stronger emphasis upon the obedience of slaves to white persons and the constituted authorities revealed a severe hardening of the attitudes of the master group toward their slaves. Two significant omissions in the code of 1842 were the leniency toward all women, and the equality in the punishment meted out to slaves and persons of color. The general impression conveyed by the slave laws of 1842, then, was one of increased repression. Any further attempt to explain this change would probably have to take into account the increased European racism and ideas of social engineering which manifested themselves in sharper lines of separation between people of European stock and others. These tendencies were most cogently expressed in the positivist ideas that found their way into the thinking of most erudite Latin Americans at this time. Yet in the absence of a detailed study of their effect on the Cuban people at this time we can merely speculate.

But in part the diminishing liberality of the Cuban slave laws can be laid definitely to the sugar revolution, which brought an increased number of Africans to the island as slaves. In the late eighteenth century, more than 60 percent of the population were white. By 1842 the percentage had declined to a little more than 40 percent, and events elsewhere in the Caribbean had further increased the uneasiness about the longevity of slavery in the area. Indeed, by 1842 the Cubans were forced to defend slavery in their land, as slaveholding societies became steadily more scarce in the Western world. British opposition to the slave trade was powerful and persistent.

British naval interceptions of slave ships bound for Cuba led to serious labor problems. To deny the Cuban planters their slaves at that time was like bleeding their lifeblood.

Yet many Cubans failed to realize that slavery was slowly changing the traditional pattern of their society. The sugar revolution and slavery had brought to the fore of the society a new landowning and slaveholding oligarchy who were keenly interested in making money and running profitable plantations. If they knew about the old patriarchal relationship between masters and slaves, they could no longer accommodate it within the new system of plantation agriculture, which tended to destroy personal relations between masters and slaves. For one thing, the new system changed the ratio of the races on the estates, and demanded a more regimented organization of the labor force than the previous systems. For another thing, the new plantation owners, particularly in the sugar areas, lived in the towns, and used intermediaries recruited from among the lower levels of the white element to assume most of the onhand, upper managerial tasks of the estates. And as the number of slaves increased, the white supervisors in particular and the white caste in general feared violent, physical retaliation by their slaves, as well as the loss of their "property" and, of course, their laborers. This increasing fear of a body of oppressed men did not permit a more lenient attitude toward the slaves, and the slave laws of 1842 reflected this change.

Slavery was an institution which affected the entire Cuban society. While the majority of white persons were by no means large landholders requiring a great number of African workers, almost every family desired or possessed slaves of some sort. Owning a slave was a significant social index: the more slaves any person had, the more social prestige accrued to him. José de la Concha claimed that even the poor whites (*guajiros*) who worked in the fields along with the slaves strongly aspired to be slaveowners themselves some day. They were the most overtly racist group in the island and in the minor positions of responsibility which they attained they often sharpened racial tensions by their attitudes.

A very wide difference existed between the numbers of slaves owned by urban white people, under better conditions, and those held by rural planters. According to the census data, the slaves of the towns were either domestics or hired hands. But more important than occupation was the pattern of slaveholding: in the towns, the individual master held far fewer slaves than in the plantation areas.

In 1857, there were 372,943 slaves in the island and 49,111 owners—a mean holding of 7.59 per owner. Broken down further, however, the figures of Cuban slaveholding emphatically expose the imbalance between the number of slaves in the towns and those of the rural plantation zones of the island. The census of 1857 gave 22,753 persons owning 65,568 urban slaves, a mean holding of nearly

3 slaves per owner. Havana, the capital city, had 29,420 slaves, owned by 9,421 persons—a mean holding of 3.1, not significantly different from the urban pattern throughout the island. The median holding was close to the mean, for the only owner to have an unusually large number was the firm of Irias and Company, Successors, which had 155 slaves, of which only 6 were registered as urban slaves.

The total of 307,375 registered slaves in the rural areas had 26,358 owners, an island-wide average holding of 11.6 slaves per owner. But the picture was very different in the plantation areas: 483 rural owners had more than 80 slaves each, yielding a total of 95,523 slaves for a mean holding of 197 slaves each. In other words, less than 1 percent of the slaveowners of Cuba held more than 25 percent of all the slaves in the island.

These slaveowners in the middle of the nineteenth century were very influential men in political affairs, and owned the largest sugar estates. . . . Julian Zulueta, the acknowledged political boss of Cuba and certainly one of the richest men in the island, owned more than 1,475 slaves in Cárdenas.

While it would quite obviously be a gross distortion to say that the planters in Cuba made the slave laws of 1842, yet the laws clearly could not ignore them. The facts speak for themselves. Slave population and plantation production formed corresponding patterns. The nine largest provinces in terms of slave population—Cárdenas, Cienfuegos, Guanajay, Güines, Matanzas, Pinar del Río, Sagua la Grande, San Antonio, and Santiago de Cuba—held 62 percent of all the slaves in the island, accounted for 80 percent of all agricultural products, and produced 80 percent of the total sugar crop. Moreover, a very small number of slaveowners held a disproportionately large number of slaves.

Cuban society and economy in the middle of the nineteenth century were, it is clear, heavily dependent on, indeed dominated by, the plantation, and by extension, the plantation owners. In trying to deduce the relation of the masters and the slaves from the slave laws, therefore, one must consider this aspect. For it was not the efficiency or laxity of the administrative bureaucracy (or, as some writers would have it, the Roman Catholic Church) which most weightily affected the conditions of the slaves. Rather, these conditions were determined by whether or not the slave found himself on the plantation or in the city, and by the unwritten laws of the individual, often very powerful, owner. Clearly the laws did have some humanitarian elements acquired from the earlier days and more relaxed atmosphere of slavery in the island. Yet bearing in mind the strains placed upon laws and tradition by changes in the economic basis of the society, we must consider the laws themselves as a very misleading index of the relations between masters and slaves.

Carl N. Degler
SLAVERY COMPARED

Carl N. Degler continues the challenge to Tannenbaum by comparing slavery in Brazil and the United States. He concludes that whatever differences there were in the practices of slavery in the two countries can be explained by economic and demographic developments, not by differences in laws, tradition, and religion. He believes the same economic and demographic patterns account for what he considers the crucial difference between the two slave societies—their diverging attitude toward the free black person. Professor Degler of Stanford University won the Bancroft Award for his 1971 publication, Neither Black Nor White: Slavery and Race Relations in Brazil and the United States.

Perhaps the most frequently stressed difference between Latin American and United States slavery is the amount of manumission. Generally it is said that in Latin America manumission was both more common and easier than in the United States. Yet, even in this area of comparison the contrast is less sharp than is often said; manumission in Brazil was not without restriction and in the United States it was not absolutely denied. Moreover, the purchase of freedom by the slave himself, so much emphasized in discussions on the nature of Brazilian slavery, was far from rare in the United States. Sumner Matison, for example, found several hundred examples of self-purchase. James Hugo Johnston, searching the governors' papers in

Virginia, came across at least ninety-one instances of free Negroes who had purchased their own freedom, a number of them being assisted in the accumulation of money by whites. Luther Jackson, studying self-purchase in three cities of Virginia, uncovered twenty examples even at the height of the sectional tensions of the 1850s and despite a law requiring removal of manumitted slaves out of the state. Kenneth Stampp cites instances, too, of slaves buying their own time, and on occasion, one buying his freedom by installments.

On the Brazilian side of the comparison it needs to be said that prior to 1871, despite tradition and the assertions of some historians, there was no law requiring a master to permit a slave to buy his freedom, though many undoubtedly did. One American historian of Brazil made a search for such a law, but found none prior to 1871, when emancipationists insisted upon it, a fact that in itself suggests the practice of self-purchase was not as firmly protected as often is alleged. It is true, nevertheless, that Brazilian law contained none of the limitations on manumission that prevailed in the southern United States, especially after 1830. All of the southern states, for instance, threw obstacles in the path of the master who sought to free his slave, not the least of which was the requirement that all newly freed slaves must leave the state. Under Brazilian law, on the other hand, emancipation was legal in almost any form, whether by letter, by will, or by simple but explicit statement at baptism. The law in Brazil, however, did contain a curious qualification to its otherwise open-handed attitude toward emancipation. It provided that freedom might be revoked by the master for ingratitude on the part of the freedman, even if that ingratitude was expressed only orally and outside of the presence of the former master! Perdigão Malheiro, who reports this provision of the law, doubted that it was still valid in 1866. But in 1871 this power to revoke freedom was explicitly withdrawn by an antislavery law, suggesting that the old provision was not such a dead letter that opponents of slavery wanted it to remain on the statute books.

The provision also raises a question as to whether the law in Brazil was in fact helping to preserve the Negro's moral personality under slavery, as has sometimes been argued. At the very least such a provision encouraged masters to think of their Negroes as minors or wards rather than as persons on an equal footing with themselves. At worst, the provision perpetuated in the Negro that sense of subordination and inferiority derived from the degraded status of slavery. To the extent that such a sense of subordination was inculcated in blacks it would tend to nullify whatever sense of independence and hopeful expectations that the generally easy and open opportunities for manumission might have encouraged in Negro slaves.

Some commentators on slavery in the United States and Latin America assert that the slave's right to hold property in South America, as contrasted with the lack of such a right in the United States, made it easier for him to buy his freedom in Brazil than in the United States. Actually, the law in Brazil did not permit slaves to possess property—or a peculium—until near the end of the slave era. For as Perdigão Malheiro wrote in his treatise on slave law in 1866, "among us, no law guarantees to the slave his peculium." However, he goes on, most masters permitted slaves to keep whatever property they gathered, letting them use it as they saw fit. Generally, the same situation in law and in practice prevailed in the United States. Slaves' property was neither recognized nor protected by law in any of the southern states, but in practice most slaveowners permitted their slaves to keep whatever property they earned from work on their own time. It was a cruel as well as a rare master in the United States, as in Brazil, who deliberately, if legally, confiscated earnings that his slave may have accumulated. Occasionally in the United States, on the other hand, the courts would throw a protective arm around the peculium, as in a South Carolina case in 1792. The court held that a slave was capable of possessing property separate from that of his master. On the basis of that decision, fifty years later the South Carolina high court concluded that though the earlier case "goes further than I desire to go . . . it is ample authority to prove that by the law of this state a slave might acquire *personal property*."

Finally, in trying to put into perspective the argument that man-umission was much easier in Brazil than in the United States, a remark of Joaquim Nabuco, the great Brazilian abolitionist, is appro-priate. Writing in 1881, Nabuco noted that between 1873 and that date some 87,000 slaves had been privately manumitted in the coun-try. Although admitting that such a number testified to the generosity of some Brazilians, Nabuco pointed out that most of the manumis-sions, even at that late date in the history of slavery, were mostly by small, urban holders, not by large planters. With some irony, he pointed out that in the province of Rio de Janeiro over the previous ten years, death "freed" 51,269 slaves whereas masters freed only 12,849 in a province that counted 333,000 slaves.

Yet, after making all these qualifications to the usually optimistic picture of the opportunities for manumission in Brazil, the balance must still come down on the side that sees that country as more liberal in this regard than the United States. In this aspect of slavery lies one of the principal differences between the two systems. The chief reason for drawing that conclusion is the considerably higher proportion of free Negroes in nineteenth-century Brazil than in the United States. Although there is some reason to believe that the disparity may not have been as great in the colonial period, the paucity of even reasonably accurate figures prior to 1800 compels us to confine the comparison to the nineteenth century. According to the traditional estimates, in 1817–18 the number of slaves in Brazil was about three times that of free Negroes and mulattoes. This ratio may be compared with that in the United States in 1860, when the number of free Negroes reached its maximum under slavery. At that date there were eight times as many slaves as free Negroes in the whole of the United States and sixteen times as many slaves as free blacks if the comparison is made in the slave states alone. After abolition in the United States, the number of free Negroes in Brazil grew enormously. Thus in 1872 the number of free Negroes and colored was more than double the number of slaves! Here is certainly a striking difference between the two slave societies. How might one account for it?

Two explanations are worth looking at. One of these is that Brazilian masters freed the sick and the old in order to relieve themselves of responsibility and financial loss. Frequent denunciations in newspapers and laws seeking to stop such practices leave no doubt that some masters were indeed freeing their infirm, aged, and incurably sick slaves. Yet it is difficult to believe that such practices, even as widespread and common as the sources lead us to believe them to be, could have been the principal source of the relatively large free colored population. Infirm, aged, or sick slaves simply would not have been numerous enough themselves or have been able to produce offspring in sufficient numbers to account for the great number of free Negroes and mulattoes in the society.

A more persuasive explanation is derived from the different processes of settlement and economic development in the two countries. As we have noticed already, Negroes and mulattoes made up a majority of the population of Brazil prior to the last quarter of the nineteenth century. Whether as slaves or as free men, Negroes and mulattoes had a place in a society that was only sparsely populated and in a slave economy that concentrated upon staple production. The free blacks and mulattoes were needed to raise cattle, grow food, to serve as shopkeepers, craftsmen, peddlers, boatmen, and for a thousand other tasks. They filled the innumerable petty jobs, the interstitial work of the economy, that the constraints of slavery would not permit the slave to perform and that white men were insufficient or unwilling to man.

Furthermore, the booms and busts so characteristic of the colonial economy in Brazil provided incentives for manumission during the busts and jobs for freed slaves during the booms. Thus when the sugar economy of the northeast, where many slaves were concentrated, declined at the end of the seventeenth century, many planters escaped the burden of excessive slaves by freeing them or letting them support themselves as *negros dos ganhos*, or self-hired slaves. The discovery of gold and diamonds in Minas Gerais in the early eighteenth century (the second boom and bust cycle) opened a new frontier, which in turn created a new demand not only for slaves to work as miners, but also for cooks, shopkeepers, muleteers, and skilled and unskilled workers. Free and slave Negroes and mulattoes could and did fill these jobs. In the mining towns hired Negro slaves were exploited as never before, Edison Carneiro points out, leaving the Negro "more autonomous, more independent of the master, more responsible, personally, for his labor and for his behavior." A lucky find of gold or diamonds might also give a slave a chance to buy his freedom. Then, when the mines were largely worked out, masters of slaves once again escaped the burden of excess labor by freeing their slaves or letting them support themselves. In short, in colonial Brazil the master sometimes had good reason to free his slaves—to be rid of their expense in bad times—while the under-manned society and economy had a place and a need for the former slave.

In the United States the economic and demographic patterns worked in the opposite direction. It is true that many plantations in the South also concentrated their slave labor on staple production and imported food and other supplies rather than growing or fashioning themselves. But the food and the supplies were produced by a large number of nonslaveholding whites in the South itself and in the Old Northwest. From the beginning of settlement in the South, much less in the United States as a whole, there had always been more than enough white men to perform all the tasks of the society *except* that of plantation worker. In a society with much empty land, few white men could be found to work for others. By the end of the eighteenth century white indentured servitude was fast dying out and the tobacco and rice plantations of the southern colonies had come to depend upon the labor of black slaves. In the nineteenth century perhaps three-fourths of the cotton grown in the South came from plantations on which black slaves supplied the labor. Indeed, it seems clear now that without black slaves the great Cotton Kingdom of the South simply could not have developed as rapidly as it did. Off the plantations, however, unlike the situation in Brazil, white labor was more than ample for the needs and expansion of the economy. Indeed, throughout the antebellum years, as for years afterward, the South actually exported white people to the rest of the nation.

In the nineteenth-century Cotton Kingdom there was little need or compelling economic reason for emancipation, for generally the economy prospered. The boom and bust pattern of Brazil did not occur in the cotton South. The only time that the slave economy of the United States came close to the boom and bust cycle was just after the Revolutionary War. At that time indigo production in South Carolina was failing rapidly because of the withdrawals of the British subsidy and tobacco markets were depressed by the loss of British markets and by the competition from other tobacco-producing areas in the New World. Furthermore, the English demand for cotton had not yet brought the Cotton Kingdom into being. Not surprisingly, during this period of transition, before cotton gave slavery a new lease on life, several thousand slaves were manumitted in Virginia and slavery was abolished in all the states north of the Mason and Dixon line. At the time many men, both north and south of the line, honestly believed that slavery would be abolished throughout the nation within a short time. In fact, of course, abolition made no more progress for another three-quarters of a century, but that story is not our concern here. The point is that for a brief period in the United

States a decline in a staple product had affected masters' willingness to emancipate in much the same way as a comparable economic situation had affected Brazilian masters.

Shifts in the late-eighteenth-century economy of the United States may have provided a brief and inadequate inducement to emancipation, but at no time did the United States economy provide a place for those who might be manumitted. Slaves in the United States supplied a unique, yet important kind of labor, as we have seen; one that was in high demand in a society in which land was plentiful but hired labor expensive. All other forms of labor, however, were easily and quickly taken care of by the large free white population, which was steadily increased by an ever-growing white immigration from Europe. In Brazil, on the other hand, the small size of the white population and relatively small amount of free white immigration (at least until the European immigration in the last quarter of the nineteenth century) meant that Negroes and mulattoes served as settlers, in the broadest sense of the word, as well as slaves. . . .

What may we conclude from this examination of slavery in Brazil and the United States? That there were in fact differences in the practices of slavery in the two countries there can be no doubt. That Brazil kept the foreign trade open longer than the United States was not only a difference, but a cause for several other differences, as we have seen. The two countries also differed markedly in their attitudes toward arming slaves and toward defending slavery on grounds of race. The explanations for these differences, however, are not to be found in differences in the laws of the two home governments nor in the attitudes and practices of the respective national religious persuasions. Neither the church nor the state in Brazil displayed any deep concern about the humanity of the slave and, in any event, neither used its authority to affect significantly the life of the slave. . . . Even when the Portuguese Crown sought to provide some protection for the Negro as a human being, it was not always obeyed by white masters in Brazil. Much more persuasive as explanations for the differences are the demographic and economic developments and geographic circumstances in the two countries, that is, the differences in their respective historical experiences.

At the same time, there is yet something else that might be gained from this comparison. For there is a pattern behind some of the differences that becomes clear only as the individual differences are viewed together. Behind several of the divergencies in practice and ideology is the clear implication that in Brazil the slave may have been feared, but the black man was not, whereas in the United States both the slave and the black were feared. Thus the willingness of Brazilians to manumit slaves much more freely than North Americans is a result of their not fearing free blacks in great numbers, regardless of the fears they may have entertained about slave uprisings. Thus Brazilians did not feel it necessary to restrict manumission as North Americans did. In the United States, slavery was always a means of controlling dangerous blacks as well as a way of organizing labor. That is why most plans for emancipation, prior to the great abolitionist crusade, looked to expatriation to Africa or some other place once the Negroes were freed. Winthrop Jordan, in *White Over Black*, points out that the "earliest American suggestion of colonization included an observation that it was not safe to have Negroes free in America." The "warning" was published in 1715. As late as the Civil War, President Abraham Lincoln was still seriously considering the founding of a settlement in Central America for the blacks who would be freed by the war. Only the impracticality of resettling four million people caused him to give up the idea.

United States fear of Negroes is also highlighted in the contrast between the willingness of Brazilian slaveholders to use blacks as slave-catchers and overseers, whereas in the United States, few white men, much less slaveholders, were prepared to put Negroes in such positions of authority. Nor is it accidental that a racial defense of slavery was developed in the United States and largely absent from Brazil. Such a defense followed almost logically from the fear of blacks and was quite consonant with the refusal to permit free blacks to be overseers and slave-catchers. Although when one looks at the United States experience alone the development of a racial defense of slavery seems quite natural, the Brazilian experience compels us to realize that the development of such a defense was not a simple function of slavery, but the result of a special attitude on the part of whites toward blacks—an attitude derived from a particular history. It would be difficult for Brazilians to develop a racial defense of slavery when they used these same blacks as overseers and slave-catchers, that is, as defenders of the system.

Finally, the fear of Negroes on the part of North Americans emerges nowhere more forcefully than when one asks why the slave trade remained open in Brazil down to 1851, but was closed in most of the United States before the end of the eighteenth century. If one examines official explanations for the closing of the slave trade, the fear of being overwhelmed by blacks stands out as a significant, if not the chief motive.

Long before the Revolution, Englishmen in North America had been seeking ways to limit the number of blacks in their midst, both slave and free. As early as 1735, the Governor and Council of South Carolina petitioned the Crown: "The Importation of Negroes we crave leave to Inform your Majesty is a Species of Trade, that is exceedingly increased of late in this Province where many Negroes are now Train'd up to be Handycraft Tradesmen; to the great Discouragement of your Majesty's white Subjects who came here to Setle [*sic*] with a view of Employement [*sic*] in their several Occupations but must often give way to a People in Slavery, which we daily discover to be a great Obstruction to the Settlement of this Frontier with white People." Then in February 1750 a report of a committee in charge of security, health, and convenience of the people of Charleston recommended that in view of the excessive number of slaves "some proper Restraint may be put to this growing Evil, to reduce the present number, And that all due encouragement may be given to white Inhabitants to reside in the said Town, it is proposed that all White Persons who will accept of servile Labour, such as Porter, etc. shall have the preference to all Jobs that offer and be entitled to an additional Hire per Diem." The next year the legislature passed a law to raise revenue to encourage white immigration. "The best way to prevent the mischief that may be attended by the great importation of negroes into the province," the law read, "will be to establish a method by which such importation should be made a necessary means of introducing a proportionate number of white inhabitants."

South Carolina was not alone in its concern. In 1772 the Virginia Legislature begged the Crown to permit it to stop the slave traffic into the province because "the importation of slaves into the colonies from the coast of Africa hath long been considered as a trade of great inhumanity, and under its *present encouragement*, we have too much reason to fear, *will endanger the very existence* of your majesty's American dominions." After the Revolution, in 1786, North Carolina placed a tax on slaves on the ground that "the importation of slaves into this state is productive of evil consequences, and highly impolitic." The widespread fear of Negroes also explains why all but one of the North American slave states had already prohibited the importation of slaves before the federal prohibition was enacted in 1808.

In Brazil, on the other hand, the slave trade came tc an end not only much later, but only after great pressure had been applied from outside the society. Although there were also some Brazilians in the nineteenth century who advocated the closing of the infamous traffic, the principal force came from the British government. In 1827, on pain of commercial restrictions, Britain compelled the Brazilian government to agree to the closing of the trade. But from the outset the Brazilians showed that they were not going to stop a traffic so important to them and especially when agreement to do so was exacted under duress. Thus for almost a quarter of a century thereafter the British navy harassed Brazilian shipping while the foreign office harassed the Imperial government in an effort to put teeth into the treaty of 1827. Success was meager. As we have seen already, it was during that twenty-year period that several hundred thousand fresh slaves entered Brazil from Africa.

The trade was definitely ended in 1851 by Brazilian action. Behind that decision lay twenty years of British harassment and humiliating violation of Brazilian sovereignty. At times the Royal Navy, in its zealous suppression of the hated traffic, actually chased slavers through the harbors and inlets of Brazil. It was not fear of being inundated by blacks that wrote an end to the trade in Brazil, but the desire on the part of Brazilians to put a stop to British hectoring and to have their country take its place among those nations that refused to participate in a business no longer considered civilized. Besides, in a country in which most of the people were black or brown, fear of being overwhelmed by colored people could hardly have been an important consideration.

The overall conclusion that emerges from this comparison of slave systems is that the differences are not fundamental to an explanation of differences in contemporary race relations. It is evident that differences in the practices of slavery in Brazil and the United States can be quite adequately accounted for by the accidents of geography, demography, and economy and the underlying differences in attitudes toward Negroes rather than by differences in the laws and practices of church and state regarding slavery. In short, the differ-

ences were a result of historical circumstances in the New World, not
of inherited moral intent or law. As a part of the whole complex of
interacting events and circumstances, to be sure, the practices of
slavery certainly played a part. But as a causal factor in the shaping
of race relations slavery was itself a consequence of deeper differences rather than a primary explanation. If we seek the basic origins
of the diverging racial patterns of Brazil and the United States,
clearly we must look behind the practices of slavery. . . .

Thomas E. Skidmore

TOWARD A COMPARATIVE ANALYSIS OF RACE RELATIONS

*Thomas E. Skidmore of the University of Wisconsin examines Brazil's multi-
racial society, what Degler calls the "mulatto escape hatch," and speculates
on why the United States never followed the Brazilian example. He suggests
we must study a complex set of political, socioeconomic, and demographic
circumstances if we hope to know what determines race relations and racial
prejudice.*

Essays in comparative history are risky ventures. Nowhere has this
become more evident than in the literature on slavery. Yet comparisons continue to be made, implicitly if not explicitly. Post-abolition
race relations is an area in which comparisons are equally
tempting—indeed, virtually unavoidable—and equally difficult to
handle. Perhaps by more careful attention to the framework of comparison we can begin to arrive at more testable hypotheses. In this
paper an attempt is made to compare certain features of race relations since abolition in the United States and Brazil. The emphasis
will be on differences. Since more readers are probably more familiar
with the American case, it may be preferable to begin with a brief
description of race relations in Brazil since final abolition in
1888. . . .

Reprinted from Thomas E. Skidmore, "Toward a Comparative Analysis of Race Relations since Abolition in Brazil and the United States," *Journal of Latin American
Studies* 4, No. 1 (1972): 1–28. Reprinted by permission. Footnotes omitted.

In order to understand post-abolition race relations in Brazil one must first note two factors: (1) how abolition came about, and (2) the size of free colored population before abolition.

Unlike the United States, Brazil abolished slavery by gradual steps. The first national law, liberating children born of slave mothers, came in 1871. Another fourteen years passed before the next law (1885) emancipated slaves of sixty years and older. The masters were compensated in both cases. Final and unconditional abolition, with the slaveholders receiving no compensation, came only in 1888.

As the abolitionist campaign continued, the slave population dwindled from a million and a half in 1872 to half a million in 1888. This drop in the number of slaves paralleled an increase in the free colored population which had been growing rapidly in the nineteenth century. Although no reliable census figures were collected before 1872, free coloreds have been estimated to have been 10–15 percent of the total population in the early nineteenth century. By 1872 they comprised 42 percent of the national total and outnumbered the slave population in every region of the country. Sixteen years before final abolition, there were 1.5 million slaves, and almost three times as many free colored. . . .

Final abolition did not, therefore, suddenly transform the context of race relations in Brazil. On the contrary, the half-million slaves who were freed in 1888 entered a complex social structure that included free men of color (of every shade). What was this system? How has it changed since 1888?

First, by the nineteenth century Brazil had a well-developed pattern of racial classification which was pluralistic, or multiracial. Physical characteristics such as skin color, hair texture, and facial characteristics were very important in indicating the racial category into which a person would be placed by those whom he met. The perception of those physical characteristics might vary according to the region, the era, or the observer. Nonetheless, the sum of such characteristics (the 'phenotype') has invariably been of great importance. The apparent wealth or status of the person being observed (indicated by his clothes or his immediate social company) would also influence the observer's reaction, as indicated by the Brazilian adage "money whitens." But these were exceptional cases, most often found among light mulattoes.

The multiracial classificatory system applied by Brazilians has often confused and misled foreign visitors, including professional sociologists and anthropologists. We might begin by explaining what the system has *not* been. Brazil has never, at least since late colonial times, exhibited a rigidly bi-racial system. There has been always a middle category (called mulatto or mestiço) of racial mixtures. The strict observation of color-based endogamy, sanctified by law in the United States, has apparently never existed in Brazil. Brazil has been, instead, a multiracial system, with social classification based, among other factors, on one's perceived physical racial characteristics.

Was family origin completely irrelevant in this system? Professor Marvin Harris, in his polemical essay *Patterns of Race in the Americas*, argues that Brazil escaped the rigid application of the "descent rule," by which ancestry, not physical appearance (unless one "passes" for white), determines racial classification. Seen in comparison with bi-racial societies, this is certainly true. Yet origin could still be thought important in Brazil. We need only remember that upwardly mobile mixed bloods often took great pains to conceal their family origins. Such behavior suggests that a mulatto, whose phenotypical features had given him social access about which he felt insecure, might find this mobility endangered by having his social status redefined through the exposure of his family origin.

The result was a subtle and shifting network of color lines, which created ambiguity and tension for all mixed bloods. Evidence of this tension can be found in the large Brazilian folklore about the "untrustworthy" mulatto. His neuroses have been poetically pictured in Freyre's *The Mansions and the Shanties.* He is the central figure in Brazil's "racial democracy," because he is granted limited entry into the higher social establishment. The limits on his mobility depend upon his exact appearance (the more "Negroid," the less mobile) and the degree of cultural "whiteness" (education, manners, wealth) he has been able to attain. The successful application of this multiracial system has required Brazilians to develop an intense sensitivity to racial categories and the nuances of their application.

This pluralistic scale of social classification rested on racist assumptions. The "Caucasian" was considered to be the natural and inevitable summit of the social pyramid. Brazilians therefore believed that the whiter the better. In the language of H. Hoetink, the white European represented the ideal "somatic norm image." This value system led naturally to the ideology of "whitening," articulated both in elitist writings and popular folklore. The ideology has expressed itself in both individual and collective terms. Individually, Brazilians have deliberately sought sexual partners who are lighter than themselves, hoping by such sexual selection to make their children lighter. Socially, the "whitening" ideology has led Brazilians to promote "eugenic improvement" by such government actions as the promotion of white immigration and the suppression, at intervals, of African cultural survivals. Both individually and collectively, therefore, Brazilians have sought to "bleach" themselves in order to approach the white ideal.

Interestingly enough, the ideology seems to have been successful. . . . There was a rapid increase in the "white" population of Brazil between 1890 and 1950. As defined by the official census, the percentages of whites grew from 44 percent in 1890 to 62 percent in 1950. The concomitant decline in the colored population was sharpest in the mulatto category between 1890 and 1940, falling from 41 percent to 21 percent, although it rose again to 27 percent by 1950.

Admittedly, the census figures must be viewed with caution. The definition of racial categories must have varied according to the historical era when the census was taken, the instructions of the census-taker, and the social attitudes prevailing among census-takers and respondents. There were, for example, evidently sharp discrepancies in the instructions given to census-takers between 1940 and 1950. Furthermore, one must assume that the social definitions of racial phenotypes changed over time. Even allowing for these factors, however, we cannot escape the conclusion that there has been a dramatic whitening of the population in the last hundred years. What could account for this process?

First, there was immigration, which was overwhelmingly white. The three million Europeans who have settled in Brazil since 1890 significantly increased the white racial element. Second, the black population apparently had a low rate of net natural increase. There is empirical evidence to support this in the census figures for the city of São Paulo, where observers by the 1920s were documenting a "negro deficit." This low reproduction rate was due to several factors. The slave imports (ended only in 1850—although a few slaves were landed thereafter) were largely men; and this, as long as it lasted, created a continuing sexual imbalance in the free colored population. The miserable living conditions of most of the colored population must have further depressed the survival rate of their children. This has also been confirmed in the vital statistics for the city of São Paulo.

There is a final explanation for the whitening effect: the way in which miscegenation occurred. If Freyre's portrait is to be believed—and there is much corroboration from other sources—we may assume that white males must have fathered many mixed bloods, thereby increasing the proportion of lighter-skinned offspring in the next generation. The ideal of whitening, as well as the traditionalistic social system, helped to prevent dark-skinned men from being such active progenitors as white men. As least equally important, black women have chosen lighter partners. Thus, the system of sexual exploitation which gave upper-class (and even lower-class) white men sexual license, helped to make the social reality conform increasingly to the ideal of "whitening."

This apparent lightening of the population has reassured Brazilians and reinforced their racial ideology. They concluded that miscegenation had worked to promote their declared goal, thus leading to the popular notion that the white genes were "stronger." Furthermore, during the high period of scientific racism—1880 to 1920—the "whitening" ideology gained scientific legitimacy because Brazilians interpreted the racist doctrines to mean that the "superior" white race would prevail in the process of racial amalgamation.

It should be added that the "whitening" ideology has met occasional resistance from black and mulatto intellectuals. In the 1920s a black nationalist movement emerged, centered primarily in São Paulo. Roger Bastide, the French sociologist who studied this movement, has argued that the black nationalist reaction was provoked by the new limits to occupational mobility of men of color in the competitive urban industrial economy. In any case, the movement was snuffed out by Vargas's dictatorship in 1937, and has never reappeared in significant form, despite the continuing urbanization and industrialization of the center-south region. One must conclude, therefore, that the ideology of "whitening" has remained overwhelmingly predominant since abolition.

Finally, Brazilian race relations must be seen in their total socioeconomic context. First, slavery existed nation-wide. Slaves were originally imported to furnish labor in an agrarian export economy, just as elsewhere in the South Atlantic colonial system. In

Brazil, however, slaves were used everywhere—the sugar plantations of the Northeast, the gold and diamond mines of the Center-West, the cattle ranches of the South, and the coffee plantations of the Center-South. By the nineteenth century slaves worked in virtually every sphere of economic activity in every region of the Empire. . . . Thus slavery had become a national, not a regional institution.

Secondly, Brazil was still a predominantly agrarian economy when abolition came. Its paternalistic system of social relations prevailed even in the urban areas. Thus the system of social stratification gave the landowners (white, and occasionally mulatto) a virtual monopoly of power—economic, social, and political. The lower strata, including poor whites as well as most free coloreds, were well-accustomed to submission and deference. This paternalistic hierarchy, in which social classification correlated highly with color, had developed as an integral part of the slave based colonial economy. But by the time of final abolition it was *not* dependent upon slavery for its continuation. At exactly what point the dependence ceased is a question to be answered by thorough research in Brazilian history. The important point here is that the majority of Brazilian planters, especially those in the prosperous coffee regions, came to understand that abolition need not endanger their economic and social dominance. This analysis proved correct. The newly freed slaves moved into the paternalistic multiracial social structure that had long since taught free men of color the habits of deference in their relationships with employers and social superiors in general. It is within this context, termed "pre-industrial" by Bastide, that race relations have proceeded over most of Brazil in most of the era since abolition. . . .

It is not difficult to describe the main contrasts in Brazilian and American race relations since abolition. It is far less simple to find an explanation for these differences. Rather than claim to have found such an explanation, I shall suggest several key factors that deserve further examination. A brief discussion of these factors may help to stimulate lines of research and analysis that would not come from the study of one society alone. If so, then perhaps in this case comparative history can begin to enjoy the heuristic value for which it is so often praised.

First, a word about the wide range of questions which this paper might attempt to cover. An explanation of the differing race relations might be sought by investigating at least three different areas of pre-abolitionist history: (l) the respective slave systems; (2) the process of abolition in each country; (3) the respective pattern of race relations among freemen during slavery. Finally, one might focus on the contrasting socioeconomic contexts since abolition—were they industrial or agrarian, urban or rural?

This paper cannot possibly explore all these areas, important as they may be. I have therefore chosen to concentrate on certain factors which cut across several of these areas. Some areas, such as a comparison of slave systems, have been recently analyzed in detail. What follows is therefore merely a partial catalog of explanatory factors. They can only be listed and discussed briefly.

1. Demography. The contrast here is striking, both in the slave-to-free ratio and for the "colored"-to-white ratio.

Brazil already had a large number of freemen of color before final abolition. By 1872 there were almost three times as many free as slave among the colored population. . . . The free colored population had apparently grown very rapidly in the nineteenth century. In 1819 the total population of approximately 3.6 million was almost one-third slave. . . . Probably only about 10–15 percent of the total population was free colored. During the intervening half-century the free colored population grew to 42 percent of the total population, while the slaves dwindled to less than 16 percent. Slaves probably outnumbered freemen (white and colored) in Brazil in the seventeenth century, whereas they were never a majority in the United States. Colored outnumbered whites in Brazil until at least the early twentieth century, whereas they never outnumbered whites in the United States. Even regionally in America, there were few states where either slaves outnumbered freemen or colored outnumbered whites, although in certain regions within states they did. These ratios do not in themselves explain anything, but they point to the fact that the whites were in a comfortable majority everywhere in the United States except within certain states of the deep South. Such was hardly the case anywhere in Brazil, until immigration markedly altered the racial balance in several states of the South and Center-South. The rapid growth of the free colored in Brazil has not yet been adequately documented, much less explained, and it offers a challenge to social historians.

What was the effect exerted in Brazil by the large free class of color on the pattern of race relations? For one thing, it created omnipresent models of free colored existence. As a result, by the time of final abolition, Brazil already had decades of experience with millions of free colored; and it had had an even longer tradition stretching into earlier centuries of upward mobility by a small number of free colored. Second, there were established patterns of movement from slavery to freedom. Professor Marvin Harris has offered an ingenious explanation for the Brazilian experience in this area. He argues that there was a long-standing shortage of skilled and semiskilled white labor in colonial Brazil. Out of necessity the European colonizers legitimized the creation of a category of freemen of color who could perform these tasks. His economic explanation contrasts sharply with the cultural and institutional emphases given by such well-known authorities as Professor Frank Tannenbaum and Gilberto Freyre. If Harris's argument is valid for the colonial era, perhaps it also applies to the nineteenth century.

2. Fertility. The rate at which different racial groups replace themselves obviously has great influence on the pattern of race relations. Rapidly increasing groups will be regarded differently from those which appear to be dying out. Fertility ratios were indeed an important factor in the formation of racial ideologies in Brazil and the United States. Yet it is a factor too seldom studied in comparative terms. Admittedly, it is a subject fraught with difficulties because the measurement of racially differential fertility can be easily distorted by untraceable shifts in the racial classification of the offspring. Nevertheless, the apparent findings are so striking as to warrant examination.

We know that the American slave population grew at a relatively rapid rate during the nineteenth century. Census figures showed that it increased at an average rate of about 23 percent each decade between 1830 and 1860. Since the slave trade in the United States had ended in 1808, the increase could only be accounted for by a net natural increase among the existing slave population. In Brazil, however, the trend was exactly the opposite. Although firm statistics are lacking, it appears that the sharp drop in the slave population after the end of the slave trade in 1850 (a few slaves were landed as late as the mid-1850s) was caused both by manumissions and by natural decrease (i.e. excess of deaths over births). Such a phenomenon was apparently common in those slave economies that continued to depend upon the slave trade. Philip Curtin, in his recent study of the

Atlantic Slave Trade, notes that "as a general tendency the higher the proportion of African-born in any slave population, the lower its rate of natural increase—or, as was more often the case, the higher its rate of natural decrease." Thus the large stock of Brazilian slaves began to shrink rapidly when the slave trade ended in 1850.

If Curtin's generalization is correct, how can it be explained? Several answers are possible. First, the morbidity and mortality rates among newly imported slaves were likely to be greater than among native-born slaves because the former had entered a new "disease climate," exposing them to health hazards against which they had no immunities, unlike the native-born slaves. Secondly, the sex ratio among new slave imports was usually highly distorted, frequently including a male ratio of 60–85 percent. Although systematic surveys are yet to be done for Brazil, Professor Stein's analysis of the slave population of Vassouras shows that the ratio of males in the total African-born population remained between 74 percent and 71 percent over the decades from 1830 to 1888. Among the total slave population of Vassouras, however, the male-female ratio dropped from 77 percent in the 1820s to 56 percent in the 1880s. The latter decline reflected the natural tendency of any unbalanced sex ratio to correct itself in the next generation, other facts being equal.

Is it also possible that the risks to slave life were greater in economies such as that of Brazil which continued to depend upon the slave trade, greater than in economies such as that of the United States, whose slave population had already achieved a healthy rate of net natural increase? Could the greater risks have been due to un-controllable factors such as disease, or perhaps because the working and living conditions were harsher? The latter suggestion would, of course, turn the entire Tannenbaum-Elkins interpretation on its head. Might an additional factor be the master's decision on whether to encourage or discourage child-bearing by slave women? It seems apparent that some Southern slaveholders welcomed slave births and even rewarded the mothers. Some regions, such as Virginia and the entire upper South, became slave exporters to the Deep South. Did Brazilian masters calculate that the replacement cost of slaves was low enough to justify their discouraging the bearing of children by slave women? Their calculation would have involved weighiing the probable cost of newly imported slaves against the cost of the lost work time of the mother and the expenses of maintaining the slave child until it was able to work. Here is a promising field for research and comparative analysis. The relative transport costs were, of course, a factor—significantly cheaper to Brazil than to the United States.

Given the above analysis, one would have expected the abnormal factors resulting from the slave trade (distorted sex ratio, high morbidity and mortality) to have disappeared after the end of the trade in 1850. One might expect to find native-born blacks exhibiting a fertility ratio similar to the general population, as occurred in the United States. This did not turn out to be the case in Brazil. Even allowing generously for the inaccuracies inherent in the Brazilian data (such as the classification of mixed-blood children differently from their mother), demographers have concluded that the black population has been reproducing at a slower rate than the mulatto and the white since abolition. Some spot checks suggest that the trend (considering here free blacks, not slaves) can be traced back at least to the early nineteenth century.

This lower fertility rate for blacks has apparently contributed significantly to the "whitening" process whose promotion is the heart of the Brazilian racial ideology. The causes of this low fertility rate remain a matter for conjecture. One of the likeliest hypotheses is the disadvantage in mating encountered by black women.

What have been the trends in fertility ratios in the United States? First, the data have been collected primarily for only two racial categories: white and Negro. We therefore cannot distinguish between black and mulatto, as can be done in Brazil. Given this limitation, it is still worth noting that the Negro birth rate has consistently exceeded the white birth rate according to statistics gathered since 1910.

3. Sectionalism. Slavery became a regional institution in the United States . . . , whereas it was truly national in Brazil. The shift of the economic center of Brazil away from the sugar-producing Northeast of the seventeenth century began with the gold and diamond boom of the Center-South in the eighteenth century, then continued southward with the coffee boom of the nineteenth century. As a result, every major geographical region had a significant percentage of slaves among its total population. In 1819, according to one unofficial estimate, no region had less than 27 percent slave out of its total population. . . . By the time the abolitionist campaign began, the national slave population was concentrated—from the standpoint of absolute numbers—in the three major coffee-growing provinces of São Paulo, Minas Gerais, and Rio de Janeiro. Seen as a percentage of the overall population within each region, however, slaves continued to be distributed throughout the Empire at a remarkably uniform rate. In 1872, when slaves made up 15.2 percent of the national population, no region had less than 7.8 percent of its total population still in slavery, and the highest ratio was only 19.5 percent. . . . Slavery had entrenched itself to a notably similar degree in every region of the country.

Brazil, therefore, never experienced the regional political tensions over slavery comparable to those which led to civil war in the United States. Although several provinces did manage to achieve total abolition four years before the final national law of 1888, race relations did not become the plaything of regional politics. It was not possible for any province to claim that its economic interests or its social structure had been undermined by the imposition of hostile forces from other parts of the country.

4. Role of the free colored before abolition. Herbert Klein has effectively demonstrated the large and important social position occupied by the Brazilian free colored before final abolition. His figures confirm and amplify Marvin Harris's thesis that the free colored had found a secure status long before the end of slavery in Brazil. Harris's analysis stopped in the early nineteenth century, and was based on the national population estimates which are by nature speculative. Klein is able to document more precisely the rapid growth of the free coloreds in the nineteenth century. Thus by 1872, the date of the first national census, but sixteen years before final abolition, freemen counted for 74 percent of the total population of color.

This free colored class had long since succeeded in gaining entry into skilled occupations, and even occasionally prominent positions as artists, politicians, and writers. The essential point to note is that the free coloreds established a considerable degree of occupational mobility—and social mobility—while slavery was still dominant *throughout* the country. These economic and social opportunities enjoyed by free coloreds furnish proof that the multiracial pattern of racial categorization was well established before final abolition. It is hard to conceive how the mobility for free coloreds could have been reduced after abolition, had any legal attempt been made.

In the United States, on the other hand, there had never been a large free colored population, either as a percentage of the total population, or even as a percentage of the overall colored population. In 1860 only 11 percent of the 4,442,000 colored Americans were free. . . . That free colored group, in turn, was only 1.6 percent of the total United States population of slightly more than 31 million. Furthermore, this free colored category, very small in relative numbers, had never established a secure economic position, with the exception of those in a few cities such as Charleston and New Orleans. This virtual absence of the free man of color before abolition made it possible for white Americans to avoid the question of what his social and economic role might be, especially in the North. When it had to be faced, the freeman was subjected to many special regulations, depriving him of full citizenship as well as of economic opportunity. This was generally true even in the North, with the apparent exception of a few states such as Massachusetts. As Leon Litwack and Eugene Berwanger have shown, there was a strong tradition of racist thought, even where there were few or even no Negroes.

When abolition came in the United States, therefore, the suddenly emanicpated slaves had no ready model for the social and economic role of the colored freeman. Since there had been so few before abolition, and since they had not succeeded in establishing an economic "place" for the free coloreds, the ex-slaves stepped into a hostile ethos where economic competition *could* immediately be defined in color terms. Furthermore, abolition came at a time when competition was at a high point in American history. The result, after an interval, was the post-Reconstruction repression of the Negro by the politicians who played on the economic fears of the poor Southern whites. The repressive pattern established was in fact nationwide, although its legal expression was most rigid in the South. The national character of the problem became obvious, however, when the two World Wars shifted the Negro population northward.

What of the political role of the free coloreds? Significantly, they were not considered mobilizable as a *separate* political cadre in Brazil. The very low degree of political participation continued after final abolition in Brazil, unlike in the United States, where white

Southern politicians eagerly sought Negro votes during Reconstruction. The subsequent disfranchisement of the Southern Negro, therefore, had no parallel in Brazil.

These factors are merely suggested as potentially useful in future comparative research. Obviously the essential task for historians will be to decide *how* these factors have fitted together. New data will be needed but it will prove most useful if it is gathered in the light of specific questions.

Slavery and American Society

Stanley M. Elkins

THE DYNAMICS OF UNOPPOSED CAPITALISM *and* SLAVERY IN CAPITALIST AND NONCAPITALIST CULTURES

Though Professor Elkins accepts Tannenbaum's distinction between Anglo- and Latin-American slavery, he sees capitalism as the key to American black chattel slavery. In his opinion capitalist values—the exploitative values of individual profit-seeking—shaped the fundamental character of Southern society. Elkins's analysis implies a general criticism of the impact of American capitalism on social values. He believes that the slave South was more capitalistic than the North, and that plantation slavery was the natural consequence of applying capitalist principles to agricultural production.

THE DYNAMICS OF UNOPPOSED CAPITALISM

Before reviewing in greater detail the legal aspects of this servitude, we should note that the most vital facts about its inception remain quite unaccounted for. The reasons for its delay have been satisfactorily explained—but why did it occur at all? Why should the drive to establish such a status have got under way when it did? What was the force behind it, especially in view of the prior absence of any sort of laws defining slavery? We may on the one hand point out the lack of any legal structure automatically compelling the Negro to become a slave, but it is only fair, on the other, to note that there was equally little in the form of such a structure to prevent him from becoming one. It is not enough to indicate the simple process whereby the interests of white servants and black were systematically driven apart: what was its dynamic? Why should the status of "slave" have been elaborated, in little more than two generations following its initial definition, with such utter logic and completeness to make American slavery unique among all such systems known to civilization?

Was it the "motive of gain"? Yes, but with a difference. The motive of gain, as a psychic "fact," can tell us little about what makes men behave as they do; the medieval peasant himself, with his virtually marketless economy, was hardly free from it. But in the emergent agricultural capitalism of colonial Virginia we may already make out a mode of economic organization which was taking on a purity of form never yet seen, and the difference lay in the fact that here a growing system of large-scale staple production for profit was free to develop in a society where no prior traditional institutions, with competing claims of their own, might interpose at any of a dozen points with sufficient power to retard or modify its progress. What happens when such energy meets no limits?

Here, even in its embryonic stages, it is possible to see the process whereby capitalism would emerge as the principal dynamic force in American society. The New World had been discovered and exploited by a European civilization which had always, in contrast with other world cultures, placed a particularly high premium on personal achievement, and it was to be the special genius of Englishmen, from Elizabeth's time onward, to transform this career concept from its earlier chivalric form into one of economic fulfillment—from "glory" to "success." Virginia was settled during the very key period in which the English middle class forcibly reduced, by revolution, the power of those standing institutions—the church and the crown— which most directly symbolized society's traditional limitations upon personal success and mobility. What the return of the crown betokened in 1660 was not so much "reaction" as the fact that all society had by then somehow made terms with the Puritan Revolution. Virginia had proven a uniquely appropriate theater for the acting-out of this narrower, essentially modern ideal of personal, of *economic,* success. Land in the early days was cheap and plentiful; a ready market for tobacco existed; even the yeoman farmer could rise rapidly if he could make the transition to staple production; and above all there was a quick recognition of accomplishment, by a standard which was not available in England but which was the only one available in Virginia: success in creating a plantation.

The decade of the 1660s inaugurated by the restoration of the Stuart monarchy, marked something of a turning point in the fortunes of the colony not unrelated to the movement there and in Maryland to fix irrevocably upon the Negro a lifetime of slavery. It was during this decade that certain factors bearing upon the colony's economic future were precipitated. One such factor was a serious drop in tobacco prices, brought on not only by overproduction but also by the Navigation Acts of 1660 and 1661, and the market was not to be fully restored for another twenty years. This meant, with rising costs and a disappearing margin of profit, that commerical production on a small-scale basis was placed under serious disabilities. Another factor was the rise in the slave population. Whereas there had been only about 300 in 1650, by 1670 there were, according to Governor Berkeley, 2,000 slaves in a servant population of 8,000. This was already 25 percent of the servants, and the figure was even more significant for the future, since the total white servant population in any given period could never by counted on to exceed their average annual immigration multiplied by five or six (the usual term in years of their indenture), while the increase of slaves over the same period would be cumulative. Such a development would by now be quite enough to stimulate the leaders of the colony— virtually all planters—to clarify in law once and for all the status of lifetime Negro servitude. The formation in 1662 of a Royal Company of Adventurers for the importation of Negroes symbolized the crown's expectation that a labor force of slaves would be the coming thing in the colonies.

It was thus in a period of relatively hard times that it became clear, if the colony of Virginia were to prosper, that capitalism would be the dynamic force in its economic life. "Success" could no longer be visualized as a rise from small beginnings, as it once could, but must now be conceived as a matter of substantial initial investments in land, equipment, and labor, plus the ability to undertake large annual commitments on credit. With the fall in tobacco prices, and with the tiny margin of profit that remained, the yeoman farmer found it difficult enough to eke out a bare living, let alone think of competing with the large planter or of purchasing slaves' or servants' indentures. Success was still possible, but now its terms were clearer, and those who achieved it would be fewer in numbers. The man who managed it would be the man with the large holdings—the man who could command a substantial force of laborers, white or black—who could afford a sizable yearly investment in the handling of his crop: in short, the capitalist planter.

The period beginning in the 1680s and ending about 1710 marked still a new phase. It saw, now under conditions of comparative prosperity, the full emergence of the plantation as the basic unit of capitalist agriculture. By about 1680 the market for Virginia and Maryland tobacco had been restored, though it is important to note that this was accompanied by no great rise in prices. It was rather a matter of having recaptured the European market by flooding it with cheap tobacco and underselling competitors. Returning prosperity, therefore, meant something far more concrete to the man with resources, who could produce tobacco in large enough amounts to make a slim profit-margin worthwhile, than to the one whose productivity was limited by the acreage which he and his family could work. These years also witnessed the initial exploitation of the Carolinas, a process which moved much more directly toward large agricultural units than had been the case in Virginia. The acceleration of this development toward clarifying the terms of commerical production— large plantations and substantial investments—had a direct connection with the widening of the market for slaves during this same period. Hand in hand with large holdings went slaves—an assumption which was now being taken more or less for granted. "A rational man," wrote a South Carolina colonist in 1682, "will certainly inquire, 'when I have Land, what shall I doe with it? What commoditys shall I be able to produce, that will yield me money in other countrys, that I may be inabled to buy Negro-slaves, (without which a planter can never doe any great matter)?' " The point had clearly passed when white servants could realistically, on any long-term appraisal, be considered preferable to Negro slaves. Such appraisals were now being made in terms of capitalized earning power, a concept appropriate to large operations rather than small, to long-term rather than short-term planning.

It was, of course, only the man of means who could afford to think in this way. But then he is the one who most concerns us—the man responsible for Negro slavery. Determined in the sixties and seventies to make money despite hard times and low prices, and willing to undertake the investments which that required, he could now in the eighties reap the fruits of his foresight. His slaves were more valuable than ever—a monument to his patience and planning. What had made them so? For one thing he, unlike the yeoman farmer, had a large establishment for training them and was not pressed by the need, as he would have been with white servants on limited indenture, to exploit their *immediate* labor. The labor was his permanently. And for another thing, the system was by now just old enough to make clear for the first time the full meaning of a second generation of native-born American Negroes. These were the dividends: slaves born to the work and using English as their native tongue. By the 1690s the demand for slaves in the British colonies had become so great, and the Royal African Company so inefficient in supplying them, that in 1698 Parliament revoked the company's monopoly on the African coast and threw open the traffic to independent merchants and traders. The stream of incoming slaves, already of some consequence, now became enormous, and at the same time the annual flow of white servants to Virginia and the Carolinas dropped sharply. By 1710 it had become virtually negligible.

What meaning might all this have had for the legal status of the Negro? The connection was intimate and direct; with the full development of the plantation there was nothing, so far as his interests were concerned, to prevent unmitigated capitalism from becoming unmitigated slavery. The planter was now engaged in capitalistic agriculture with a labor force entirely under his control. The personal relationship between master and slave—in any case less likely to exist on large agricultural units than on smaller ones—now became far less important than the economic necessities which had forced the slave into this "unnatural" organization in the first place. For the plantation to operate efficiently and profitably, and with a force of laborers not all of whom may have been fully broken to plantation discipline, the necessity of training them to work long hours and to give unquestioning obedience to their masters and overseers superseded every other consideration. The master must have absolute power over the slave's body, and the law was developing in such a way as to give it to him at every crucial point. Physical discipline was made virtually unlimited and the slave's chattel status unalterably fixed. It was in such a setting that those rights of personality traditionally regarded between men as private and inherent, quite apart from the matter of lifetime servitude, were left virtually without defense. The integrity of the family was ignored, and slave marriage was deprived of any legal or moral standing. The condition of a bondsman's soul—a matter of much concern to church and civil authority in the Spanish colonies—was here very quickly dropped from consideration. A series of laws enacted between 1667 and 1671 had systematically removed any lingering doubts whether conversion to Christianity should make a difference in status: henceforth it made none. The balance, therefore, involved on the one side the constant pressure of costs, prices, and the problems of management, and on the other the personal interests of the slave. Here, there were no counterweights: those interests were unsupported by any social pressures from the outside; they were cherished by no customary feudal immunities; they were no concern of the government (the king's main interest was in tobacco revenue); they could not be sustained by the church, for the church had little enough power and influence among its own white constituencies, to say nothing of the suspicion its ministers aroused at every proposal to enlarge the church's work among the blacks. The local planter class controlled all those public concerns which most affected the daily life of the colony, and it was thus only in matters of the broadest and most general policy that this planter domination was in any way touched by bureaucratic decisions made in London. The emergent institution of slavery was in effect unchallenged by any other institutions.

The result was that the slave, utterly powerless, would at every critical point see his interests further depressed. At those very points the drive of the law—unembarrassed by the perplexities of competing interests—was to clarify beyond all question, to rationalize, to simplify, and to make more logical and symmetrical the slave's status in society. So little impeded was this pressure to define and clarify that all the major categories in law which bore upon such status were very early established with great thoroughness and completeness. The unthinking aggressions upon the slave's personality which such a situation made possible becomes apparent upon an examination, in greater detail, of these legal categories.

SLAVERY IN CAPITALIST AND NONCAPITALIST CULTURES

The four major legal categories which defined the status of the American slave may be roughly classified as "term of servitude," "marriage and the family," "police and disciplinary powers over the slave" and "property and other civil rights." The first of these, from which somehow all the others flowed, had in effect been established during the latter half of the seventeenth century; a slave was a slave for the duration of his life, and slavery was a status which he transmitted by inheritance to his children and his children's children.

It would be fairest, for several reasons, to view the remaining three categories in terms of the jurisprudence of the nineteenth century. By that time the most savage aspects of slavery from the standpoint of Southern practice (and thus, to a certain extent, of law) had become greatly softened. We may accordingly see it in its most humane light and at the same time note the clarity with which its basic outlines remained fixed and embodied in law, much as they had been laid down before the middle of the eighteenth century.

That most ancient and intimate of institutional arrangements, marriage and the family, had long since been destroyed by the law, and the law never showed any inclination to rehabilitate it. Here was the area in which considerations of humanity might be expected most widely to prevail, and, indeed, there is every reason to suppose that on an informal daily basis they did: the contempt in which respectable society held the slave trader, who separated mother from child and husband from wife, is proverbial in Southern lore. On the face of things, it ought to have been simple enough to translate this strong social sentiment into the appropriate legal enactments, which might systematically have guaranteed the inviolability of the family and the sanctity of the marriage bond, such as governed Christian polity everywhere. Yet the very nature of the plantation economy and the way in which the basic arrangements of Southern life radiated from it, made it inconceivable that the law should tolerate any ambiguity, should the painful clash between humanity and property interest ever occur. Any restrictions on the separate sale of slaves would have been reflected immediately in the market; their price would have dropped considerably. Thus the law could permit no aspect of the slave's conjugal state to have an independent legal existence outside the power of the man who owned him. . . .

It would thus go without saying that the offspring of such "contubernial relationships," as they were called, had next to no guaranties against indiscriminate separation from their parents. Of additional interest is the fact that children derived their condition from that of their mother. This was not unique to American slavery, but it should be noted that especially in a system conceived and evolved exclusively on grounds of property there could be little doubt about how such a question would be resolved. Had status been defined according to the father's condition—as was briefly the case in seventeenth-century Maryland, following the ancient common law—there would instantly have arisen the irksome question of what to do with the numerous mulatto children born every year of white planter-fathers and slave mothers. It would have meant the creation of a free mulatto class, automatically relieving the master of so many slaves on the one hand, while burdening him on the other with that many colored children whom he could not own. Such equivocal relationships were never permitted to vex the law. That "the father of a slave is unknown to our law" was the universal understanding of Southern jurists. It was thus that a father, among slaves, was legally "unknown," a husband without the rights of his bed, the state of marriage defined as "only that concubinage . . . with which alone, perhaps, their condition is compatible," and motherhood clothed in the scant dignity of the breeding function.

Regarding matters of police and discipline, it is hardly necessary to view the typical slave's lot in the nineteenth century as one of stripes and torture. . . . Yet here again what impresses us is not the laxity with which much of the daily discipline was undoubtedly handled, but rather the completeness with which such questions, even extending to life and limb, were in fact under the master's dominion. "On our estates," wrote the Southern publicist J. D. B. DeBow in 1853, "we dispense with the whole machinery of public police and public courts of justice. Thus we try, decide, and execute the sentences in thousands of cases, which in other countries would go into the courts." The law deplored "cruel and unusual punishment." But wherever protection was on the one hand theoretically extended, it was practically canceled on the other by the universal prohibition in Southern law against permitting slaves to testify in court, except against each other, and in any case the courts generally accepted the principle that the line between correction and cruelty was impossible to determine. . . . In general, the court's primary care—not only in the killing of slaves by persons other than the master but also in cases where the slave himself had committed murder and was executed by the state—was for the pecuniary interest of the owner. Numerous enactments provided for compensation in either event. It was precisely this pecuniary interest which was at the very heart of legal logic on all such questions. Just as it was presumed to operate against "cruel and unusual punishment," so it became virtually a *non sequitur* that a man should kill his own slave. The principle had been enuniciated very early: "It cannot be presumed that prepensed malice (which alone makes murder felony) should induce any man to destroy his own estate."

The rights of property, and all other civil and legal "rights," were everywhere denied the slave with a clarity that left no doubt of his utter dependency upon his master. . . . He could neither give nor receive gifts; he could make no will, nor could he, by will, inherit anything. He could not hire himself out or make contracts for any purpose—even including, as we have seen, that of matrimony—and thus neither his word nor his bond had any standing in law. He could buy or sell nothing at all, except as his master's agent, could keep no cattle, horses, hogs, or sheep and, in Mississippi at least, could raise no cotton. Even masters who permitted such transactions, except under express arrangement, were uniformingly liable to fines. It was obvious, then, that the case of a slave who should presume to buy his own freedom—he being unable to possess money—would involve a legal absurdity. "Slaves have no legal rights in things, real or personal; but whatever they may acquire, belongs, in point of law, to their masters."

Such proscriptions were extended not only over all civil rights but even to the civic privileges of education and worship. Every Southern state except Maryland and Kentucky had stringent laws forbidding anyone to teach slaves reading and writing, and in some states the penalties applied to the educating of free Negroes and mulattoes as well. It was thought that "teaching slaves to read and write tends to dissatisfaction in their minds, and to produce insurrection and rebellion"; in North Carolina it was a crime to distribute among them any pamphlet or book, not excluding the Bible. The same apprehensions applied to instruction in religion. Southern society was not disposed to withhold the consolations of divine worship from its slaves, but the conditions would have to be laid down not by the church as an institution, not even by the planters as laity, but by planters simply as masters.

* * *

It is true that among the most attractive features of the plantation legend, dear to every Southerner with a sense of his past, were the paternal affection of the good master for his blacks and the warm sentiments entertained in Southern society at large for the faithful slave. The other side of the coin, then, might appear as something of a paradox: the most implacable race-consciousness yet observed in virtually any society. It was evolved in the Southern mind, one might say, as a simple syllogism, the precision of whose terms paralleled the precision of the system itself. All slaves are black; slaves are degraded and contemptible; therefore all blacks are degraded and contemptible and should be kept in a state of slavery. How had the simple syllogism come into being? That very strength and bulwark of American society, capitalism, unimpeded by prior arrangements and institutions, had stamped the status of slave upon the black with a clarity which elsewhere could never have been so profound, and had further defined the institution of slavery with such nicety that the slave *was,* in fact, degraded. That the black, as a species, was thus contemptible seemed to follow by observation. This assumption took on a life of its own in the attitudes of the people, and the very thought of such a creature existing outside the pale of their so aptly devised system filled the most reasonable of Southerners with fear and loathing. Quite apart from the demands of the system itself, this may account for many of the subsidiary social taboos—the increasing severity of the laws against manumission, the horror of miscegenation, the depressed condition of the free Negro and his peculiar place in Southern society: all signs of how difficult it was to conceive a nonslave colored class. Nothing in their experience had prepared them for it; such a class was unnatural, logically awry, a blemish on the body politic, an anomaly for which there was no intellectual category. . . .

The basic fact was, of course, that the slave himself was property. He and his fellow bondsmen had long since become "chattels personal . . . to all intents, constructions and purposes whatsoever."

In the slave system of the United States—so finely circumscribed and so cleanly self-contained—virtually all avenues of recourse for the slave, all lines of communication to society at large, originated and ended with the master. The system was unique, *sui generis.* The closest parallel to it at that time was to be found in the Latin-

American colonies of Spain and Portugal. But the differences between the two systems are so much more striking than the
similarities that we may with profit use them not as parallels but as
contrasts. In the Spanish and Portuguese colonies, we are immediately impressed by the comparative lack of precision and logic
governing the institution of slavery there; we find an exasperating
dimness of line between the slave and free portions of society, a
multiplicity of points of contact between the two, a confusing pro-
miscuity of color, such as would never have been thinkable in our
own country. But before attempting to establish legal and customary
classifications on the slave's condition in these places, in some manner corresponding to those we used for the United States, something
should be said about the social and institutional setting in which
slavery, in Spain and Portugal themselves, was both viewed and
practiced.

* * *

Of all the national states of Western Europe, Spain, though dynas-
tically united to a substantial degree late in the fifteenth century (and
having even absorbed Portugal in the sixteenth), remained, long into
modern times, much the most "medieval." Its agriculture retained
many of the subsistence features characteristic of manorial economy.
Its social stability was guaranteed by that standing alliance of church
and state upon which every feudal community rested; there, on a
national scale, the Inquisition maintained at extravagant cost the dual
secular-spiritual concept of society so characteristic of the Middle
Ages and so repugnant to every modern idea. Moreover, having to
deal with the Moslems on Spanish soil, the Spaniards had built
crusades and the crusading temperament into their basic experience,
where it actively remained long after the collapse of the other
crusaders' states in Asia Minor. This fact had much to do with the
failure to develop a banking and commercial class comparable to
those existing elsewhere, for the chronic persecutions of the Moors
and Jews deprived the kingdom of its most energetic and experienced businessmen. Banking services tended to be performed in very
large part by foreigners, and Spanish wealth quickly found its way to
places outside the realm. The monarchy's role in all such matters

was conceived in a highly paternal and "illiberal" way, and laissez faire was just as unacceptable in economic life as was free-thinking in religion.

This royal paternalism was especially notable in colonial affairs and shows a striking contrast to the permissive policies which allowed so wide a latitude of local autonomy in the English colonies. The royal houses of Spain and Portugal had been the first in the race for overseas colonies—the crown and grandees having been rather more oriented to "glory" than to "success"—but they in time found themselves outstripped by the English and Dutch and saw the fruits of their glory dribble away to London, Antwerp, and other successful centers of banking. This lack of economic efficiency was not unconnected with the very administrative efficiency that permitted the Spanish crown to maintain such rigid control over its American dependencies. The degree of supervision exercised over colonial life by the Council of the Indies at Madrid does not seem to have been sufficiently appreciated. Add to this the power of the church, and the resulting setting may be seen as one hardly favorable to wide-scale enterprise. Even the establishment of great plantations in Cuba, Santo Domingo, Brazil, and elsewhere in the seventeenth and eighteenth centuries did not mean unmitigated capitalism, as would be the case under the free skies of Virginia, Maryland, and the Carolinas. The great difference lay in the fact that other institutional concerns were present besides those involved with production.

No such dramatic transvaluation of social norms as occurred in seventeenth-century England to accommodate the new standards of the bourgeoisie would ever take place in Spain. And nowhere could the chivalric concept of the *hidalgo*, the man who did no work with his hands and to whom business was contemptible, persist so tenaciously as in Spain and the Spanish colonies. There, on the other hand, the concept of private property, peculiarly appropriate to the demands of an entrepreneurial class, would not develop with nearly the elaborateness that characterized it elsewhere. In at least one area—the master-slave relationship—this fact had very important consequences. For all the cruelty and bigotry of this quasi-medieval society, the balance between property rights and human rights stood in a vastly different ratio—much to the advantage of human rights—from that seen in the American South.

In the colonies of Latin America we are thus able to think of the church, the civil authority, and the property concerns of the planter-adventurer as constituting distinct and not always harmonious interests in society. . . .

The Spaniards and Portuguese had the widespread reputation by the eighteenth century—whatever may have been the reasons—for being among all nations the best masters of slaves. The standards for such a judgment cannot, of course, be made too simple. Were slaves "physically maltreated" in those countries? They could, conceivably, have been treated worse than in our own nineteenth-century South without altering the comparison, for even in cruelty the relationship was between man and man. Was there "race prejudice"? No one could be more arrogantly proud of his racial purity than the Spaniard of Castile, and theoretically there were rigid caste lines, but the finest Creole families, the clergy, the army, the professions, were hopelessly "defiled" by Negro blood; the taboos were that vague in practice. Was there squalor, filth, widespread depression of the masses? Much more so than with us—but there it was the class system and economic "underdevelopment," rather than the color barrier, that made the difference. In these countries the concept of "beyond the pale" applied primarily to beings outside the Christian fold rather than to those beyond the color line.

We are not, then, dealing with a society steeped, like our own, in traditions of political and economic democracy. We are concerned only with a special and peculiar kind of fluidity—that of their slave systems—and in this alone lay a world of difference. It was a fluidity that permitted a transition from slavery to freedom that was smooth, organic, and continuing. Manumitting slaves, carrying as it did such high social approval, was done often, and the spectacle of large numbers of freedmen was familiar to the social scene. Such opportunities as were open to any member of the depressed classes who had talent and diligence were open as well to the ex-slave and his descendants. Thus color itself was no grave disability against taking one's place in free society; indeed, Anglo-Saxon travelers in nineteenth-century Brazil were amazed at the thoroughgoing mixture of races there. "I have passed black ladies in silks and jewelry," wrote Thomas Ewbank in the 1850s, "with male slaves in livery behind them. . . . Several have white husbands. The first doctor of the city is a colored man; so is the President of the Province." Free Negroes had the same rights before the law as whites, and it was possible for the most energetic of their numbers to take immediate part in public and professional life. Among the Negroes and mulattoes of Brazil and the Spanish colonies—aside from the swarming numbers of skilled craftsmen—were soldiers, officers, musicians, poets, priests, and judges. "I am accustomed," said a delegate to the Cortes of Cádiz in 1811, "to seeing many engaged in all manner of careers."

All such rights and opportunities existed *before* the abolition of slavery; and thus we may note it as no paradox that emancipation, when it finally did take place, was brought about in all these Latin-American countries "without violence, without bloodshed, and without civil war."

The above set of contrasts, in addition to what it may tell us about slavery itself, could also be of use for a more general problem, that of the conservative role of institutions in any social structure. The principle has been observed in one setting where two or more powerful interests were present to limit each other; it has been tested negatively in a setting where a single interest was free to develop without such limits. The latter case was productive of consequences which could hardly be called, in the classical sense of the term, "conservative."

Eugene D. Genovese

CAPITALIST AND PSEUDO-CAPITALIST FEATURES OF THE SLAVE ECONOMY and THE ORIGINS OF SLAVERY EXPANSIONISM

Professor Genovese in studying Southern agricultural development concluded that slavery exercised decisive influence over not only the economic life of the region, but over its social ideals as well. It was slavery that made the South a distinct nation-within-a-nation, in conflict with the capitalist mentality of the North and West. This theory, which has the flavor of two

From *The Political Economy of Slavery,* by Eugene Genovese, pp. 19–23, 28–36, 243–51, 256–70. Copyright © 1961, 1963, 1965 by Eugene Genovese. Reprinted by permission of Pantheon Books, a Division of Random House, Inc.

civilizations locked in combat, was originally presented to counter the revisionist view that slavery was essentially plantation capitalism.

CAPITALIST AND PSEUDO-CAPITALIST FEATURES OF THE SLAVE ECONOMY

The slave economy developed within, and was in a sense exploited by, the capitalist world market; consequently, slavery developed many ostensibly capitalist features, such as banking, commerce, and credit. These played a fundamentally different role in the South than in the North. . . .

We need to analyze a few of the more important capitalist and pseudo-capitalist features of Southern slavery and especially to review the barriers to industrialization in order to appreciate the peculiar qualities of this remarkable and anachronistic society.[1]

The defenders of the "planter-capitalism" thesis have noted the extensive commercial links between the plantation and the world market and the modest commercial bourgeoisie in the South and have concluded that there is no reason to predicate an antagonism between cotton producers and cotton merchants. However valid as a reply to the naive arguments of the proponents of the agrarianism versus-industrialism thesis, this criticism has unjustifiably been twisted to suggest that the presence of commercial activity proves the predominance of capitalism in the South.[2] Many precapitalist economic systems have had well-developed commercial relations, but if every commercial society is to be considered capitalist, the word loses all meaning. In general, commercial classes have supported the existing system of production. . . .

We must concern ourselves primarily with capitalism as a social system, not merely with evidence of typically capitalistic economic practices. In the South extensive and complicated commercial relations with the world market permitted the growth of a small commercial bourgeoisie. The resultant fortunes flowed into slaveholding, which offered prestige and economic and social security in a

---

[1] This colonial dependence on the British and Northern markets did not end when slavery ended. Sharecropping and tenantry produced similar results. Since abolition occurred under Northern guns and under the program of a victorious, predatory outside bourgeoisie, instead of under internal bourgeois auspices, the colonial bondage of the economy was preserved, but the South's political independence was lost.

[2] Govan, *JSH,* XXI (Nov. 1955), 448.

planter-dominated society. Independent merchants found their businesses dependent on the patronage of the slaveholders. The merchants either became planters themselves or assumed a servile attitude toward the planters. The commercial bourgeoisie, such as it was, remained tied to the slaveholding interest, had little desire or opportunity to invest capital in industrial expansion, and adopted the prevailing aristocratic attitudes.

The Southern industrialists were in an analogous position, although one that was potentially subversive of the political power and ideological unity of the planters. The preponderance of planters and slaves on the countryside retarded the home market. The Southern yeomanry, unlike the Western, lacked the purchasing power to sustain rapid industrial development.[3] The planters spent much of their money abroad for luxuries. The plantation market consisted primarily of the demand for cheap slave clothing and cheap agricultural implements for use or misuse by the slaves. Southern industrialism needed a sweeping agrarian revolution to provide it with cheap labor and a substantial rural market, but the Southern industrialists depended on the existing, limited, plantation market. . . .

If for a moment we accept the designation of the planters as capitalists and the slave system as a form of capitalism, we are then confronted by a capitalist society that impeded the development of every normal feature of capitalism. The planters were not mere capitalists; they were precapitalist, quasi-aristocratic landowners who had to adjust their economy and ways of thinking to a capitalist world market. Their society, in its spirit and fundamental direction, represented the antithesis of capitalism, however many compromises it had to make. The fact of slave ownership is central to our problem. This seemingly formal question of whether the owners of the means of production command labor or purchase the labor power of free workers contains in itself the content of Southern life. The essential features of Southern particularity, as well as of Southern backwardness, can be traced to the relationship of master to slave. . . .

The banking system of the South serves as an excellent illustration of an ostensibly capitalist institution that worked to augment the

---

[3] An attempt was made by Frank L. Owsley and his students to prove that the Southern yeomanry was strong and prosperous. For a summary treatment see *Plain Folk of the Old South* (Baton Rouge, La., 1949). This view was convincingly refuted by Fabian Linden, "Economic Democracy in the Slave South: An Appraisal of Some Recent Views," *JNH*, XXXI (April 1946), 140–89.

power of the planters and retard the development of the bourgeoisie. Southern banks functioned much as did those which the British introduced into Latin America, India, and Egypt during the nineteenth century. Although the British banks fostered dependence on British capital, they did not directly and willingly generate internal capitalist development. They were not sources of industrial capital but "large-scale clearing houses of mercantile finance vying in their interest charges with the local usurers."[4]

The slave states paid considerable attention to the development of a conservative, stable banking system, which could guarantee the movement of staple crops and the extension of credit to the planters. Southern banks were primarily designed to lend the planters money for outlays that were economically feasible and socially acceptable in a slave society: the movement of crops, the purchase of land and slaves, and little else.

Whenever Southerners pursued easy-credit policies, the damage done outweighed the advantages of increased production. This imbalance probably did not occur in the West, for easy credit made possible agricultural and industrial expansion of a diverse nature and, despite acute crises, established a firm basis for long-range prosperity. Easy credit in the South led to expansion of cotton production with concomitant over-production and low prices; simultaneously, it increased the price of slaves.

Planters wanted their banks only to facilitate cotton shipments and maintain sound money. They purchased large quantities of foodstuffs from the West and, since they shipped little in return, had to pay in bank notes. For five years following the bank failures of 1837 the bank notes of New Orleans moved at a discount of from 10 to 25 percent. This disaster could not be allowed to recur. Sound money and sound banking became the cries of the slaveholders as a class.

Southern banking tied the planters to the banks, but more important, tied the bankers to the plantations. The banks often found it necessary to add prominent planters to their boards of directors and were closely supervised by the planter-dominated state legislatures. In this relationship the bankers could not emerge as a middle-class counterweight to the planters but could merely serve as their auxiliaries.

[4] Paul A. Baran, *The Political Economy of Growth* (New York, 1957), p. 194.

The bankers of the free states also allied themselves closely with the dominant producers, but society and economy took on a bourgeois quality provided by the rising industrialists, the urban middle classes, and the farmers who increasingly depended on urban markets. The expansion of credit, which in the West financed manufacturing, mining, transportation, agricultural diversification, and the numerous branches of a capitalist economy, in the South bolstered the economic position of the planters, inhibited the rise of alternative industries, and guaranteed the extension and consolidation of the plantation system.

The Ideology of the Master Class

The planters commanded Southern politics and set the tone of social life. Theirs was an aristocratic, antibourgeois spirit with values and mores emphasizing family and status, a strong code of honor, and aspirations to luxury, ease, and accomplishment. In the planters' community, paternalism provided the standard of human relationships, and politics and statecraft were the duties and responsibilities of gentlemen. The gentleman lived for politics, not, like the bourgeois politician, off politics.

The planter typically recoiled at the notions that profit should be the goal of life; that the approach to production and exchange should be internally rational and uncomplicated by social values; that thrift and hard work should be the great virtues; and that the test of the wholesomeness of a community should be the vigor with which its citizens expand the economy. The planter was no less acquisitive than the bourgeois, but an acquisitive spirit is compatible with values antithetical to capitalism. The aristocratic spirit of the planters absorbed acquisitiveness and directed it into channels that were socially desirable to a slave society: the accumulation of slaves and land and the achievement of military and political honors. Whereas in the North people followed the lure of business and money for their own sake, in the South specific forms of property carried the badges of honor, prestige, and power. Even the rough parvenu planters of the Southwestern frontier—the "Southern Yankees"—strove to accumulate wealth in the modes acceptable to plantation society. Only in their crudeness and naked avarice did they differ from the Virginia gentlemen. They were a generation removed from the refinement that follows accumulation.

Slavery established the basis of the planter's position and power. It measured his affluence, marked his status, and supplied leisure for social graces and aristocratic duties. The older bourgeoisie of New England in its own way struck an aristocratic pose, but its wealth was rooted in commercial and industrial enterprises that were being pushed into the background by the newer heavy industries arising in the West, where upstarts took advantage of the more lucrative ventures like the iron industry. In the South few such opportunities were opening. The parvenu differed from the established planter only in being cruder and perhaps sharper in his business dealings. The road to power lay through the plantation. The older aristocracy kept its leadership or made room for men following the same road. An aristocratic stance was no mere compensation for a decline in power; it was the soul and content of a rising power. . . .

The prevailing attitude of the aristocratic South toward itself and its Northern rival was ably summed up by William Henry Holcombe of Natchez: "The Northerner loves to make money, the Southerner to spend it."[5]

At their best, Southern ideals constituted a rejection of the crass, vulgar, inhumane elements of capitalist society. The slaveholders simply could not accept the idea that the cash nexus offered a permissible basis for human relations. Even the vulgar parvenu of the Southwest embraced the plantation myth and refused to make a virtue of necessity by glorifying the competitive side of slavery as civilization's highest achievement. The slaveholders generally, and the planters in particular, did identify their own ideals with the essence of civilization and, given their sense of honor, were prepared to defend them at any cost.

This civilization and its ideals were antinational in a double sense. The plantation offered virtually the only market for the small nonstaple-producing farmers and provided the center of necessary services for the small cotton growers. Thus, the paternalism of the planters toward their slaves was reinforced by the semipaternal relationship between the planters and their neighbors. The planters, in truth, grew into the closest thing to feudal lords imaginable in a nineteenth-century bourgeois republic. The planters' protestations of love for the Union were not so much a desire to use the Union to

[5] Diary dated Aug. 25, 1855, but clearly written later. Ms. in the University of North Carolina.

protect slavery as a strong commitment to localism as the highest form of liberty. They genuinely loved the Union so long as it alone among the great states of the world recognized that localism had a wide variety of rights. The Southerners' source of pride was not the Union, nor the nonexistent Southern nation; it was the plantation, which they raised to a political principle.

The Inner Reality of Slaveholding

The Southern slaveholder had "extraordinary force." In the eyes of an admirer his independence was "not as at the North, the effect of a conflict with the too stern pressure of society, but the legitimate outgrowth of a sturdy love of liberty."[6] This independence, so distinctive in the slaveholders' psychology, divided them politically from agrarian Westerners as well as from urban Easterners. Commonly, both friendly and hostile contemporaries agreed that the Southerner appeared rash, unstable, often irrational, and that he turned away from bourgeois habits toward an aristocratic pose. . . .

The slaveholder, as distinct from the farmer, had a private source of character-making and mythmaking—his slave. Most obviously, he had the habit of command, but there was more than despotic authority in this master-slave relationship. The slave stood interposed between his master and the object his master desired (that which was produced); thus, the master related to the object only mediately, through the slave. The slaveholder commanded the products of another's labor, but by the same process was forced into dependence upon this other.[7]

Thoughtful Southerners such as Ruffin, Fitzhugh, and Hammond understood this dependence and saw it as arising from the general relationship of labor to capital, rather than from the specific relationship of master to slave. They did not grasp that the capitalist's dependence upon his laborers remains obscured by the process of exchange in the capitalist market. Although all commodities are products of social relationships and contain human labor, they face each other in the market not as the embodiment of human qualities but as things with a seemingly independent existence. Similarly, the laborer sells his labor-power in the way in which the capitalist sells

---

[6] William M. Sanford (?), *Southern Dial*, I (Nov. 1857), 9.
[7] *Cf.* G. W. F. Hegel, *The Phenomenology of Mind* (2 vols.; London, 1910), I, 183 ff.

his goods—by bringing it to market, where it is subject to the fluctuations of supply and demand. A "commodity fetishism" clouds the social relationship of labor to capital, and the worker and capitalist appear as mere observers of a process over which they have little control.[8] Southerners correctly viewed the relationship as a general one of labor to capital but failed to realize that the capitalist's dependence on his laborers is hidden, whereas that of master on slave is naked. . . .

This simultaneous dependence and independence contributed to that peculiar combination of the admirable and the frightening in the slaveholder's nature: his strength, graciousness, and gentility; his impulsiveness, violence, and unsteadiness. The sense of independence and the habit of command developed his poise, grace, and dignity, but the less obvious sense of dependence on a despised other made him violently intolerant of anyone and anything threatening to expose the full nature of his relationship to his slave. Thus, he had a far deeper conservatism than that usually attributed to agrarians. His independence stood out as his most prized possession, but the instability of its base produced personal rashness and directed that rashness against any alteration in the status quo. Any attempt, no matter how well-meaning, indirect, or harmless, to question the slave system appeared not only as an attack on his material interests but as an attack on his self-esteem at its most vulnerable point. To question either the morality or the practicality of slavery meant to expose the root of the slaveholder's dependence in independence.

The General Crisis
of the Slave South

The South's slave civilization could not forever coexist with an increasingly hostile, powerful, and aggressive Northern capitalism. On the one hand, the special economic conditions arising from the dependence on slave labor bound the South, in a colonial manner, to the world market. The concentration of landholding and slaveholding prevented the rise of a prosperous yeomanry and of urban centers. The inability to build urban centers restricted the market for agricultural produce, weakened the rural producers, and dimmed hopes for agricultural diversification. On the other hand, the same concentration of wealth, the isolated, rural

[8] *Cf* Karl Marx, *Capital* (3 vols.; New York, 1947), I, 41–55.

nature of the plantation system, the special psychology engendered by slave ownership, and the political opportunity presented by the separation from England, converged to give the South considerable political and social independence. This independence was primarily the contribution of the slaveholding class, and especially of the planters. Slavery, while it bound the South economically, granted it the privilege of developing an aristocratic tradition, a disciplined and cohesive ruling class, and a mythology of its own.

Aristocratic tradition and ideology intensified the South's attachment to economic backwardness. Paternalism and the habit of command made the slaveholders tough stock, determined to defend their Southern heritage. The more economically debilitating their way of life, the more they clung to it. It was this side of things—the political hegemony and aristocratic ideology of the ruling class—rather than economic factors that prevented the South from relinquishing slavery voluntarily.

As the free states stepped up their industrialization and as the westward movement assumed its remarkable momentum, the South's economic and political allies in the North were steadily isolated. Years of abolitionist and free-soil agitation bore fruit as the South's opposition to homesteads, tariffs, and internal improvements clashed more and more dangerously with the North's economic needs. To protect their institutions and to try to lessen their economic bondage, the slaveholders slid into violent collision with Northern interests and sentiments. The economic deficiencies of slavery threatened to undermine the planters' wealth and power. Such relief measures as cheap labor and more land for slave states (reopening the slave trade and territorial expansion) conflicted with Northern material needs, aspirations, and morality.[9] The planters faced a steady deterioration of their political and social power. Even if the relative prosperity of the 1850s had continued indefinitely, the slave states would have been at the mercy of the free, which steadily forged ahead in population growth, capital accumulation, and economic development. Any economic slump threatened to bring with it an internal political disaster, for the slaveholders could not rely on their middle and lower classes to remain permanently loyal.[10]

[9] These measures met opposition from powerful sections of the slaveholding class for reasons that cannot be discussed here. The independence of the South would only have brought the latent intraclass antagonisms to the surface.

[10] The loyalty of these classes was real but unstable. For our present purposes let us

When we understand that the slave South developed neither a strange form of capitalism nor an undefinable agrarianism but a special civilization built on the relationship of master to slave, we expose the root of its conflict with the North. The internal contradictions in the South and the external conflict with the North placed the slaveholders hopelessly on the defensive with little to look forward to except slow strangulation. Their only hope lay in a bold stroke to complete their political independence and to use it to provide an expansionist solution for their economic and social problems. The ideology and psychology of the proud slaveholding class made surrender or resignation to gradual defeat unthinkable, for its fate, in its own eyes at least, was the fate of everything worthwhile in Western civilization.

THE ORIGINS OF SLAVERY EXPANSIONISM

Once upon a time in the happy and innocent days of the nineteenth century, men believed that Negro slavery had raised an expansionist slaveocracy to power in the American South. Today we know better. The revisionists have denied that slavery was expansionist and have virtually driven their opponents from the field. Their arguments, as distinct from their faith in the possibilities of resolving antagonisms peacefully rest on two formidable essays. In 1926, Avery O. Craven published his *Soil Exhaustion as a Factor in the Agricultural History of Maryland and Virginia,* which sought to prove that the slave economy could reform itself, and three years later Charles William Ramsdell published his famous article on "The Natural Limits of Slavery Expansion,"[1] which constituted a frontal attack on the "irrepressible conflict" school.

I propose to restate the traditional view, but in such a way as to avoid the simplistic and mechanistic notions of Cairnes and his followers and to account for the data that has emerged from the conscientious and often splendid researches of the revisionist historians. Specifically, I propose to show that economics, politics, social life,

merely note that Lincoln's election and federal patronage would, if Southern fears were justified, have led to the formation of an antiplanter party in the South.
[1] *AHR,* XVI (Sept. 1929), 151–71.

ideology, and psychology converged to thrust the system outward and that beneath each factor lay the exigencies of the slaveholding class. Each dictated expansion if the men who made up the ruling class of the South were to continue to rule.

Roots and Taproot

Antebellum Southern economic history reinforces rather than over-turns the nineteenth-century notion of an expansionist slaveocracy. That notion undoubtedly suffered from grave defects and considera-ble crudeness, for it insisted on the lack of versatility of slave labor and the steady deterioration of the soil without appreciating the partially effective attempts to reform the slave economy. Yet the revisionist work of the Craven school, which has contributed so much toward an understanding of the economic complexities, has not added up to a successful refutation.

We may recapitulate briefly the main points of the preceding studies, which lead to the economic root of slavery expansionism. At the beginning we encounter the low productivity of slave labor, de-fined not according to some absolute or purely economic standard, but according to the political exigencies of the slaveholders. The slaves worked well enough in the cotton and sugar fields, when organized in gangs, but the old criticism of labor given grudgingly retains its force.

Slave labor lacked that degree and kind of versatility which would have permitted general agricultural diversification. Slaves could and did work in a variety of pursuits, including industrial, but under circumstances not easily created within the economy as a whole. Division of labor on the plantations and in society proceeded slowly and under great handicaps. The level of technology, especially on the plantations, was kept low by the quality and size of the labor force. Mules and oxen, for example, replaced faster horses principally be-cause they could more easily withstand rough and perhaps vengeful handling. Negro laborers had been disciplined to sustained agricul-tural labor before being brought to the Americas. Their low produc-tivity arose from the human and technological conditions under which they worked, and these arose from the slave system.

An analysis of Southern livestock and the attempts to improve it reveals the complex and debilitating interrelationships within the slave economy. The South had more than enough animals to feed its population but had to import meat. A shortage of liquid capital made acquisition of better breeds difficult, and the poor treatment of the animals by the slaves made maintenance of any reasonable standards close to impossible. As a further complication, the lack of urban markets inhibited attention to livestock by depriving planters of outlets for potential surpluses. The South boasted an enormous number of animals but suffered from their wretched quality.

Slavery provided a sufficient although not a necessary cause of soil exhaustion. It dictated one-crop production beyond the limits of commercial advantage and in opposition to the political safety of the slaveholders. Planters could not easily rotate crops under the existing credit structure, with a difficult labor force, and without those markets which could only accompany industrial and urban advance. The sheer size of the plantations discouraged fertilization. Barnyard manure was scarce, commercial fertilizers too expensive, and the care necessary for advantageous application unavailable. The shortage of good implements complicated the operation, for manures are easily wasted when not applied properly.

Craven insists that the existence of a moving frontier, north and south, brought about the same result, but as we have seen, the special force of slavery cannot so easily be brushed aside. The North confronted the devastating effects of soil exhaustion and built a diversified economy in the older areas as the frontier pushed westward. The South, faced with the debilitating effects of slavery long after the frontier had passed, had to struggle against hopeless odds.

These direct effects of slavery received enormous reinforcement from such indirect effects as the shortage of capital and entrepreneurship and the weakness of the market. Capital investments in slaves and a notable tendency toward aristocratic consumption had their economic advantages but inhibited the rise of new industries. The Southern market consisted primarily of the plantations and could not support more than a limited industrial advance. The restricted purchasing power of the rural whites, of the urban lower classes, and indirectly of the slaves hemmed in Southern manufacturers and put them at a severe competitive disadvantage relative to Northerners, who had had a head start and who had much wider markets in the free states to sustain production on an increasing scale. The barriers to industrialization also blocked urbanization and thereby undermined the market for foodstuffs. . . .

The South made one form of agricultural adjustment while slavery remained. The great agricultural revival in the Upper South overcame the most serious effects of slavery by reducing the size of slaveholdings, converting surplus slaves into cash, and investing the funds in the supervision, fertilization, and reconversion of smaller estates. This process threatened the economic and ideological solidity of the slaveholders' regime and had other drawbacks, but most important, it broke on an imminent contradiction. The sale of surplus slaves depended on markets farther south, which necessarily depended on virgin lands on which to apply the old, wasteful methods of farming. Reform in one region implied exhaustive agriculture in another. Thus, the process of agricultural reform had narrow limits in a closed slave system and had to be reversed when it pressed against them. No solution emerged from within the system, but one beckoned from without. The steady acquisition of new land could alone guarantee the maintenance of that interregional slave trade which held the system together. . . .

The economic process propelling the slave South along expansionist paths had its political and social parallels, the most obvious being the need to reestablish parity in the Senate or at least to guarantee enough voting strength in Washington to protect Southern interests. In an immediate political sense the demand for more slave-state Congressmen was among the important roots of expansionism, but in a deeper sense it was merely a symptom of something more fundamental. Had the South not had a distinct social system to preserve and a distinct and powerful ruling class at its helm, a decline of its political and economic power would have caused no greater alarm than it did in New England.

A second political root was the need to protect slavery where it was profitable by establishing buffer areas where it might not be. Just as the British had to spend money to secure ascendancy in Tibet so that they could make money in India, the South had to establish political control over areas with dubious potentialities as slave states in order to protect existing slave states. The success of the Texas cause removed the fear of Mexican tampering with slaves in Louisiana, much as annexation removed potential British-inspired tampering. "Texas must be a slave country," wrote Stephen F. Austin to his sister. "The interest of Louisiana requires that it should be; a population of fanatical abolitionists in Texas would have a very pernicious and dangerous influence on the overgrown population of the state."[2] . . .

The warning of the Louisville *Daily Courier* in 1860 that Kentucky could afford to remain in the Union but that the Lower South could not touched the central issue. Suppose, it asked, Kentucky sold its slaves south. "And then what? Antislavery will not be content to rest. . . . The war will be transferred to the Cotton States."[3]

The need to push forward in order to ward off concentrations of hostile power arose from the anachronistic nature of the slave regime. By 1850, if not much earlier, world opinion could no longer tolerate chattel slavery, and British opposition in particular was both formidable and implacable. The transformation of the Caribbean into a slaveholders' lake and an alliance or understanding with Brazil held out the only hope of preventing a dangerous and tightening containment.

Slaveholders also sought additional territory to reduce the danger of internal convulsion. Lieutenant Matthew F. Maury, who helped bring about the American exploration of the Amazon Valley in the 1850s, discussed the eventual absorption of much of Latin America by the United States:

> *I cannot be blind to what I see going on here. It is becoming a matter of faith—I use a strong word—yes a matter of faith among leading Southern men, that the time is coming, nay that it is rapidly approaching when in order to prevent this war of the races and all its horrors, they will in self-defense be compelled to conquer parts of Mexico and Central America, and make slave territory of that—and that is now free.[4]*

Representative Thomas L. Clingman of North Carolina told the House that Northerners were "too intelligent to believe that humanity, either to the slave or the master, requires that they should be pent up within a territory which after a time will be insufficient for their subsistence, and where they must perish from want, or from collision that would occur between the races."[5] Southerners always kept the West Indian experience in front of them when they discussed the racial proportions of the population.

[2] Quoted in Herbert Aptheker, *American Negro Slave Revolts* (New York, 1963), pp. 32–33.
[3] Dec. 20, 1860 in Dwight L. Dumond (ed.), *Southern Editorials on Secession* (New York, 1931), p. 360.
[4] Quoted in Aptheker, *Slave Revolts,* p. 34.
[5] Clingman, *Speeches,* p. 239.

Probably, steady infusions of new land were also needed to placate the nonslaveholders, but we know little about slaveholder-nonslaveholder relationships as yet and little can be said with certainty.

The psychological dimension of slavery expansionism has been the subject of various essays and has, for example, emerged from interpretations of Southern frustration and resultant aggression. We need not pursue esoteric lines of inquiry, especially with formulas so broad as to be able to encompass almost every society in any age, to appreciate that a psychological dimension did exist. As Southerners came to regard slavery as a positive good and as they came to value the civilization it made possible as the world's finest, they could hardly accept limits on its expansion. To agree to containment meant to agree that slavery constituted an evil, however necessary for the benefit of the savage Africans. That sense of mission so characteristic of the United States as a whole had its Southern manifestation in the mission of slavery. If slavery was making possible the finest society the world had ever known, the objections to its expansion were intolerable. The free-soil argument struck at the foundations of the slaveholder's pride and belief in himself.

*   *   *

When the more intelligent and informed Southerners demanded the West for slavery they often, perhaps most often, spoke of minerals, not cotton or even hemp. Slavery, from ancient times to modern, had proved itself splendidly adaptable to mining. Mining constituted one of the more important industries of the Negroes of preconquest Africa, and slave labor had a long history there. . . .

Closer in time and place to the South, Brazil afforded an impressive example of the successful use of slave labor in mining. In the middle of the eighteenth century diamond mining supplemented gold mining in Minas Gerais and accounted for a massive transfer of masters and slaves from the northeastern sugar region.[6] Southern leaders knew a good deal about this experience. "The mines of Brazil," reported *De Bow's Review* in 1848, "are most prolific of iron,

[6] João Pandía Calógeras, *A History of Brazil* (tr. Percy Alvin Martin; Chapel Hill, N.C., 1939), pp. 40–41; C. R. Boxer, *The Golden Age of Brazil, 1695–1750* (Berkeley, Cal., 1962) devotes a chapter and additional space to a splendid discussion.

gold, and diamonds. . . . The operation is performed by negroes . . . 30,000 negroes have been so employed."[7] The eastern slave states had had experience with gold mining, and although the results were mixed, the potentialities of slave labor had been demonstrated.[8] Planters in the Southwestern states expressed interest in gold mines in Arkansas and hopefully looked farther west.[9] "If mines of such temporary value should, as they may, be found in the territories, and slaves could be excluded from these," wrote A. F. Hopkins of Mobile in 1860, "it would present a case of monstrous injustice."[10]

During the Congressional debates of 1850, Representative Jacob Thompson of Mississippi, later to become Secretary of the Interior under Buchanan, expressed great concern over the fate of the public domain of California if she were to be hastily admitted to the Union and expressed special concern over the fate of the gold mines.[11] Ten years later, after a decade of similar warnings, pleas, hopes, and threats, S. D. Moore of Alabama wrote that the South was "excluded from California, not pretendedly even by 'isothermal lines,' or want of employment for slave labor, for in regard to climate and mining purposes the country was admirably adapted to the institution of African slavery."[12] Had it not been for the antislavery agitation, Representative Clingman told the House in 1850, Southerners would have used slaves in the mines of California and transformed it into a slave state.[13] Albert Gallatin Brown, one of the most fiery and belligerent of the proslavery extremists, wrote his constituents that slave labor was admirably suited to mining and that California could and should be made into a slave state.[14] Even as a free state California demonstrated the usefulness of slave labor. In 1852 the state legislature passed a mischievous fugitive slave law that could be and was interpreted to allow slaveholders to bring slaves into the state to work in the mines and then send them home.[15]

---

[7] "The South American States," *DBR*, VI (July 1848), 14.
[8] Cf. Fletcher M. Green's articles on gold mining in Georgia, North Carolina, and Virginia: *GHQ*, XIX (June 1935), 93–111 and (Sept. 1935), 210–28; *NCHR*, XIV (Jan. 1937), 1–19 and (Oct. 1937), 357–66. Significantly, the Southeastern developments were discussed in relation to California. See *DBR*, XVIII (Feb. 1855), 241–50.
[9] See, e.g., Francis Terry Leak Diary, July 7, 1855.
[10] *DBR*, XXVIII (March 1860), 281.
[11] *Congressional Globe*, XIX, Part 2, 31st Congress, 1st Session, HR, Sept. 7, 1850.
[12] "The Irrepressible Conflict and the Impending Crisis," *DBR*, XXVIII (May 1860), 535.
[13] Clingman, *Speeches*, p. 239 (Jan. 22, 1850).
[14] *Speeches, Messages, and Other Writings* (ed. M. W. Cluskey; Philadelphia, 1859), p. 181.
[15] Delilah L. Beasley, "Slavery in California," *JNH*, III (Jan. 1918), 40–41.

Similarly, a Texan wrote in 1852 that a Mississippi and Pacific railroad would secure the New Mexico territory for the South by opening the mining districts to slave labor.[16] During the War for Southern Independence, Jefferson Davis received a communication from his Southwestern field commander that a successful drive to California would add "the most valuable agriculture and grazing lands, and the richest mineral region in the world."[17]

Southerners had long cast eyes toward Mexico and looked forward to additional annexations. "I want Cuba," roared Albert Gallatin Brown. "I want Tamaulipas, Potosí, and one or two other Mexican states; and I want them all for the same reason—for the planting or spreading of slavery."[18] Throughout the 1850s, *De Bow's Review* printed articles about Mexico and particularly about Mexican mines.

It is one thing to note that Southerners sought to expand slavery into Mexico's mining districts or that they lamented the political barriers to the expansion of slavery into New Mexico's; it is another for us to conclude that their hopes and desires were more than wishful thinking. Allan Nevins has presented a formidable case to suggest that slavery had little room even in the mining districts of the Southwest and Mexico. He shows that even in the Gadsden Purchase the economic exigencies of mining brought about the quick suppression of the enterprising individual by the corporation. Western mining, as well as transportation, lumbering, and some forms of agriculture, required much capital and became fields for big business. High labor costs led to a rising demand for labor-saving machinery, but Nevins does not consider that this very condition might, under certain circumstances, have spurred the introduction of slave labor.[19] He writes:

> For three salient facts stood out in any survey of the Far West. First, this land of plain and peak was natural soil for a free-spirited and highly competitive society, demanding of every resident skill and intelligence. It was, therefore, even in that Gadsden Purchase country which had been bought at the behest of the slave states, a country naturally inhospitable to slavery. Second, when so much energy was steadily flowing into western expansion, and such wide outlets for more effort existed there, it was

[16] "Public Lands of Texas," *DBR*, XIII (July 1852), 54.
[17] Quoted in W. H. Watford, "Confederate Western Ambitions," *SHQ*, XLIV (Oct. 1940), 168.
[18] Brown, *Speeches, Messages*, p. 595; speech at Hazlehurst, Miss., Sept. 11, 1858.
[19] *The Emergence of Lincoln* (2 vols.; New York, 1950), I, 330–31.

> *impossible to think of the country turning to Caribbean areas for a heavy thrust southward. Its main forces moved naturally toward the sunset, where rich opportunities were hardly yet sampled. The cotton kingdom, which realized that the West gave little scope for its peculiar culture, might plan grandiose Latin American adventures; but it would get little support from other regions. And in the third place, conditions in the West demanded capital and organization on a broad scale; if it was a land for individualists, it was even more a land for corporate enterprise—a land for the businessman. Those who pondered these three facts could see that they held an ominous meaning for the South. The nearer Northwest had already done much to upset the old sectional balance, and the Far West, as it filled up, would do still more.*[20]

On economic grounds Nevins's analysis has much to offer, but his remarks on the competitive struggle in the Southwest and on the inability of Southerners to get national support for Caribbean adventures do not prove nearly so much as he thinks. At most, they suggest that the North was strong enough to block slavery expansionism into the Southwest and frustrate Southern ambitions, elsewhere. If so, the case for secession, from the proslavery viewpoint, was unanswerable.

Nevins's remarks illustrate the wisdom of other Southern arguments—that the South had to secure new land politically, not by economic advance, and that the South had to have guarantees of positive federal protection for slavery in the territories.[21] The *Charleston Mercury*, climaxing a decade of Southern complaints, insisted in 1860 that slavery would have triumphed in California's gold mining areas if Southerners had had assurances of protection for their property. . . .

The Southern demand for federal guarantees made sense, but even that did not go far enough. Ultimately, the South needed not equal protection for slave property but complete political control. If a given territory could be organized by a proslavery party, then slaveholders would feel free to migrate. Time would be needed to allow the slave population to catch up; meanwhile, free-soil farmers had to be kept out in favor of men who looked forward to becoming slaveholders. Under such circumstances the territory's population might grow very slowly, and the exploitation of its resources might

---

[20] Ibid., I, 342.
[21] I find it strange that Nevins attacks this late antebellum demand as an abstraction; his own evidence indicates that it was of central importance to the slavery cause.

lag far behind that of the free territories. Nothing essential would be lost to the South by underdevelopment; the South as a whole was underdeveloped. In short, the question of political power necessarily had priority over the strictly economic questions. . . .

For the moment let us consider Kansas as solely and inevitably a wheat state. Large slave plantations have not proved well-adapted to wheat growing, but small plantations were doing well in the Virginia tidewater. In open competition with Northwestern farmers the slaveholders probably would have been hurt badly. They knew as much. When, for example, Percy Roberts of Mississippi maintained that Negro slavery could thrive in the Northwest grain belt, he simultaneously maintained that the African slave trade would have to be reopened to drive down the cost of labor and put the slaveholders in a favorable competitive position.[22] Historians like Nevins and Paul W. Gates have expressed confidence that slavery could not have triumphed in Kansas even if it had been allowed a foothold. They may be right, but only if one assumes that the South remained in the Union. Slavery expansionism required fastening proslavery regimes in such territories, but ultimately it required secession to protect the gains. Had Kansas joined a Southern Confederacy as a slave state, its wheat-growing slaveholders could have secured the same internal advantages as the sugar planters of Louisiana, and Union wheat could effectively have been placed at a competitive disadvantage in the Southern market.

Ramsdell's dismissal of Southern interest in Cuba and Central America, however necessary for his argument, does not bear examination. Southern sugar planters, who might have been expected to fear the glutting of the sugar market should Cuba enter the Union, spoke out for annexation. They seem to have been convinced that suspension of the African slave trade to Cuba would raise the cost of production there to American levels and that they would be able to buy Cuban slaves cheaply.[23] Besides, as Basil Rauch points out, Louisiana sugar planters were moving to Cuba during the 1850s and looking forward to extending their fortunes.[24] . . .

---

[22] "African Slavery Adapted to the North and Northwest," *DBR*, XXV (Oct. 1858), 379–85.
[23] J. S. Thrasher, "Cuba and the United States," *DBR*, XVII (July 1854), 43–49.
[24] *American Interest in Cuba, 1848–1855* (New York, 1948), p. 200; James Stirling, *Letters from the Slave States* (London, 1857), pp. 127 ff; John S. C. Abbott, *South and North; or Impressions Received during a Trip to Cuba* (New York, 1860), pp. 52, 53.

Opposition to territorial expansion by many Southerners has led some historians to deny the existence of an "aggressive slaveocracy" or to assert, with Ramsdell, that Southerners were too individualistic to be mobilized for such political adventures, which were often contrary to their private interests. No conspiracy theory is required. That there were many Southern leaders who sensed the need for more territory and fought for it is indisputable. That individual Southerners were not always willing to move when the interests of their class and system required them to merely indicates one of the ways in which slavery expansionism proved a contradictory process. Southerners opposed expansion for a variety of reasons, but mostly because they feared more free states. Expansion southward had the great advantage of not being cotton expansion, and the economic argument against it was weak. On the other hand, many feared that the annexation of Cuba would provide an excuse for the annexation of Canada or that the annexation of Mexico would repeat the experience of California. This opposition should be understood essentially as a preference for delaying expansion until secession had been effected, although there were, of course, many who opposed both.[25]

The Anguish of Contradiction

If the slave South had to expand to survive, it paradoxically could not do so when given the opportunity. Unsettled political conditions prevented the immigration of slave property, much as the threat of nationalization or of a left-wing or nationalist coup prevents the flow of American capital to some underdeveloped countries to which it is invited.

"Where," asks Allan Nevins when discussing Kansas, "were proslavery settlers to come from? Arkansas, Texas, and New Mexico were all calling for slaveholding immigrants, and the two first were more attractive to Southerners than Kansas."[26] Slave property necessarily moved cautiously and slowly. So long as it had to move at the pace set by Northern farmers, it would be defeated. The mere fact of competition discouraged the movement of slaveholders, and if they

---

Texans, too, wanted Cuba. See Earl W. Fornell, "Agitation in Texas for Reopening the Slave Trade," *SHQ*, LX (Oct. 1956), 245–59.
[25] *SQR*, XXI (Jan. 1852), 3; see the arguments advanced by William Walker for avoiding an attempt to link Nicaragua with the Union, *The War in Nicaragua*, Chap. VIII.
[26] *Ordeal of the Union*, II, 304.

were willing to move, they could not hope to carry enough whites to win.

An area could be safely absorbed by the slave regime only by preventing Northern free-soilers from entering. Danhof has demonstrated that farm making was an expensive business.[27] Northern farmers had a hard time; Southern farmers, without slaves or minimal savings, found it much harder. Traditionally, the more energetic nonslaveholders moved into new land first and cleared it; the planters followed much later.[28] If those early settlers had to secure the territory against free-soilism before the planters and slaveholders moved in, the struggle could not ordinarily be won. Many Southern nonslaveholders could be and were converted to the antislavery banner once they found themselves away from the power and influence of the slaveholders. . . . Their allegiance to the system rested ultimately on the ability of the slaveholders to retain political power and social and ideological leadership and to prevent these men of the lower classes from seeing an alternative way of life. Yet, by 1860 even Missouri had become a battleground because of its special geographic position and Northern and foreign immigration. Kansas could never be secured for slavery unless the slaveholders had political control and the migrating Southern farmers were isolated from corrupting influences. . . . Only if a territory shut out free-soil immigration, quickly established the political hegemony of the slaveholders, and prepared for a much slower development than Northerners might give it, could it be secured for slavery. These conditions negated slavery expansionism, but only so long as the South remained in the Union.

Invitation to a (Self-Inflicted) Beheading

The South had to expand, and its leaders knew it. "There is not a slaveholder in this House or out of it," Judge Warner of Georgia declared in the House of Representatives in 1856, "but who knows

[27] Clarence H. Danhof, "Farm-making Costs and the 'Safety Valve,'" *JPE*, XLIX (June 1941), 317–59. Cf. Nevins, *Emergence of Lincoln*, I, 159, on Kansas in the 1850s. Thomas Le Duc has argued that many farmers could and did squat in squalor while slowly building a farm: "Public Policy, Private Investment and Land Use in American Agriculture, 1825–1875," *Agr. Hist.*, XXXVII (Jan. 1963), 3–9. Even with this qualification, capital and resources were a big factor, and the competitive advantage of Northern farmers over Southern is beyond doubt. Only when circumstances permitted the massive movement of planters and slaves could the result be different.
[28] Yarbrough, *Economic Aspects of Slavery*, p. 104.

perfectly well that whenever slavery is confined within certain specified limits, its future existence is doomed."[29] The Republican party,
said an editorial in *The Plantation* in 1860, denies that it wants to war
on slavery, but it admits that it wants to surround it with free states.
To do so would be to crush slavery where it now exists.[30] Percy L.
Rainwater's study of sentiment in Mississippi in the 1850s shows how
firmly convinced slaveholders were that the system had to expand or
die.[31] . . . The extinction of slavery would have broken the power of
the slaveholders in general and the planters in particular. Ideologi-
cally, these men had committed themselves to slaveholding and the
plantation regime as the proper foundations of civilization. Politically,
the preservation of their power depended on the preservation of its
economic base. Economically, the plantation system would have tot-
tered under free labor conditions and would have existed under
some intermediary form like sharecropping only at the expense of
the old ruling class. . . . The slaveholders knew their own power and
could not help being suspicious of sweeping changes in their way of
life, no matter how persuasively advanced. Their slaveholding psychology, habit of command, race pride, rural lordship, aristocratic
pretensions, political domination, and economic strength militated in
defense of the status quo. Under such circumstances an occasional
voice warning that a conversion to tenantry or sharecropping carried
serious dangers to their material interests sufficed to stiffen their
resistance. . . .

Those who, like Max Weber, Ramsdell, even Phillips, and count-
less others, assume that the South could have accepted a peaceful
transition to free labor gravely misjudge the character of its ruling
class. . . .

The slaveholders, not the South, held the power to accede or
resist. To these men slaves were a source of power, pride, and
prestige, a duty and a responsibility, a privilege and a trust; slavery
was the foundation of a special civilization imprinted with their own
character. The defense of slavery, to them, meant the defense of their
honor and dignity, which they saw as the essence of life. They could
never agree to renounce the foundation of their power and moral

[29] Quoted in George M. Weston, *The Progress of Slavery in the United States* (Washington, D.C., 1857), p. 227.
[30] *The Plantation* (March 1860), pp. 1–2.
[31] "Economic Benefits of Secession: Opinions in Mississippi in the 1850s," *JSH,* I (Nov.
1935), 459 and *passim.*

sensibility and to undergo a metamorphosis into a class the nature and values of which were an inversion of their own. Slavery represented the cornerstone of their way of life, and life to them meant an honor and dignity associated with the power of command. When the slaveholders rose in insurrection, they knew what they were about: in the fullest sense, they were fighting for their lives.

Eric Foner
THE REPUBLICANS AND RACE

In this selection from Free Soil, Free Labor, Free Men, *Eric Foner explores the racial attitudes of the Republicans. He finds that the Republicans knew that slavery debased black people and that it menaced Northern free institutions, in particular the right to work. Yet they could not escape their long-held associations of slavery with Americans of African descent. Many Republicans believed that a black person was incapable of competing in a mobile, white society. Professor Foner teaches at the City College of New York.*

On his visit to the United States in the 1830s, Alexis de Tocqueville made his justly famous observation that racial prejudice seemed to be stronger in the North than in the South, and was most intense in the western states which had never known slavery. Several recent historical studies have shown that racial prejudice was all but universal in antebellum northern society. Only five states, all in New England, allowed the black man equal suffrage, and even there he was confined to menial occupations and subjected to constant discrimination. In the West, Negroes were often excluded from the public schools, and four states—Indiana, Illinois, Iowa, and Oregon—even barred them from entering their territory. This pervasive prejudice made the question of the proper place of the black man in American society the most troublesome and perplexing one the Republicans faced before the Civil War. Like the Democrats, Republicans often

From *Free Soil, Free Labor, Free Men: The Ideology of the Republican Party before the Civil War*, by Eric Foner, pp. 261–67, 295–300. Copyright © 1970 by Eric Foner. Reprinted by permission of Oxford University Press, Inc. Footnotes omitted.

made use of electoral appeals which smacked of racism, and some historians have interpreted this as proof that there existed no fundamental differences between the two parties' racial attitudes. Yet the Republicans did develop a policy which recognized the essential humanity of the Negro, and demanded protection for certain basic rights which the Democrats denied him. Although deeply flawed by an acceptance of many racial stereotypes, and limited by the free-labor ideology's assumption that the major responsibility for a person's success or failure rested with himself, not society, the Republican stand on race relations went against the prevailing opinion of the 1850s, and proved a distinct political liability in a racist society.

Nowhere did race present more political difficulties than in the Northwest. Why was this area, which some historians have seen as the very breeding ground of democracy and egalitarian individualism, marked by such intense racial prejudice? Clearly one important reason was the large population of southern origin—men and women who had migrated to escape the influences of slavery, but had brought with them the anti-Negro outlook of slave society. As one Republican of southern background put it, "It is not probable, sir, with the prejudices of my early education, that I would be likely to have too great sympathy for negroes." However, states like Michigan and Wisconsin, whose population came largely from the East, also revealed racial prejudice, although to a lesser degree than Indiana, Illinois, and Ohio. It may be that the greater social mobility of western society helped make fear of the Negro—and therefore prejudice—more severe. In the East, no one questioned that the free black should occupy a subordinate position in society, even where he had substantial legal equality. In the more fluid social structure of the West, however, free Negroes might be able to rise socially and economically. This fear had an especially potent appeal in the lower West, which foresaw an influx of freedmen, ready to challenge the status and prerogatives of white men, should emancipation take place. Where the social order was least stratified—as in the frontier states of Kansas, California, and Oregon—legal discrimination was most severe. Thus, paradoxically, the very social mobility for which the West has been celebrated may have tended to exaggerate racial prejudice.

Although many Republicans agreed with the black abolitionist Frederick Douglass that racism was "the greatest of all obstacles in the way of the anti-slavery cause," they also knew that advocacy of the free Negro's rights might prove politically disastrous. Horace Greeley, for example, explained in 1846 that though he favored equal suffrage for New York Negroes, a proposal to establish it would certainly be defeated in a popular referendum. Prejudiced voters were to blame, Greeley wrote: "You know how numerous and potent this class is." When Democrats charged in the 1850s that the Republicans favored Negro equality, an Indianan informed Salmon P. Chase that unless the claim were refuted, "we shall be beaten not only in Ind. but in the Union from this time forward." Those Republicans who defended the rights of black men found themselves subjected to ridicule and insult. "I know, sir, it is an ungracious task," Henry Wilson told the Senate, ". . . to maintain even the legal rights of a proscribed race; I am not insensible to the gibes and jeers, the taunts and misrepresentations of a corrupted public opinion. . . ." And Oliver Morton said that the reason the Republicans did not carry every township in the North in 1860 was that many voters associated anti-slavery with the prospect of "turning the negroes loose among us."

At times during the 1850s it seemed that the only weapon in the Democrats' political arsenal was the charge that the Republicans were pro-Negro. "Whenever we resist the expansion of slavery into the territories," Wilson complained, "we have a lecture about the equality of the races. When we propose the homestead policy . . . we have lectures about the equality of the races." Such attacks had always been a problem for anti-slavery men, but in the 1850s they were greatly increased. In the Lincoln-Douglas campaign of 1858, the organ of the Democratic party urged readers to "Keep it before the people of Illinois that the Abolition-Republican party headed by Abraham Lincoln are in favor of negro equality. . . ." Francis P. Blair later described this charge as the "incessant theme" of Douglas's campaign. The Wisconsin Democracy labeled the Republicans the "Nigger party," and in Indiana, a Democratic parade featured a group of young ladies carrying the banner, "Fathers, save us from nigger husbands." Though most frequent in the West, such charges were not confined to that section. The New York Democratic platform of 1857, for example, charged the Republicans with favoring Negro suffrage. During the campaign of 1860, Democrats spread the rumor that the Republican vice-presidential candidate, Hannibal Hamlin, was a mulatto. The most intense Democratic attacks were reserved for Republicans who had records of support for Negro rights. When Salmon P. Chase ran for Governor of Ohio in 1855, he was accused of believing that "one negro of the South was of more importance to our state government, than all the white people of the State." Two years later, a Republican reporting on a speech by Chase's Democratic opponent concluded, "this part of the speech was an appeal to the lowest prejudices of caste." It is not surprising that Chase complained that Democrats had little interest in any issue but race. All they wanted, he said, was "simply to talk about the universal nigger question, as they call it. All that they seem to say is 'nigger, nigger, nigger.' "

Republicans revealed the variety of their racial attitudes in the ways in which they responded to these Democratic charges. Some Republicans denounced appeals to prejudice on principled grounds. One Ohio Congressman dismissed Democratic charges as "an appeal to that low, vulgar prejudice which wages war against the negroes because the lowest man in society is always anxious to find some one lower than himself. . . ." Others felt the Democrats could best be answered by ridicule. Democrats, the Cincinnati *Gazette* observed, seemed to fear that "the Caucasian type of manhood" was "in imminent danger of disappearing from this continent." And at the Iowa Constitutional Convention of 1857, the prolonged debates about the rights of free Negroes led a Republican delegate to remark, "The gentlemen over the way are more sensitive in regard to the negro than any men I have ever seen in my life." More often, however, Republicans took the approach that the question of Negro rights was irrelevant to their party's policies. The *National Era*—the organ of the Liberty and Free Soil parties which later served as a spokesman for radical Republicans—pointed out that many Americans opposed the extension of slavery out of concern for "the national honor and prosperity," rather than an interest in Negro rights. A man who advocated abolition in the District of Columbia, the *Era* observed, was not bound "to admit a black man to his table for the sake of consistency." The editor of the Chicago *Evening Journal*, Charles Wilson, said much the same thing. "It [does not] necessarily follow," he wrote, "that we should fellowship with the negroes because our policy shakes off their shackles." Often, Republican politicians tried to keep the race issue out of politics altogether. As Lyman Trumbull warned Lincoln when the Republican state platform was under consideration in Illinois, "It will not do, of course, to get mixed up with the free negro question. . . ."

The use of the race issue as a potent political weapon by the Democrats led many Republicans to reply in kind. Especially in the West, Republican spokesmen insisted that they, not the Democrats, were the real "white man's party," and they often vehemently denied any intention of giving legal or social equality to free Negroes. The astute politician David Davis, Lincoln's friend and adviser, insisted during the 1858 campaign that Republican orators "distinctly and emphatically disavow *negro suffrage*, negroes holding office, serving on juries and the like." When Democrats charged that anti-slavery spokesmen subordinated the rights of whites to those of Negroes, Republicans responded that they hoped to keep the territories open to free white settlers by barring slavery. It required no effort to show, an Iowa Congressman wrote, that the Democratic, not the Republican party, "exalts and spreads Africans at the expense of the white race." Because they opposed Democratic plans to "flood Kansas and the other Territories with negro slaves," Republicans claimed "that we are the only white man's party in the country." And when Democrats accused them of favoring the intermixing of the races, Republicans responded that keeping the races separate by barring slavery from the territories would prevent this very intermixing. Said a leading Iowa Republican, "It is the institution of slavery which is the great parent of amalgamation. Gentlemen need not fear it from those opposed to that institution."

To a large extent, these expressions of racism were political replies to Democratic accusations rather than gratuitous insults to the black race. Few Republicans were as blatantly prejudiced as the New York *Tribune*'s associate editor James S. Pike, who so despised the Negro race that he hoped the South would secede, taking its black population with it. Some Republicans who insisted they were advocating the rights of the white race made sure to add that they did not wish "to disclaim any sympathy" for Negroes. Yet inherent in the anti-slavery outlook of many Republicans was a strong overtone of racism. For the whole free-labor argument against the extension of slavery contained a crucial ambiguity. Was it the institution of slavery, or the presence of the Negro, which degraded the white laborer? Sometimes Republicans clearly stated that the institution itself, not the race of the slave, was to blame. An Ohio Congressman declared that while he agreed that a black population represented a nuisance, "a free white man could live where there are negroes, and maintain his freedom; but no white non-slaveholder can live where slave laws, customs, and habits pertain, and retain [his] rights. . . ." The radical *National Era* informed the South, "We are not opposed to the extension of either class of your population, provided it be *free*, but to the existence of slavery and migration of *slaves*." More often, however, Republicans indicated that they made little distinction between free Negroes and slaves, and felt that association with any black degraded the white race. "I want to have nothing to do, either with the free negro or the slave negro . . . ," said Lyman Trumbull. "We wish to settle the Territories with free white men." And Simon Cameron of Pennsylvania stated that he wished to keep Negroes out of the territories, because the white laborer "must be depressed wherever the Negro is his competitor in the field or the workshop."

Although this kind of argument was resorted to throughout the Republican party, it was used most frequently by the former Democrats. These men, particularly the New York Barnburners and their followers like Wilmot and the Blairs, came from a political tradition hostile to Negro rights and accustomed to the use of race prejudice as a political weapon. During the fight for free soil in the 1840s, they had linked racism and anti-slavery in a way which was repeated in the prewar decade. David Wilmot, for example, insisted that his Proviso of 1846 was the "White Man's Proviso," and he told the House that by barring slavery from the Mexican Cession he intended to preserve the area for "the sons of toil, of my own race and own color." An astute abolitionist observer noted that Wilmot's speeches often contrasted "black labor" and "free labor," "as though it were the negro and not slavery which degraded labor." Similarly, the *National Era* pointed out that the New York Barnburners tended to place their opposition to slavery extension "on the ground of an abhorrence of 'black slaves,' " rather than of slavery itself. And during the 1850s, the former Democrats took the lead in racist appeals. They represented in the most extreme degree the racism from which no portion of the Republican party could claim total freedom. . . . During the 1850s, a good number of abolitionists and black leaders remained aloof from the Republican party because of its racist elements. An influential Negro newspaper charged in 1860 that antislavery meant little more to the Republicans than "opposition to the black man," and the black orator H. Ford Douglass told a Massachusetts abolitionist audience that no party deserved their votes "unless that party is willing to extend to the black man all the rights of a citizen." On the other hand, prominent blacks like Frederick Douglass and Dr. John Rock actively supported Frémont and Lincoln, and colored conventions throughout the North endorsed Republican candidates. These men recognized that the basic fault of the Republicans' racial attitude was not simple racism but ambivalence. Even Republicans who attacked racial prejudice and defended Negro rights were not free from prejudice, for almost all accepted in some degree the racial stereotypes of their time. Even Seward and Chase, with their long records of advocacy of Negro rights, had this problem. Seward could lecture a Michigan audience during the campaign of 1856 on the necessity for giving blacks the rights to vote—a position which could hardly be of political advantage—but at the same time, he viewed the Negro as a "foreign and feeble" element of the population which, unlike European immigrants, could never be assimilated and would eventually "altogether disappear." And Chase could insist during the gubernatorial campaign of 1857, at great political hazard, that one of his aims was to have it acknowledged "that colored people have rights and privileges which they have not now." But he also believed that an eventual separation of the races was both inevitable and necessary.

To a large extent, the ambivalence and contradictions in the Republican attitude towards the Negro stemmed from the fact that their racial outlook was part of their larger free-labor ideology. The Republicans' affirmation of the Negro's natural rights included the right to participate as a free laborer in the marketplace, and, as we have seen, they demanded that he be protected in such legal rights as were essential to that participation, such as holding property and testifying in court. In 1857, Lincoln defined the irreducible minimum of the Negro's natural rights in economic terms. Speaking of a black woman, he declared, "In some respects she is certainly not my equal, but in her natural right to eat the bread she earns with her own hands without asking leave of anyone else, she is my equal, and the equal of all others." As a free laborer, moreover, the Negro was entitled to compete for economic advancement. "Give every man a fair and equal chance upon the arena of human endeavor," Chase demanded in 1853, and in the debate on education in the District of Columbia, Henry Wilson urged the Senate to "educate, if we can, these poor colored children, and enable them, as far as possible, to improve their condition in life." And Edward Wade of Ohio insisted that the free Negro be allowed to participate in the homestead bill's benefits, so he could "locate himself where he can have the opportunity to prove his equality with the whites, or make his inequality manifest beyond controversy."

Wade's statement makes manifest the central ambiguity of the free-labor attitude towards the Negro. On the one hand, it sought to strike down discriminatory legislation and provide an opportunity for economic advancement; on the other, there lingered the nagging doubt whether the Negro was indeed capable of making use of the opportunities offered him. Some Republicans, to be sure, thought the Negro "amenable to the Law of Progress," as the *National Era* put it, and they insisted that discrimination, not inferiority, was to blame for his lowly social position. "It is nonsense to talk about the inferiority of the negro race, whilst at the same time they are kept in a state of degradation, which renders mental and moral improvement an impossibility," said a New York Congressman. And a Minnesotan agreed that "the temporary condition of a people" was a poor measure of what they might achieve in the future. To most Republicans, however, the Negro, free or slave, was a poor prospect for social advancement. They accepted the stereotype of the black man which pictured him as lazy, unenterprising, and lacking in the middle-class, Puritan qualities of character so essential for economic success. "As a class," the New York *Tribune* complained in 1855, "the Blacks are indolent, improvident, servile, and licentious." Greeley argued that while black men, because of prejudice, could hardly be expected to gain economic parity with whites, they "ought to be more industrious, energetic, thrifty, independent, than a majority of them are." The Philadelphia *North American* agreed that the reason for the Negro's confinement in menial jobs was not merely discrimination but "something deeper . . . the constitution of the negro himself."

Republican spokesmen also attributed the reluctance of free Negroes to take part in colonization projects to their lack of initiative. Negroes "must become possessed with the same spirit of self-relying enterprise" as the whites, the *National Era* complained. "Were we a colored man, we would never rest from our wanderings till we had found a place where our children might grow up into the dignity of a noble manhood." The influential Springfield *Republican* declared that a black colony would long since have been established in Central America, "if they had any pluck—if the best of them had a particle of spirit of the white man." Reports about southern slaves told the same story. Olmsted reported that the great majority of field hands appeared "very dull, idiotic, and brute-like," and lazy besides. Cassius M. Clay of Kentucky insisted that Negroes could never achieve anything in the South because they lacked self-reliance, and a visitor to the South from Vermont wrote his Republican Congressman that although slavery was an evil, the blacks would starve if set free, since "labor is not connected with their ideas of freedom." In vain did some radicals argue that the free Negroes of New England and Western Reserve were industrious, intelligent, self-reliant, and literate. Most Republicans would agree with the *National Era* that "It is the real evil of the negro race that they are so fit for slavery as they are."

A good number of the ambiguities in Republicans' racial attitudes stemmed from the contradiction between their political outlook, which stressed civil rights and some kind of legal equality, and the free labor ideology. For even those Republicans most active in efforts to extend the legal rights of free Negroes insisted that black men must prove themselves capable of economic advancement before they could expect full recognition of their equality. Greeley, for example, criticized black leaders for devoting their time to the struggle for political rights. Instead, he insisted, they should concern themselves with self-improvement and character-building, by having black men withdraw from menial trades, form separate communities, and prove that they could acquire wealth and manage business. "One negro on a farm which he has cleared or bought," the New York editor wrote, ". . . is worth more to the cause of Equal Suffrage than three in an Ethiopian (or any other) convention." The *New York Times* agreed. "It matters little," it advised colored citizens, "whether a man is black, white, or mingled. If he is respectable, he will be respected." Horace Mann, Ben Wade, and Cassius Clay gave the same answer to an Ohio colored convention which solicited their advice in 1852. Negroes should wait for political rights, and concentrate on learning trades, forming their own communities, and acquiring "habits of self-respect and independence." Just as the free-labor ideology insisted that a white man must have an independent economic existence to be truly free, it demanded that blacks prove, by economic advancement, that they deserved legal equality. "White people," said Wade, "while poor and ignorant, are no more respected than you are. I say again, color is nothing. When you have attained intelligence and independence, you will soon be admitted to your social and political rights."

Many of the Republican criticisms of free Negroes were shared by black leaders. "The colored people," Frederick Douglass told Harriet Beecher Stowe, "are wanting in self-reliance," and he deplored their tendency to remain in menial occupations. Some colored conventions advised Negroes to leave the cities and take jobs on farms as a means of self-improvement, and other spokesmen insisted that frugality, self-reliance, and a "better regulation of our domestic habits," were essential preconditions to social advancement. The black leaders insisted, however, that the Negro's deficiencies in character and achievement were wholly the result of prejudice and discrimination, and they objected to the "tone of assumed superiority and arrogant complacency," with which Republicans like Greeley criticized black citizens. But black spokesmen accepted the free-labor idea that independence was the key to respectability, and that "to be dependent is to be degraded." And they insisted that they desired not any special privileges or aid, but merely equality of opportunity. "Remove all obstacles, and give the black man an equal chance," the black spokesmen said, ". . . and then should he not succeed, he will not ask you or anyone else to mourn over his failure."

During the 1850s, Republicans accepted the idea that the Negro should be given an "equal chance" to prove himself capable of economic advancement, and their actions in state legislatures and in Congress had the effect of breaking down some of the legal inequalities which surrounded the black citizen. "I want every man to have the chance—and I believe a black man is entitled to it—in which he *can* better his condition . . . ," Lincoln insisted in 1860. The limitations of the Republican outlook did not become fully manifest until the tragic failure of Reconstruction. Given the long history of slavery and the continuing fact of discrimination, the mere granting of civil equality was not enough to guarantee real equality of opportunity for northern Negroes, much less for newly freed southern slaves. Many Republicans, of course, never expected the Negro to attain complete equality. Greeley had written before the war that, free or slave, Negroes would always occupy an inferior social position, and during Reconstruction, Seward observed philosophically, "They are God's poor; they always have been and always will be everywhere." But even the more radical Republicans, who sincerely hoped that the Negro could rise to economic and social equality, shrank from a long period of federal protection of Negro rights and a redistribution of southern property. The free-labor ideology, based on the premise that all Americans, whatever their origins, could achieve social advancement if given equal protection of the law, was only an incomplete version of the full commitment which would have been necessary to make these hopes fully realized.

Suggestions for Additional Reading

The body of historical literature treating slavery is immense. These suggestions for additional reading will identify some bibliographic aides as well as key historiographic debates and crucial topics in the literature on American slavery.

Two indispensable bibliographic aides for coping with the writings on slavery are James McPherson et al., *Blacks in America: Bibliographic Essays* (New York, 1971), and Elizabeth Miller and Mary L. Fisher, *The Negro in America: A Bibliography* (Cambridge, Mass., 1970). Though both bibliographies cover all of Afro-American history and culture, nearly half of the titles listed in both deal with some feature of American slavery. A more comprehensive and earlier bibliography is Monroe N. Work, *A Bibliography of the Negro in Africa and America* (New York, 1928; reprinted New York, 1966). John Hope Franklin, *From Slavery to Freedom*, 4th ed. (New York, 1974) is a standard textbook on black history and contains an extensive bibliography. Two anthologies that provide useful bibliographies are Nathan I. Huggins et al., eds., *Key Issues in the Afro-American Experience*, 2 vols. (New York, 1971), and Allan Weinstein and Frank O. Gatell, eds., *American Negro Slavery* (New York, 1973). Gary B. Nash, *Red, White, and Black: The Peoples of Early America* (Englewood Cliffs, N.J., 1974), and Robert William Fogel and Stanley L. Engerman, *Time on the Cross: Evidence and Methods—A Supplement* (Boston, 1974) are two secondary works that have particularly fine bibliographic essays. Leslie H. Fishel and Benjamin Quarles, *The Negro American: A Documentary History* (Glenville, Ill., 1967), and Willie Lee Rose, *A Documentary History of Slavery in North America* (New York, 1976) are useful collections of documents.

In examining how Americans have interpreted slavery and its impact on American life, students should consult published primary materials. Two insightful contemporary appraisals of plantation slavery are by a sympathetic foreign visitor, Alexis de Tocqueville, *Democracy in America*, ed. Richard D. Hefner (New York, 1956), and by a critical northerner, Frederick Law Olmsted, *The Cotton Kingdom* (New York, 1861). A savage indictment of slavery is the abolitionist Theodore Weld's *American Slavery As It Is*, ed. Richard O. Curry and Joanna Cowden (Itasca, Ill., 1972). Eric McKitrick, *Slavery Defended*

(Englewood Cliffs, N.J., 1963) presents some of the views of the proponents of American slavery.

There are numerous published slave autobiographies and narratives. The most famous is by the ex-slave and black abolitionist Frederick Douglass, *A Narrative of the Life of Frederick Douglass* (Boston, 1845). A comprehensive collection of slave narratives is George P. Rawick's multivolume *The American Slave: A Composite Autobiography* (Westport, Ct., 1972). See also B. A. Botkin, ed., *Lay My Burden Down: A Folk History of Slavery* (Chicago, 1945); Robert S. Starobin, ed., *Blacks in Bondage: Letters of American Slaves* (New York, 1974); C. Vann Woodward, "History from Slave Sources," *American Historical Review* 79 (April 1974): 470–81.

Much of the historical literature on slavery focuses on the life and economy of the slave plantation. Among the earliest studies that present the basic outlines of the slave plantation are the general histories prepared by nineteenth-century scholars, such as James Ford Rhodes, *History of the United States from the Compromise of 1850* (New York, 1893–1906), and John Bach McMaster, *A History of the People of the United States from the Revolution to the Civil War* (New York, 1883–1913). In particular, Rhodes and McMaster wanted to highlight the unsavory effects that slavery had on American life and refute the claims of the antebellum defenders of slavery. Ulrich B. Phillips, in *American Negro Slavery* (New York, 1918), and *Life and Labor in the Old South* (Boston, 1929), challenged those general histories. Phillips, the first scholar to use extensively plantation records, portrayed slavery as a benign social institution that served as a useful training ground for the racially inferior and culturally deprived black slave. Phillips remained the authority on American slavery for three decades. Two scholarly studies influenced by Phillips are James B. Sellers, *Slavery in Alabama* (University, Ala., 1950), and Charles B. Syndor, *Slavery in Mississippi* (New York, 1933).

With changes in the social and scientific attitudes of mid-twentieth-century Americans, Phillips's conclusions became unacceptable to the academic community, and scholars sought to refute his findings. In an important essay, "U. B. Phillips and the Plantation Legend," *Journal of Negro History* (April 1944), Richard Hofstadter charged that Phillips had used an unrepresentative sample of sources and that he had been racially biased in selecting his facts. In 1950 Oscar and Mary Handlin followed Hofstadter's critique with their

"Origins of the Southern Labor System," *William and Mary Quarterly* 6 (April 1950) in order to prove that there was nothing unique about black people that led to their enslavement. And the refutation of Phillips culminated with Kenneth Stampp's *The Peculiar Institution* (New York, 1956). Surpassing Phillips in both the scope and depth of his research, Stampp presented slavery as a harsh, repressive system for the exploitation of cheap labor.

During the last two decades, historians of slavery have focused on two issues: the effect of slavery on the slave and the economics of slavery. In the controversial study, *Slavery: A Problem in American Institutional and Intellectual Life* (Chicago, 1959), Stanley Elkins argued that in the United States the institution of slavery was more repressive than in other societies and that this "closed" system reduced the slave to a fawning, dependent, childlike "Sambo." Almost all recent publications on slavery in some way confront Elkins's thesis. For refutations of Elkins, see Ann J. Lane, ed., *The Debate Over Slavery: Stanley Elkins and His Critics* (Urbana, 1971), and John W. Blassingame, *The Slave Community* (New York, 1972). Studies of slave resistance are Herbert Aptheker, *Negro Slave Revolts* (New York, 1943), and Gerald W. Mullin, *Flight and Rebellion: Slave Resistance in Eighteenth-Century Virginia* (New York, 1972).

Robert W. Fogel and Stanley L. Engerman's *Time on the Cross: The Economics of American Negro Slavery* (Boston, 1974) has provoked intense debate over the profitability of slavery. Fogel and Engerman depict slavery as a rational business enterprise that was considerably more efficient than the family farms of the North. An important critique of their work is Herbert G. Gutman, *Slavery and the Numbers Game* (Urbana, 1975). Other criticisms are summarized in Thomas Haskell, "The True and Tragical History of 'Time on the Cross'," *New York Review of Books* 22 (October 2, 1975). Alfred H. Conrad and John R. Meyer, *The Economics of Slavery and Other Econometric Studies* (Chicago, 1964) is another significant work on slavery as an economic system. Eugene D. Genovese, *The Political Economy of Slavery* (New York, 1961) believes that slavery was "pre-capitalist." Julia Floyd Smith, *Slavery and Plantation Growth in Antebellum Florida, 1821–1860* (Gainesville, Fla., 1973) disputes Genovese's conclusions.

Scholars have studied slavery in various temporal contexts. On the origins of slavery, Winthrop Jordan, *White Over Black* (Chapel Hill,

N.C., 1968) is a standard interpretation. Jordan has outlined other interpretations in his historiographic essay, "Modern Tensions and the Origins of American Slavery," *Journal of Southern History*, 28 (February 1962). On the Atlantic slave trade, Phillip D. Curtin, *The Atlantic Slave Trade: A Census* (Madison, 1969), and Daniel P. Mannix, *Black Cargoes: A History of the Atlantic Slave Trade, 1518–1865* (New York, 1962) are important. Key studies of slavery and race relations in the colonial era are Herbert S. Klein, *Slavery in the Americas: A Comparative Study of Virginia and Cuba* (Chicago, 1967); Gary B. Nash, *Red, White, and Black* (Englewood Cliffs, N.J., 1974); Edmund S. Morgan, *American Slavery, American Freedom: The Ordeal of Colonial Virginia* (New York, 1975); Thad W. Tate, *The Negro in Eighteenth-Century Williamsburg* (Williamsburg, Va., 1964); Peter H. Wood, *The Black Majority* (New York, 1974). Duncan J. Macleod, *Slavery, Race, and the American Revolution* (New York, 1974) and Benjamin Quarles, *The Negro in the American Revolution* (Chapel Hill, N.C., 1961) relate slavery to the Revolution. Eugene Genovese's monumental study, *Roll, Jordan, Roll: The World the Slaves Made* (New York, 1974), undoubtedly will be a focal point for all future research on slavery in the antebellum South. Ira Berlin, *Slaves Without Masters: The Free Negro in the Antebellum South* (New York, 1974) explores a crucial area in social relations.

Slavery and race affected more than just the Southern plantation. The interaction between slavery and urban life is examined in Robert S. Starobin, *Industrial Slavery in the Old South* (New York, 1970) and Richard C. Wade, *Slavery in the Cities: The South, 1820–1860* (New York, 1964). Studies of Northern slavery are Lorenzo J. Greene, *The Negro in Colonial New England* (New York, 1942); Edgar J. McManus, *Black Bondage in the North* (Syracuse, 1973); Arthur Zilversmit, *The First Emancipation: The Abolition of Slavery in the North* (Chicago, 1967). Eugene H. Berwanger, *The Frontier Against Slavery: Western Anti-Negro Prejudice and the Slavery Extension Controversy* (Urbana, 1967), Eric Foner, *Free Soil, Free Labor, Free Men* (New York, 1970), and Leon Litwack, *North of Slavery* (Chicago, 1961) all probe the racial attitudes of Northerners. William H. and Jane Pease delineate the prejudices of antislavery people in "Antislavery Ambivalence: Immediatism, Expediency, Race," *American Quarterly* 17 (Winter 1965). A study of one racial equalitarian, William Lloyd Garrison, is Aileen Kraditor's *Means and Ends in Abolitionism*

(New York, 1969). Racism is further explored in George M. Fredrickson, *The Black Image in the White Mind: The Debate on Afro-American Character and Destiny, 1817–1914* (New York, 1971); Thomas Gosset, *Race: The History of an Idea in America* (Dallas, 1963); William R. Stanton, *The Leopard's Spots: Scientific Attitudes toward Race in America, 1815–1959* (Chicago, 1960).

There is a wealth of scholarship available comparing slave systems. Some of the newest and most influential studies are David W. Cohen and Jack B. Greene, eds., *Neither Slave Nor Free: The Freedman of African Descent in the Slave Societies of the New World* (Baltimore, 1972); Carl N. Degler, *Neither Black Nor White* (New York, 1971); Stanley L. Engerman and Eugene D. Genovese, eds., *Race and Slavery in the Western Hemisphere: Quantitative Studies* (Princeton, 1975); Harmannus Hoetink, *Slavery and Race Relations in the Americas: Comparative Notes on Their Nature and Nexus* (New York, 1973). Laura Foner and Eugene D. Genovese, eds., *Slavery in the New World: A Reader in Comparative History* (Englewood Cliffs, N.J., 1969) is a useful collection of essays, and John V. Lombardi, "Comparative Slave Systems in the Americas: A Critical Review," in Richard Graham and Peter H. Smith, eds., *New Approaches to Latin American History* (Austin, 1974), surveys the historiographic battles. David Brion Davis in his two award-winning studies, *The Problem of Slavery in Western Culture* (Ithaca, 1966) and *The Problem of Slavery in the Age of Revolution* (Ithaca, 1975) contrasts various concepts of slavery in Western culture. Jack P. Greene, "Society and Economy in the British Caribbean during the Seventeenth and Eighteenth Centuries," *American Historical Review* 79 (December 1974) identifies new studies on Caribbean slavery. Ann M. Pescatello, ed., *The African in Latin America* (New York, 1975) and Rolando Mellafe, *Negro Slavery in Latin America* (Berkeley, 1975) will introduce the student to the history of Latin American slavery.